SAN JUAN
ADVENTURE GUIDE

SAN JUAN
ADVENTURE GUIDE

a guide to hiking, biking,
and skiing in southwestern colorado

≈

JEFF LA FRENIERRE

Printed in the United States of America

09 08 07 06 05 04 03 02 01 00   5 4 3 2 1

Library of Congress Cataloging-in-Publication Data

La Frenierre, Jeff.
    San Juan adventure guide : a guide to hiking, biking, and skiing
in southwestern Colorado / Jeff La Frenierre.
        p.   cm.
    Includes index.
    ISBN 0-87108-909-2 (alk. paper)
    1. Hiking—San Juan Mountains (Colo. and N.M.)—Guidebooks. 2. All terrain cycling—San Juan Mountains (Colo. and N.M.)—Guidebooks. 3. Skis and skiing—San Juan Mountains (Colo. and N.M.)—Guidebooks. 4. San Juan Mountains (Colo. and N.M.)—Guidebooks. I. Title.
    GV199.42.S26 L24 2000
    917.88'30433—dc21   99-087507

Cover and book design by Julie Noyes Long
Book composition by Lyn Chaffee
Cover photographs by Jeff La Frenierre

To Paula—Thank you for being my companion

Climb the mountains and get their good tidings;
Nature's peace will flow into you as sunshine into
flowers; the winds will blow their freshness into
you and the storms their energy; and cares will
drop off like autumn leaves.

—John Muir

Wilderness. The word itself is music.

—Edward Abbey

I have been to only a few other places in my life
that boast an amount of sensory input that comes
even close to that which dwells in the San Juans.
This is the mountain version of the Grand Canyon.
No matter which way I face, there is something not
only beautiful, but uniquely beautiful.

—M. John Fayhee

CONTENTS

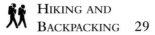

HIKING AND BACKPACKING 29

MOUNTAIN BIKING 115

PREFACE

Enveloped by the icy breeze of an alpine dawn, I stand atop a rocky San Juan peak, one of the innumerable summits in the sprawling mountain range. From my lofty perch, I gaze in all directions and see an ocean of sweeping mountains, serrated ridges, and imposing cliffs. Beneath the impossibly blue skies of this autumn morning, the landscape is a tapestry of color: brilliant snowfields swirl across somber, gray rock; the muted browns of frosty tundra commingle with patches of hunter-green spruce forest and golden aspen groves. The sparkle of a tundra pond catches my eye, and the distant roar of a long cascade captures my ear. I glimpse a herd of elk grazing on a nearby mountain slope, and I stare down into a shaded valley and see the silent remains of a frontier boomtown gone bust.

Calling the San Juans "Colorado's most beautiful mountains" is a pretty audacious statement, but I can think of no other place that deserves such praise. The granite spires of Rocky Mountain National Park are magnificent, absolutely; the reflection of Aspen's Maroon Bells in a crystalline lake is sublime. However, there is something more to the San Juans. Few other places in the state—in the world, I think—have so many wonderful features complementing one another so perfectly. Simply put, the San Juans are more rugged, wild, and awe inspiring than any other group of mountains in the southern Rockies.

San Juan Adventure Guide was written to provide accurate information for devotees of self-propelled recreation—hiking, mountain biking, and backcountry skiing—in the San Juan Mountains. It was also my intent that it serve as a tool to increase the understanding and appreciation of this unique region. I have fought a difficult internal struggle in determining whether this book should have been written at all. Haven't overly enthusiastic proponents who have instigated a recreational stampede despoiled enough places? Look no further than the Moab area, which has recently undergone a dramatic transformation from lonely desert outpost to bustling—and ecologically threatened—recreation destination. However, in the five years it has taken to develop this book from abstract concept to reality, it is clear that the people are already coming. San Juan trailheads that were empty a few years ago are now often crowded. Yesterday's lonely meadows and quiet forests are rapidly becoming today's exclusive subdivisions.

I have come to the realization that the publication of this book is not a bad thing. Not only does it provide an opportunity to share beautiful places and exciting adventures, it gives me a medium through which I can encourage people to view these mountains as something more than a playground—to see them as a reservoir of ecological diversity; a time machine to our region's geologic, prehistoric, and frontier past; and a sanctuary for self-discovery. The paradox of Moab gives me hope. While serious questions have risen concerning the effect the recreation explosion is having on the canyon country's ecosystems, it is also obvious that this explosion has resulted in a greater awareness concerning the protection of the wilderness that still exists on the Colorado Plateau. The national groundswell of support for the preservation of Utah's red-rock wilderness can be directly attributed to the fact that people, in increasing numbers, are experiencing the landscape for themselves.

It is fortunate that large tracts of the San Juans have been designated official wilderness areas and so are protected from civilization's encroachment; however, many threats remain. It is my fervent hope that you, the reader, will come to appreciate the magnificent scenery and dramatic history of the region. But more so, I hope that you will become an advocate for its preservation. Ultimately, the onus is on each one of us, as individuals, to not only tread lightly, but to fight those who would exploit this wondrous landscape.

In appreciation of those who fight to ensure the region's ecological health and of those who work to promote responsible wilderness travel, I am donating a percentage of my royalties from the sale of this book to the San Juan Mountains Association and the San Juan Citizens Alliance. It is but a small token, but without the efforts of these and other groups and individuals, the San Juans would be a much less wild place. A donation will also be made to the Colorado Avalanche Information Center, an organization whose work makes winter backcountry travel a much safer experience.

ACKNOWLEDGMENTS

A hearty "thank you" is extended to everyone who lent their support to this project: Chet and Hope Williams, for editing portions of the manuscript and offering excellent suggestions, not to mention companionship and some really good meals; Linda, Bob, and Tammy La Frenierre, for their unending support and welcome company on several San Juan adventures; Ed Butts, for reviewing portions of the manuscript and offering excellent suggestions about wording and tone; Cathy Zack, for performing an exhaustive review of the manuscript's original incarnation; Carol Nugent, Ann Thompson, Dwight Hyde, Brian Franke, and Steve Kirin, for joining us on various hikes, rides, and tours; and our trusty Nissan Pathfinder, for keeping us moving through countless blizzards, over treacherous passes, and through the raging waters of Pole Creek.

And finally, the biggest "thank you" goes out to my wife, Paula, who devoted so much time and energy to what must have seemed for so long to be a pipe dream. Without her ideas and corrections, this book would not exist. As a team, we gasped for air at the summit of Uncompahgre, dodged lightning and bruising hail near Wetterhorn Basin, explored the depths of Cottonwood Gulch on a -20°F morning, and bolted from the terrifying roar of the Hermosa Creek mystery beast. Her presence on each of the book's hikes, rides, and tours made the flowers brighter, the sunsets more colorful, and the snow closer to perfect. May our adventures continue for a lifetime.

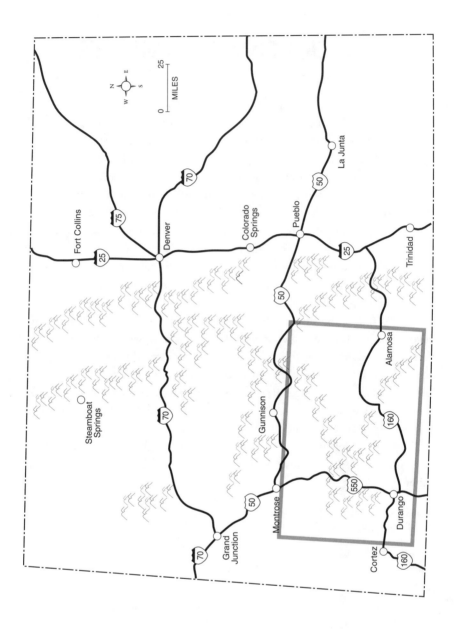

THE SAN JUAN LANDSCAPE

San Juan Geography

Located at the southern end of the Rocky Mountains, the San Juans are one of the most complex mountain systems on the North American continent. Unlike other ranges, which are often composed of a long, linear group of peaks and an easily recognizable crest, the San Juans are more like a massive, crumpled blanket. For more than 10,000 square miles, the land has been thrust skyward into a mosaic of castellated peaks, high plateaus, deep canyons, and narrow valleys, creating an alpine setting as sublime as any in America.

Although the timeline of geologic events that affects their structure exceeds a billion years, the San Juans are considered young compared to the world's other mountain ranges and have appeared in their present form for only the last ten thousand years. Reading like an epic disaster tome, the story told by these rock formations is one of massive volcanic explosions, vast ice fields, repeated floods, countless earthquakes, and great landslides. As they have done throughout the world, these geologic events have created the landscape we recognize today.

Taken as a whole, the San Juans are Colorado's largest mountain group, stretching 120 miles east to west and 90 miles north to south. Within the greater San Juans are several distinct "subranges." Included among these are the Sneffels Range, which forms the San Juans' northern abutment; the colorful San Miguel Range; the Rico Mountains; the somewhat isolated La Plata Range; the craggy Needle Mountains; the small but dramatic West Needle Mountains; and the La Garita Range, which stretches northeast toward the remainder of Colorado's Rockies.

Perhaps the most remarkable feature of the San Juans is their exceedingly high altitude. It is said that no other mountain range in the United States (outside of Alaska) has a higher average elevation. There are more than one thousand summits greater than 12,000 feet in the San Juans, with thirteen of those exceeding 14,000 feet. The vertical relief is impressive, with the highest summits rising between 6,000 and 7,000 feet above the surrounding valleys. Even in the heart of the range, vertical relief from valley floor to summit typically exceeds 0.5 mile. One of America's most recognizable mountain features, the Continental Divide, runs across the top of the La Garitas, makes a hundred-mile horseshoe bend around the headwaters of the Rio Grande, then continues down the crest of the South San Juans. Even the passes are at sky-scraping altitudes: None are lower than 10,000 feet, and several of the highest exceed 12,000 feet.

The San Juans are the headwaters for more than a dozen rivers, which radiate outward like the spokes of a wheel. The mightiest of these is the Rio Grande, which flows eastward from the heart of the range before turning south to flow through the San Luis Valley, the length of New Mexico, and eventually into the Gulf of Mexico, some 1,800 miles later. Rio Grande tributaries include the Alamosa, Conejos, and Chama Rivers. The San Juan River and its tributaries, which include the Navajo, Rio Blanco, Piedra, Los Pinos, Animas, La Plata, and Mancos Rivers, drain the southern flank of the range. Two rivers have their headwaters in the western San Juans: the Dolores and the San Miguel. The north flank of the range is drained by the Uncompahgre, Cimarron, and Lake Fork Rivers, all of which contribute their waters to the Gunnison River—itself an important tributary of the Colorado River.

The San Juans have a vertical relief of roughly 8,000 feet, which translates to an ecological range of nearly 2,500 miles. More simply put, the ecosystems found here are similar to those found in both Mexico and Canada. This means that the region is astonishingly diverse, ecologically speaking. The San Juans encompass as many as eight major biotic communities, or ecosystems, each of which provides just the right living conditions for certain species of plants and wildlife. Frequent visitors to the San Juans come to know the region as much by the plants and animals as the names of the trails. These biotic communities are mostly determined by altitude.

San Juan Ecosystems

The *semidesert shrubland* is found at the lowest elevations flanking the San Juans and features hot summers, cold winters, and very little precipitation. As you might expect, trees are rarely found (except near watercourses), with shrubs such as rabbitbrush and sage being the predominant vegetation. Belying its seeming desolation, the ecosystem teems with wildlife, particularly during winter, when snow drives many creatures down from the high elevations. Pronghorn antelope, mule deer, coyote, and jackrabbit are among the common mammals of the shrublands, as well as an impressive number of birds. Look for sage grouse, sparrow, hawk, and golden eagle, to name a few. Examples of this ecosystem are found in the Lake Fork Valley north of Lake City, in the San Luis Valley east of the San Juans, and in the valleys of the lower Dolores and San Miguel Rivers.

The *pinon-juniper woodland* is found throughout the San Juan foothills, especially between elevations of 5,000 and 7,000 feet, and is one of the most easily recognized biotic communities in the region. Also called the "pygmy forest," this ecosystem is named after the dominant conifers of the ecosystem. These short, often gnarled-looking trees thrive in arid climates and coarse soils and are usually widely spaced, with little in the way of forest-floor ground cover. Like the semidesert shrubland, this ecosystem is an important winter wildlife habitat and is home to many of the same animal species. Pinon nuts and juniper berries are especially important food sources for them. Excellent examples of this ecosystem are found in the Ridgway vicinity, the mesa country southwest of the La Plata Range, and on the lowest slopes of the La Garita Range above the San Luis Valley.

A *riparian* ecosystem, unlike any other, is not determined by elevation but by its proximity to water. While the climates of different riparian areas may vary significantly, they share one common feature: a moister environment than that of the surrounding landscape. Regardless of elevation, riparian ecosystems are critical wildlife habitats, especially for migrating birds. An unfortunate paradox is that humans are also attracted to riparian landscapes, and as a whole, they are the most threatened ecosystems in the region. There are few San Juan adventures where you will not be near some sort of riparian ecosystem, be it a cottonwood-lined river, beaver pond, meadow brook, or tundra marsh.

Great thickets of Gambel oak and mountain mahogany dominate the *montane shrubland* ecosystem, which is common in the foothill areas of the San Juans, particularly on the south and west sides of the range. Mountain lion, black bear, mule deer, and coyote are common in this ecosystem, as are numerous birds, including scrub jay, rufous-sided towhee, and the Colorado state bird, the lark bunting. Montane shrublands are especially beautiful in autumn, when the leaves of the oak turn rich shades of orange and crimson. To see for yourself, try exploring the lower Hermosa Creek drainage, or the lower slopes on the west side of Owl Creek Pass during autumn.

The *montane forest,* commonly found between 7,000 and 9,000 feet, is home to ponderosa pine and Douglas fir, the dominant trees in this ecosystem. Extensive stands of aspen also appear in this ecosystem, particularly in disturbed areas such as old burns. You'll also see an occasional lodgepole pine, especially on the northern slopes of the La Garitas. Most of the large mammals that winter in the lower ecosystems work their way into the montane forests during summer, where they forage on abundant grasses, shrubs, and tree bark. When you come across a ponderosa (easily identified by its beautiful, reddish bark), inhale deeply near its trunk, and you'll be enveloped in a sweet vanilla (or butterscotch) aroma. Ute Indians used to harvest the cambium from ponderosa bark to use as a culinary sweetener. Though the montane forest is widespread, there is little old-growth left—look along the Piedra and Los Pinos Rivers and on the lower few miles of the Treasure Mountain Trail for some of the best examples. Among the region's many great aspen groves, those in the Cimarron Valley and along the Dolores River are especially beautiful.

The dark, somber realm of the *subalpine forest* ecosystem is one of the Rocky Mountain's signature landscapes. Composed primarily of Engelmann spruce and subalpine fir, these are the wettest landscapes in the San Juans. Copious summer rains and exceptionally deep winter snows result in average annual precipitation totals often in excess of 50 inches (compared to the 10–15 inches common in the semidesert shrubland). Subalpine meadows are also verdant, and dozens of wildflower varieties grow in close proximity to one another. The deep snowpack relegates this ecosystem as a summer-only range for most species of wildlife, with the region's great elk herds migrating to lower elevations during winter and its healthy black bear population hibernating in shallow caves and hollows. The conifers of this ecosystem are distinct from those of the montane: Compare the tapered crown of an Engelmann spruce to the broad crown of a ponderosa and determine which species has adapted to withstand heavy loads of snow. Almost any outing in a San Juan wilderness area will be within the subalpine ecosystem; Ivy Creek and the Conejos Headwaters are particularly good places to visit.

Though often seen as an abrupt boundary between the subalpine forest and the alpine tundra, *treeline* is actually a distinct ecosystem with several unique features. Treeline, or "timberline," is the highest point at which trees can grow before the bitter cold and high winds of the higher elevations eliminate any further forest colonization. Treeline altitude is largely dependent upon latitude. In Washington's North Cascades, treeline is roughly 6,000 feet—an elevation below which most trees can thrive in the southern

Rockies. In the San Juans, treeline ranges between 11,500 and 12,000 feet, depending on local topography and microclimates. Hike through treeline, and you'll never fail to find the stunted, gnarled trees known as *krummholz*— a German word that means "crooked wood." Krummholz can be any tree species—it simply refers to those pioneering trees that grow at the extreme limits of their range, where hugging the ground is the only means by which to survive the brutal alpine winds. The bristlecone pine is a unique tree sometimes found at treeline in the more arid eastern San Juans. This species, which is often identified with the mountain ranges of the Great Basin, have proven to be the longest-lived entities on Earth: One bristlecone in California was determined to be more than five thousand years old. You'll find bristlecone en route to Conejos Peak, among other places.

Though *alpine tundra* is widespread across the highest ranges of the western United States, few places can match the extent and beauty of the tundra found in the San Juans. Surviving in a climate too cold and windswept for any tree, the various plant species of the tundra hug the ground, tolerate intense solar-radiation, and reproduce in a growing season that averages about six weeks in length. One of the most beautiful San Juan features is its tundra wildflower gardens. Places like Indian Trail Ridge, Yankee Boy Basin, and American Basin, where great bouquets of columbine, bluebell, and paintbrush grow, are home to some of the densest, most colorful displays of wildflowers found anywhere in the world. The drier tundra communities of the eastern San Juan Mountains, which feature dainty patches of forget-me-not, moss campion, and alpine avens, are different but no less interesting. Though very few mammals live year-round in the tundra ecosystem, you may spot ptarmigan, marmot, pika, bighorn sheep, elk, and mountain goat during your summer tundra travels. There is no better place to examine this amazing biotic community than at the Powderhorn Wilderness's Calf Creek Plateau, which is the largest single expanse of alpine tundra in the contiguous United States.

San Juan Climate

An old saw popular among Coloradans is "If you don't like the weather, just wait ten minutes." It is true that Colorado in general, and its mountains in particular, experience varied and extreme weather throughout the year. Depending on where in the state you happen to be, severe thunderstorms, intense blizzards, beautiful sunny days, and blistering winds are all common weather phenomena at anytime of the year, sometimes all occurring within the same week.

The San Juans are a semiarid region, with generally warm summers and cold winters; however, the weather and temperature vary significantly from one place to another. Compare, for example, the climate of Durango with that of Red Mountain Pass, some 60 miles to the north and 5,000 feet higher in elevation. Durango's average high temperature in July is 85°F, while the average at the pass is only 64°F. The highest temperature ever recorded in Durango is 102°F, while in forty years of climate study at Red Mountain Pass, the temperature has never climbed higher than 77°F. Annual precipitation in Durango is about 19 inches, with a winter snowfall total averaging about 70 inches. On Red Mountain Pass, the annual precipitation is twice as much, and the estimated annual snowfall exceeds 500 inches. The number of days with precipitation is also significantly different, with about 80 the norm in Durango and 145 typical of the pass.

A San Juan winter is something to behold. Fierce winds, bitterly cold temperatures, and frequent, heavy snowfalls mark the overall winter climate. Moderate snowstorms, often tracking from the northwest, occur on a regular basis and can be expected at least once per week throughout the winter. Below approximately 7,000 feet, the snow will usually melt in time for the next storm. Above that altitude, however, the snow piles onto a snowpack that grows ever deeper throughout the season, making the possibility of avalanches an ever-present danger.

As temperatures begin to warm in late winter and early spring, moisture-laden storms surge in from the southwest, and more intense snowfalls can be expected. March and April are the region's snowiest months, at which time the winter snowpack reaches its greatest depth and the mountains are most prone to avalanches. By late April, rainstorms become more common than snow at the lower elevations. Despite their tempestuous nature, the spring months can be the best in which to plan that overnight ski adventure—if you get a clear weather window, the temperatures, lighter winds, and increased hours of sunlight can make for magical conditions. Just remember to expect a warmer, mushier snowpack than that of the colder months.

In late spring, a few winterlike snowstorms may batter the higher terrain, but generally precipitation totals begin to drop significantly, and temperatures consistently stay above freezing at all but the highest elevations. By the

Summer on the Calf Creek Plateau—an afternoon thunderstorm builds in the distance.

end of May, the snowpack should be completely melted below 10,000 feet, while areas above this elevation remain buried for another four to six weeks, keeping the alpine region's hiking trails inaccessible. June is the month with the best weather; the days are at their longest while the weather is at its driest.

By mid-July, the snows are typically melted throughout the San Juans—except in drifted areas and avalanche gullies, where it may never completely melt—and the tundra is decorated with a dazzling collection of wildflowers. Temperatures are at their warmest, though people camped above treeline can still expect subfreezing nighttime temperatures. This season also marks the arrival of the southwest monsoon, a steady flow of moisture from Mexico's Pacific coast. Violent afternoon thunderstorms become an almost daily event, and during the wettest years, prolonged periods of rainy weather can be expected. These summer storms can be quite severe, with dangerous lightning and intense hail. Fortunately, most are short-lived, and many evenings turn out to be refreshingly cool and clear.

The beauty of a summer day notwithstanding, the golden days of September and early October are the best time to visit the San Juans. By Labor Day, the often torrential rains of the summer monsoon have shut off, and most days are crisp and clear. Scattered storms may pass through the region, but most are minor and move quickly to the east. The first dusting of snow on the highest peaks can be expected sometime in mid- to late September, often followed by a several week–long period of Indian summer.

By the second or third week of October, the winter pattern of weekly storms begins once more, and the snow again begins to accumulate on the mountain slopes. Higher-elevation trails become inaccessible, and lakes and streams begin to freeze. Daytime temperatures drop into the chilly range, and nighttime temperatures, especially in the mountain communities, become downright cold. This is sort of a "lost season" for exploring the San Juans, as most hiking trails are snow covered but have too little snow to allow much in the way of skiing or snowshoeing. As a result, few people travel to the region at this time, and those that do experience greater solitude than during other times of the year.

So what does all of this mean to the San Juan adventurer? Come prepared for any weather possibility! I have been snowed upon in July and snowshoed in a T-shirt in January. The weather here is fickle and can change dramatically and rapidly at anytime of year. It goes without saying that this variable climate will play an important role in your San Juan travels.

San Juan History

Though civilization has encroached upon the San Juans only within the last century, the region has a human history that dates back some ten thousand years. The earliest inhabitants of the area, likely following the retreating glaciers of the Ice Age, were foragers that hunted game and gathered berries and roots. Little research has been done regarding these Archaic peoples, and the extent of their travels into the alpine heart of the region remains unknown. Artifacts have been found in several areas, including Piedra Pass and in the Elk Creek drainage near Silverton.

When the foragers began cultivating their food roughly two thousand years ago, they also planted the seeds for a more advanced civilization. By growing maize, beans, and squash, the Ancient Puebloans—better known as the Anasazi—had more time to develop the engineering and artistic skills that resulted in the cliff dwellings, pottery, and rock art for which they are now famous. The Anasazi flourished in the canyons, valleys, and mesas to the south and west of the San Juans, never inhabiting the mountains themselves (with the exception of the religious site at Chimney Rock). Researchers believe that they traveled into the higher terrain in search of game and timber, as pottery shards have been found near Kennebec Pass in the La Platas. Due to some combination of resource depletion, war, and drought, the Anasazi migrated farther south between A.D. 1250 and 1300, leaving behind the ruins at which we continue to marvel.

Around A.D. 1500, another group of people migrated into the San Juan region from the northwest. Known as the Utes, these nomadic hunters ranged throughout the region, following the seasonal migrations of fauna and the seasonal ripening of berries and roots. At first the Utes lived in small groups of extended families; however, once they acquired horses from the Spanish, they were able to better utilize their resources and congregate in larger bands. Ute bands inhabited much of present-day Colorado and Utah, with three groups calling the San Juans home: the Capotes, who inhabited the San Luis and Chama Valleys; the Tabeguache (pronounced TAB-a-wash), who roamed the Uncompahgre and Gunnison Valleys; and the Weminuche (WEM-in-ooch), of the central San Juans. Hunting with bow and arrow (and guns obtained from the Spanish) and living in tepees adopted from the Plains tribes, the Utes enjoyed dominion throughout the San Juans.

Some 250 years after arriving in North America, the Spanish left their colonies in New Mexico and began exploring southwestern Colorado. The first official expedition was in 1765 and was led by Juan Maria de Rivera, who skirted the La Plata and San Miguel ranges and entered the Gunnison River valley. Another group, the Dominguez-Escalante expedition, departed Santa Fe in 1776 in an unsuccessful attempt to reach Monterey, California. Following much the same route as Maria de Rivera's expedition, they bestowed many of the place-names we recognize today, including *El Rio de la Piedra Parada* ("River of the Rock Wall"), *El Rio de las Animas Perdidas* ("River of Lost Souls"), and *El Rio de Nuestra Senora de las Dolores* ("River of Our Lady of Sorrows"). Following in their footsteps came other groups, who sought trade with the Utes as well as furs and gold.

The first American to see the San Juans was probably Zebulon Pike, who in 1806 illegally entered the San Luis Valley, which was Spanish territory at that time. His expedition was arrested and taken to Santa Fe before being released. Control of the region passed to Mexico in 1821 when it declared its independence from Spain; however, the United States soon gained title to the land (as with all of the Southwest) as a result of the Mexican-American War in 1848. Within a year, John C. Fremont led the first official

U.S. government expedition into the region. He reached the San Juans that winter and almost starved and froze to death after attempting a winter traverse of the La Garita Range.

In 1860, prospectors began fanning out across the southern Rockies from the new boomtown of Denver, with Charles Baker leading the first American prospectors into the San Juans. Traveling up the Rio Grande, they crossed Stony Pass and arrived in "Baker's Park" (the present-day site of Silverton), where they discovered promising amounts of gold. Returning a year later with a larger group, Baker continued prospecting but was generally less successful due to hostile Utes, severe weather, and the region's profound isolation. The onset of the Civil War precluded further exploration and set back the eventual San Juan gold rush for another decade.

In the meantime, the Utes had signed a number of treaties—including one in 1868—that had whittled away at their territory but allowed the tribe to retain nearly all of the San Juans as their exclusive domain. This legal status did little to prevent a new influx of prospectors once the war had ended, and soon pressure to push the Utes out of the region began to mount. In 1873, the government offered the Utes the Brunot Treaty, which the Utes thought would only transfer title of the mines to the government, but in fact released all Ute rights to the San Juan Mountains. There is historical evidence that this treaty was an intentional deception on the part of the U.S. government. Ute chief Ouray recognized that his tribe could not win a war against the U.S. Army, and he peacefully led his people from their generations-old home onto a small reservation on the Colorado–New Mexico border.

With the San Juans now fully open to American prospectors, the gold rush began in earnest. The Hayden Survey traversed the region in 1874 to collect detailed geographical and geological data, information that was of great importance to the prospectors flooding the area. Within months, the first settlements were founded, including Lake City in 1874 and Telluride, Silverton, and Ouray the following year. By the end of the decade, dozens of towns—most of which are now nothing but a memory—had sprung up in every corner of the region. The railroads quickly followed, with the Denver and Rio Grande arriving at Durango in 1880, Silverton in 1882, Ouray in 1887, Lake City in 1889, and Telluride in 1890. The boom continued, and new strikes in the Rio Grande drainage led to the 1890 founding of Creede.

Though it had been gold that had lured the first San Juan prospectors, it was silver that fueled the region's economic development. When silver was devalued in 1893, the resulting national economic crisis was especially damaging to the San Juan mining industry. Many mines closed, and some of the smaller towns were abandoned. The region survived through other prosperous discoveries—including the 1896 discovery of the Camp Bird claim—and most of the larger communities continued to bustle for another two decades. By the onset of World War I, mining production began to diminish as ore became depleted and mineral values fell. The Great Depression caused the further curtailment of the industry, and the fifty-year boom, in which the region had produced hundreds of millions of dollars' worth of gold, silver, lead, and zinc, finally came to a close.

Though sporadic mining continued for many years, the ranching and logging industries supported the San Juans' economy until the 1960s. Since that time, tourism, spurred by the region's beautiful scenery, varied attractions, and resort development, has become the most important industry in the San Juans. A new boom has taken place in recent years, with the region's high quality of life attracting many new residents. Because of this, skyrocketing property values and dramatic growth are now among the San Juans' greatest threats.

HOW TO USE THIS GUIDE

Combining hiking, mountain biking, and backcountry skiing into one book, *San Juan Adventure Guide* is probably a little different than other guides you may have previously read. The format is based upon a pair of assumptions: The first is that most people enjoy dabbling in a number of different sports, such as devoted hikers who spend much of the winter on snowshoes, or rabid backcountry skiers who turn to mountain biking when the snow melts. The second is that there are few people who spend anytime hiking, biking, or skiing in the San Juans who are not eager to return again and again throughout the year.

Deciding which routes to include and which to leave out was one of the most difficult aspects of creating this book. In doing so, my main goal was to highlight trails that offer a broad range of experiences and scenery in all corners of this diverse region. You will find easy bike rides on country roads and wild single-track rides in remote drainages; short hikes easily completed in a morning and weeklong wilderness expeditions; and gentle valleys perfect for ski touring and steep terrain that is considered some of Colorado's best telemarking.

Each of the descriptions in this guide includes two components: a section of "vital statistics," and a detailed trail narrative. The vital statistics include:

- *Distance:* The mileage for each activity. In some instances, the mileage has been generalized, though the distances should be accurate to within 0.25 mile.
- *Elevation Range:* The high and low elevations of the activity, which are a tool for determining potential weather and access problems. For example, the higher the elevation, the greater the likelihood that there will be summer snowfields and gusty winter winds.
- *Total Elevation Gain:* The amount of elevation to be gained, with out-and-back totals included for activities described as round-trip adventures. This information is critical when you determine the fitness level required of a given activity and compare it to your level of skill and stamina.

❧ *Trail Conditions:* An overview of the normal conditions that can be expected on a given trail or route. This includes its relative steepness; the condition of the tread (rocky, muddy, smooth, etc.); and whether there are streams to ford, snowfields to cross, or particularly difficult terrain features to navigate. This also includes information pertaining to potential weather hazards and difficult route-finding situations.

❧ *Avalanche Hazard (skiing only):* This describes the overall potential that a given tour has in being exposed to avalanche-prone terrain. A hazard rating of *None* means that there is no avalanche-prone terrain found on that route. *Low* means that there are few areas of hazard, each of which is avoidable with careful route selection. *Moderate* means that there are numerous areas of hazard, some of which may be unavoidable. *High* means that there is significant hazard over large portions of the tour, and that most of these areas are unavoidable. These ratings only take into account the type of terrain, not the actual snow conditions on a given day. If the snowpack is unstable, even a tour with a moderate hazard rating can be extremely dangerous to do.

❧ *Skill Level (biking and skiing only):* This pertains to the relative experience *(novice, intermediate, advanced)* required of the adventurer in order to have a safe and enjoyable time on a given trail. This is subjective, as skill level sometimes relates to bravery as much as experience. This rating does *not* reflect the overall difficulty of a particular activity. There are numerous instances of bike rides and ski tours that are long and steep but that do not require well-honed skills.

❧ *Season:* A general range of months in which the trails or routes are accessible (i.e., snow-free for hikes and bike rides, sufficient snowpack for ski tours). Because of the highly irregular weather patterns that the San Juans experience from year to year, it is best to check locally before setting your heart upon a certain adventure.

❧ *United States Geological Survey (USGS) Maps:* Lists the specific maps that you should carry. Most descriptions will list the 7.5-minute quadrangles that cover the trail, though the USGS County Topographic series is more appropriate for some bike rides.

❧ *Administration:* Identifies either the U.S. Forest Service ranger district or Bureau of Land Management (BLM) resource area responsible for the route. Phone numbers are listed in the Resources and Information section.

☙ *Trailhead Information:* Includes concise directions from an easy-to-locate point, such as a major intersection or town. *Trailheads* refer to specifically signed and constructed parking facilities; *Access* refers to a specific but otherwise unmarked starting point. An alternate trailhead is supplied for those with two-wheel-drive vehicles when four-wheel-drive access is required. Note that many roads remain icy or snowpacked throughout much of the winter and thus may require snow tires or chains for safe travel.

HAZARDS AND PRECAUTIONS

The key to safe outdoor travel is preparation. Knowing how to handle yourself when difficult situations arise is part of the spirit of adventure, and only through familiarization with potential hazards can you ensure a safe and comfortable experience. But a word of caution: No guidebook can completely describe the potential hazards of the outdoor world. Ultimately, the actions you take and the decisions you make are your responsibility alone, and accepting the consequences is part of assuming the inherent risk when hiking, biking, skiing, or enjoying any other outdoor activity. Remember: The mountains show no mercy.

The Mountain Environment

In general, the ambient air temperature of a mountain environment decreases by three degrees Fahrenheit for every thousand feet of elevation gained, which means that staying warm is critical to staying safe. The lofty San Juans often experience arctic conditions even though they are at a temperate latitude. Once you are above treeline, you'll find that even the warmest summer days rarely top 60°F, and strong winds are common. Because of this, *hypothermia* is perhaps the most common affliction suffered by outdoor recreationists. A lowering of the body's core temperature, hypothermia is greatly exacerbated by wind and wetness. Ironically, it is most likely to occur during summer storms, at temperatures between 30°F and 50°F, when you may be exposed to wet and windy conditions with inadequate apparel. Symptoms of hypothermia include exhaustion, uncontrolled shivering, slurred speech, memory lapses, and a stumbling gait. If these symptoms are observed, get the victim out of the weather, remove wet clothing, provide something warm to drink, and put him or her in a warm sleeping bag. Beware: Most hypothermia victims are unaware that they have a problem.

Altitude sickness is also a concern, especially if you are unaccustomed to the 8,000- to 14,000-foot elevations of the San Juans. It is definitely a good idea to take a day or two to acclimate yourself before undertaking any strenuous activity. Symptoms include lightheadedness, nausea, and loss of appetite, and the only effective treatment is descending to a lower elevation. Because altitude sickness can lead to more serious illnesses like pulmonary

Because altitude sickness can lead to more serious illnesses like pulmonary edema (a potentially fatal condition), it should not be taken lightly.

Your susceptibility to *sunburn* and *dehydration* increases at higher elevations, where the thinner atmosphere permits more intense ultraviolet radiation. Sunburn can occur in as little as fifteen minutes, particularly on sunny winter days when the snow serves as a giant reflector. Dehydration also occurs quickly, because of intense ultraviolet radiation and because persistent alpine winds wick moisture away from your body. Always carry and use sunscreen, sunglasses, and lip balm, and drink plenty of fluids.

Unfortunately, *giardia* is found in all San Juan surface water, even in the tiniest brooks at the highest elevations in the most remote wilderness. Giardia, which thrives in cold, clear waters that appear pristine, is a nasty little cyst that causes severe intestinal distress. Unless your water source is coming directly from the earth (and even then not on the ground, but from a cliff), you will need to treat your water before drinking it. Treatment methods include boiling the water for at least five minutes, chemically treating it with iodine or chlorine tablets, or using a pump filter.

Stream crossings and *steep snowfields* can both be dangerous. Many hikes are simply impossible until after the spring runoff season of late May though early July because of high stream flows. When you do attempt a stream crossing, be sure to avoid areas just above waterfalls or rapids so that you have a recovery area should you lose your footing. Use a stick for support and to probe for holes in the riverbed, and be sure to unbuckle and loosen pack straps so that shedding the extra weight is easy in case of a fall. As for snowfields, skirt them if a safe, nondestructive alternate route is easily located; otherwise, do not cross them unless you have an ice ax and know how to self-arrest.

Finally, be sure to avoid the many *abandoned mines* that are common in the San Juans. They are susceptible to cave-ins and can have pockets of "bad air." Many mine structures are on the verge of collapse, and their sites are often littered with rusty nails, sharp pieces of metal, and broken glass.

Filing a trip plan with a person not coming along with you will allow a rescue attempt to be initiated more quickly should you become lost or injured. If you do become lost, remember to stay in one place and let the searchers come to you. Don't rely on a cellular phone to get you out of trouble, as service is often spotty in this remote and rugged country. Also, consider purchasing a Colorado hiker's certificate or fishing license, both of which provide search-and-rescue insurance. While most Colorado search-and-rescue organizations do not usually charge for their services, rules for when charges are levied are not hard and fast. Should you require a more extensive rescue operation, you may be billed. The hiker's certificate insures you against that possibility and is a small price to pay for financial peace of mind.

Mountain Weather and Avalanches

More often than not, it is the fickleness of mountain weather that turns otherwise innocuous excursions into calamities. The San Juans, like most mountain environments, are renowned for their highly changeable weather, and outdoor recreationists must be prepared for a variety of conditions. Many warm summer days turn stormy in the afternoon, while winter days that start out sunny can easily become wracked with blizzards within a few hours. San Juan adventurers are strongly advised to always keep one eye to the sky.

Thunderstorms occur on the majority of summer afternoons in the San Juans. Though their pattern of development is very predictable, the speed at which they build often surprises the unwary. Most storms last less than a half hour; however, they can produce heavy rain and hail and are usually accompanied by gusty winds and frequent lightning. Temperatures often plummet during these storms (sometimes by as much as 20 degrees in one hour), making hypothermia a very real threat. Being caught above treeline during a thunderstorm can be very dangerous. If a storm approaches, make your way into a forested area as quickly as possible. If you cannot and you feel the signs of an imminent lightning strike (tingling skin and hair standing on end), crouch as low as possible with only the soles of your shoes touching the ground. Standing on a piece of foam padding may provide additional insulation from nearby strikes. In forested areas, look for shelter in a dense growth of small trees, and avoid isolated trees and lakeshores. The best prevention is to plan for the weather by starting early and returning below treeline by noon.

The secret to safe winter adventures in the San Juans is staying dry and being prepared for any weather possibility. It is critical that you do not allow yourself to become soaked by perspiration since you can become seriously chilled once it dries. Strong winds amplify the cold-weather hazard, as the air temperature does not have to be particularly low for dangerous conditions to develop. A sunny 20°F can feel like a frigid -15°F if a 25 mph breeze is blowing. Frostbite can occur anytime the air is below freezing, and when the air or wind-chill temperatures are below -25°F, flesh can freeze within one minute of exposure. The best bet is to dress so that you can add and remove layers of clothing as conditions warrant. Furthermore, always carry a full complement of winter gear, regardless of how warm and sunny it is at the trailhead.

Winter travel in much of the San Juans can be very dangerous if you are unfamiliar with avalanches and how to avoid them. In the simplest terms, there are four "ingredients" to an avalanche: a steep slope, snowcover, a weakness in the snowpack, and a trigger. Slopes that range from 25 to 50 degrees in pitch are where almost all slides occur, as little snow typically accumulates on steeper terrain. A weakness in the snowpack is created when weather conditions permit the snow-crystal structure on the surface of the snowpack to lose its cohesive bond. An avalanche is triggered when the added weight of additional snow—accumulated either by new snowfall or wind drifting—exceeds the weight-bearing capacity of the unstable layer. Human-triggered slides occur because either the added weight of the person exceeds that capacity or the act of tracking across the snowpack reduces its ability to support the existing snow.

The key to avoiding avalanches is knowing when and where they are likely to occur. Avoid steep terrain during and just after a snowstorm or strong wind event. Once on your skis, intelligent route selection is critical. Avoiding obvious avalanche terrain is your best bet, but if you must traverse a danger zone, you'll need to know how to analyze the snowpack for signs of weakness. Look for recent avalanche activity on a slope of similar steepness, elevation, and aspect, and listen for "creaking" and "whomping" in the snowpack—nature's way of telling you that things are not safe. If these clues are not evident, you'll need to be able to dig a snowpit and perform a shear test—skills best learned by completing an avalanche-safety seminar. Once you have determined that it is safe to proceed, traverse danger areas one person at a time in order to minimize the risk to the group—many accidents occur when one person triggers a slide onto another.

Should an avalanche catch you or someone in your party, it is critical that an immediate rescue be undertaken. Only 50 percent of people buried in an avalanche will survive a half hour beneath the snow, so there is usually no time to contact rescue professionals. You'll have to locate the victim and dig him or her out as quickly as possible. To do so effectively, each person in your party will need to have an avalanche beacon and a collapsible shovel. A beacon, which allows you to pinpoint a victim's location, typically costs between $200 and $300, but when viewed as life insurance proves to be extremely cheap. If you choose not to invest in the proper equipment needed when traveling through avalanche terrain, you are taking a huge risk.

Before heading into the mountains, contact the Colorado Avalanche Information Center (CAIC) either by phone or via the Internet (see Resources and Information). The CAIC issues detailed forecasts of mountain weather and avalanche conditions on a twice-daily basis from November through April. It uses a four-tiered rating system to describe the relative safety of backcountry travel and issues avalanche warnings when natural avalanche activity is likely. Using these forecasts, you should be able to determine if it's a good day to head into the hills.

Wildlife

Of all the things that can "get you" in the San Juans, wildlife is probably the least worrisome. Ticks are common in grassy meadows and dense vegetation below about 9,000 feet from late May through July. They often leap onto your body from a trailside blade of grass or overhanging leaf and crawl around until finding a suitable place to attach themselves—often the scalp, armpits, or groin. If traveling in such areas, wear long pants with your socks rolled over the cuffs and a long-sleeved shirt. Check yourself regularly for ticks and remove any that you find. If one has already attached itself, use tweezers to remove the entire body in order to avoid infection.

Black bears and mountain lions are relatively common in the San Juans, though both are extremely wary of human contact and will flee if given the opportunity. It is important to bear-proof your camp to keep bruins from becoming habituated to people and people food. Always keep a clean camp and store both food and garbage in a vehicle or hung from a high branch far from reach. *Never* keep food in your tent. It is also a good idea to cook well away from your tent.

Two last critters to look out for are rattlesnakes and marmots. Rattlesnakes are sometimes seen in the dry foothills surrounding the range (rarely above 8,000 feet), but they too are not aggressive and will almost always flee. The marmot, an alpine rodent, can present a threat to your gear, as they sometimes gnaw on things with a salty residue, such as leather boots and sweaty pack straps. This is usually only a problem at popular destinations where marmots are accustomed to people. If you keep such items inaccessible, you should have no problem with them.

Mountain Driving

Many San Juan roads are rocky, steep, and narrow, and many require a high-clearance, four-wheel-drive vehicle. Colorado law stipulates that uphill traffic has the right-of-way; however, if there is a convenient pullout nearby, stop and let any oncoming traffic pass, regardless of your direction of travel. Don't be afraid to back up, if necessary, to find such a pullout. During winter, nearly all back roads are closed, and even the major highways are often restricted to vehicles with chains or snow tires, especially over the passes. If you are visiting the region between October and April, be sure you have such equipment in your vehicle. The Silverton Chamber of Commerce updates road conditions on four-wheel-drive routes throughout the area, and the Colorado Department of Transportation maintains an excellent road-conditions hot line and Web site (see Resources and Information).

The Ten Essentials

There are ten essential items that should always be carried by each person traveling in the backcountry, whether on foot, bike, or skis. Most of the time, these items will go untouched in your pack, but should you ever need them, they can be literal lifesavers:

- *Extra clothing.* Be prepared for any weather possibility, especially windy, wet conditions.
- *Food and water.* You never know when you'll have to spend an extra night outdoors, so pack extra high-energy foods that can sustain you in an emergency.
- *First-aid kit.* Make sure your first-aid kit is fully stocked and in good condition.
- *Knife.*
- *Sunglasses and sunscreen.*

- *Fire starter.* Includes waterproof matches, a striker, a lighter, and a candle.
- *Flashlight with extra batteries.* The mini headlamps now available are light, inexpensive, and convenient.
- *Signaling device.* A mirror and a whistle. Three short blasts of the whistle signals that assistance is needed.
- *Maps.* USGS 7.5-minute quadrangles are, at a scale of 1:24,000, the most detailed maps available. Unfortunately, some of the San Juan quads are more than forty years old and have outdated trail and road information. A county topographic series produced by the USGS at a scale of 1:50,000 is also useful, but some sheets are also rather outdated. USGS maps are available at sporting-goods stores throughout the region or can be ordered directly from the USGS by calling (800) HELP-MAP. Trails Illustrated also produces a set of four topographic maps that cover most of the region. These are great for travel planning, but their 1:66,667 scale is less detailed than the USGS quads.
- *Compass.* Handheld Global Positioning System (GPS) receivers are increasingly popular and can be very helpful in navigation; however, they do not eliminate the need to carry a map and compass.

Mountain bikers should add a few other essential items: a repair kit including a chain tool, tire irons, a spare tube, a patch kit, and an assortment of wrenches. Never ride without a helmet. Backcountry skiers who plan on venturing into avalanche terrain should always carry collapsible shovels and avalanche beacons and know how to use them.

TREAD LIGHTLY

Within the last few decades, the explosion of outdoor recreation's popularity combined with the shrinkage of our available wilderness has created the situation we have today: Our wilderness is being "loved to death." The time has come for everyone—whether you are a wilderness backpacker, a casual mountain biker, or a backcountry skier—to play an active role in minimizing the present impact while working to repair the damage already done. By following the guidelines suggested below, you can "leave no trace" of your backcountry travels. Consider this a challenge as critical to the success of your adventure as summiting the peak, surviving the ride, or carving the perfect turns.

Foot Travel

- When traveling on developed trails, resist the urge to walk two abreast, cut switchbacks, and skirt obstacles, all of which increase erosion, damage delicate plants, and create unsightly braided paths. This is very important on soggy paths; if you are unwilling to slog through mud or across snowfields, turn back and look for a drier hike. Do your best to climb over downed logs instead of trampling around them.

- When traveling cross-country, it is critical that you walk on bare ground, rocks, or logs as much as possible in order to minimize the trampling of vegetation. If traveling with a group, be sure to spread out so that plants that do get stepped upon are not subjected to repeated stomping. Cross-country travel is not advised in marshy and muddy areas, which are easily damaged. If you happen to be climbing a mountain, avoid the destructive practice of "skiing the scree"—sliding down loose gravel slopes, which significantly increases erosion and damages delicate plants.

- If you come across paths that are just forming, be sure to stay off of them so that they do not become unofficial (and incorrectly engineered) trails. In fact, you might even spread downed logs, brush, and rocks across them in order to discourage others from using these ersatz trails.

- Pack out everything that you bring into the backcountry, including all trash, toilet paper, and food scraps. Make a habit of carrying a trash bag and collecting litter left behind by less considerate people.
- When passing other trail users, step off the trail in a single spot— preferably at a bare area or a large rock. Walking alongside the trail to pass causes significant and long-lasting damage to adjacent vegetation.
- Walking quietly is one of the easiest ways to preserve a sense of solitude, even in popular areas—it's surprising how far shouts and whistles can carry in otherwise silent places.
- Travel in small groups; four to six people is considered the maximum for low-impact travel.
- Leave all natural features as you have found them. It is neither acceptable to pick flowers nor to carve names in trees and on rocks. All archaeological artifacts—including old mining equipment—is protected by law and should be left in place. While rockhounding on mine dumps and in other impacted areas is fine, do not dig into pristine ground.

Bike Travel

- Ride only on established roads and trails, never cross-country. Don't cut switchbacks, skirt obstacles, or ride to the side of a trail or road.
- While all public roads are open to bikers, many trails are not. It is the biker's responsibility to find out the status of a given trail *before* riding it. Biking in designated wilderness or wilderness-study areas is strictly prohibited.
- Always yield the right-of-way to other trail users. Never speed recklessly down a trail, and always anticipate that someone will be around the next bend. When passing horseback riders, dismount to avoid spooking the animals. Never ride off-trail to pass other parties.
- Though it may look "cool," splashing through mud can cause long-lasting ruts that can damage trails and increase erosion of adjacent slopes. When approaching large mud-bogs or marshy areas, dismount from your bike and carry it over the obstacle. If the trail is consistently muddy, turn back and ride elsewhere until it has had a chance to dry out. Stick to road rides during the spring and early summer melting season, as well as during rainy periods.

❧ Avoid disturbing wildlife and livestock. Because you can quietly and quickly traverse large areas, it is very common to surprise animals as you ride. Should you have such an encounter, stop at a distance sufficient to allow the animal an escape route and time to retreat without panicking.

Camping Out

❧ Where available, camp in previously impacted sites where considerate campers will cause little additional damage. In pristine areas, choose a campsite that will minimize impacts on the land, such as naturally barren areas that are at least 200 feet from water sources and trails. With pristine campsites, it is important to move camp each night so that trampled vegetation can repair itself and social trails have no time to develop. Avoid camping where discernible sites are just beginning to be established. Heed camping prohibitions, which are often in place near wilderness lakes. Never alter your campsite by trenching, cutting trees, or building "camp furniture."

❧ Try to blend in with the landscape. Staying within the aforementioned parameters, look for sites well away from trails and streams. Hide your camp behind vegetation or topographic features so that others' sense of solitude remains preserved. Avoid situating your camp in or near places that naturally draw people: viewpoints, lakeshores, waterfalls, and meadows.

❧ Cook well away from camp, using rocky or otherwise barren areas as kitchen sites. Preprocess your food supplies to remove excess packaging before your trip, and pack out all food scraps and garbage when you leave.

❧ Keep your food out of the reach of bears and rodents. Hang your food, garbage, and cooking equipment from a sturdy branch at least 10 feet above the ground, 2 feet below the branch, and as far out from the tree trunk as possible.

❧ Never clean dishes or wash with soap directly in a water source. Carry water to a site at least 200 feet away, and avoid using soap (even biodegradable soap) when possible. Strain gray water to remove larger food particles, which should then be carried out with your trash.

❧ Properly dispose of human waste by burying it in a cathole 6 to 8 inches deep, which should be located at least 200 feet from water sources, trails, and potential campsites. When finished, cover the hole with the displaced soil as well as rocks and branches. If you are camping in the same site for multiple nights, be sure to disperse your cathole locations. Urine need not be buried but should also be discarded at least 200 feet from water sources, trails, and camps. Toilet paper should be packed out with other garbage. The threat of fire precludes burning the paper, and buried paper is often unearthed by wildlife. Even better, try to find a natural substitute, such as leaves or stones.

❧ Because they heighten the potential for wildfires, scar the earth, and result in the removal of all deadfall from popular camping areas, campfires have become increasingly inappropriate in backcountry areas. Instead, use backpacking stoves when possible. If you must have a fire, use only existing fire rings or a portable fire pan in an appropriate location, such as a large area of exposed bedrock or a barren stream channel. Use only dead *and* downed wood for fuel.

In a classic San Juan autumn scene, Mt. Sneffels rises above a forest of golden aspen.

HIKING AND BACKPACKING

With a level of irreverence that only Edward Abbey himself could muster, the great wilderness sage wrote the credo by which all hikers live:

> *In the first place you can't see anything from a car; you've got to get out of the goddamned contraption and walk, better yet crawl, on hands and knees . . . When traces of blood begin to mark your trail you'll see something, maybe.*

NEEDLE MOUNTAINS CIRCUIT

DISTANCE: 35.9 miles one-way

ELEVATION RANGE: 8,200 to 12,850 feet

TOTAL ELEVATION GAIN: 8,300 feet

TRAIL CONDITIONS: Highly varied, with everything from well-constructed trail to faint footpaths; sustained, steep ascents and descents; unbridged stream crossings; muddy tread at times; potential for snowfields well into July. This journey is for fit, experienced backpackers only.

SEASON: July through September

USGS MAPS: Snowdon Peak (1972); Storm King Peak (1975); Columbine Pass (1975); Mountain View Crest (1973)

ADMINISTRATION: San Juan NF; Columbine RD; Rio Grande NF; Divide RD

TRAILHEAD: Both the Needle Creek and Elk Park Trailheads are accessible only via the Durango & Silverton Narrow Gauge Railroad or on foot. See the following description for details.

The spectacular beauty of the San Juans is no longer a secret. In greater numbers each and every year, people come by bus, car, airplane, and train to see for themselves the sculpted peaks, crashing waterfalls, and magnificent meadows of the region. Yet, as will always be the case, it is the relative few who explore on their own two feet that come away with the greatest appreciation for what they have seen. By no other mode of transportation, and at no other speed, can you intimately experience all that the San Juans have to offer.

Needle Mountains Circuit

Sprawling across more than a half million acres, the Weminuche Wilderness (by far Colorado's largest designated wilderness) ensures that the heart of the San Juans will be forever sheltered from the effects of civilization. Prized by ecologists and wilderness enthusiasts alike, the Weminuche is not only an area of astounding beauty, but is one of the southern Rockies's few primitive islands where the potential for complete biodiversity remains. It is a place where even the great—and presently extirpated—predators of the mountain ecosystems, wolves and grizzly bears, would have room to thrive should their reintroduction ever become a reality. Though the wilderness can be satisfactorily sampled by enjoying one of the many day hikes that penetrate its periphery, it takes a much longer and thorough exploration to truly experience all that the Weminuche has to offer. A weeklong circuit of the Needle Mountains highlights much of what makes the Weminuche unique, including some of the most awe-inspiring scenery to be found anywhere in the Rockies.

The morning light playing across the tundra at the foot of Hunchback Pass is reminiscent of Alaska.

The steep and sharply carved peaks of the Needles and the adjacent Grenadier Range are among the most striking in Colorado. Rising above deep valleys, these granitic horns tower as much as a vertical half mile above the surrounding alpine meadows and lakes that dot their flanks. Their sculpted masses show the quintessential effects of glacial geology: spirelike summits, deep cirques, ragged arêtes, and hanging valleys. Each valley is blanketed in coniferous forests, drained by crystalline streams and waterfalls, and is home to a wide range of wildlife, including elk, deer, black bear, mountain goat, and bighorn sheep. The Needle Mountains Circuit allows the close examination of this wilderness, as well as the personal introspection possible only by traveling one step at a time.

One of the paradoxes of the Weminuche is that this most wild of wildernesses is also one of the most popular—and threatened. Nowhere else is this so apparent as on the trails traversed by this circuit. Glowing descriptions such as those in the previous paragraphs have drawn backpackers from around the world, making this journey one of the "classics" often mentioned in books and magazine articles about Rocky Mountain hiking. Secondly, the presence of three 14,000-foot peaks (Eolus, Sunlight, and Windom) at the heart of the Needles has made this area extremely popular with weekend peak-baggers, while dozens of other summits have become well known to mountaineers attracted to the steep, smooth, stable granite found here. Furthermore, the unique attraction of taking a historic steam locomotive deep into a mountainous realm where, once debarked, wilderness surrounds you for many miles, is irresistible to many. The result is twofold: First, true wilderness solitude is almost impossible to find on much of this route, and second, environmental degradation is becoming an extremely serious concern. Campfires have already been completely banned from the Needle Creek drainage, and while a permit system has yet to be established, visitation that can amount to a hundred campers per night just in Chicago Basin during the busiest summer weekends could result in the eventual installation of some sort of regulatory program. It is imperative that you practice "leave no trace" travel and camping skills while exploring the Needles and follow all of the regulations created to keep this wilderness wild.

As with any multiday wilderness journey, there are significant physical and mental challenges to be overcome while hiking the circuit. The great distance, as well as two separate ascents of nearly 4,000 feet, will overwhelm the unprepared. Compounding the matter are those hazards presented by Mother Nature herself: raging, unbridged streams; exposure to poor weather; lingering snowfields; and high altitude. Because this country is so far removed from roads and communications, help can be a long time coming should an emergency arise. Self-sufficiency is an absolute requirement. If you are uncertain about your abilities, be conservative. Try a simple overnight trip from either of the two railroad-accessed trailheads, or test yourself on a longer journey closer to civilization.

They say that "getting there is half the fun," something that is especially true when accessing the trailheads for this circuit. The only "vehicle" access to either the Needleton Trailhead or the Elk Park Trailhead is via the Durango & Silverton Narrow Gauge Railroad (D&SNGRR), which offers a historic rail journey that is regarded as one of Colorado's prime attractions. Of course, rail transportation creates a special set of logistical issues, including making reservations, paying for tickets, and meeting the railroad's schedule. For information and reservations, contact the railroad at (970) 247-2733 or write to D&SNGRR, 479 Main Avenue, Durango, CO 81301. As a general rule, you will need to make reservations at least a month or two in advance. Typically, the railroad schedules two stops at each trailhead per day: a late morning arrival en route to Silverton from Durango and a mid-afternoon stop on the return trip. Because of this schedule, you will not have "full" hiking days on either end of your journey, so plan accordingly. Should you prefer to avoid the train ride, it is possible to access both trailheads via trails intersecting US 550. Needleton can be reached via the 11-mile Purgatory Trail (elevation loss of 1,300 feet with a gain of 500 feet), while Elk Park is accessible via the 4-mile Molas Trail (elevation loss of 1,700 feet).

Though the circuit can be hiked in either direction with equal reward, a start at Elk Park is recommended not only because it will save you about 700 feet of elevation gain, but also because the train back to Durango arrives at Needleton roughly an hour later than at Elk Park each afternoon, making the final day's hike a bit less harried. From the whistle-stop on the Animas River's bank, the trail is found at the end of a short spur track, near a large signboard. Follow the trail up a short climb until it intersects the path accessed by the Molas Trail. Bear right, passing a trailhead register, and enter the wilderness. The trail climbs moderately up the Elk Creek drainage, occasionally near to, and at other times high above, the boisterous stream. About 2 miles up the trail, the ascent steepens considerably and continues an unrelenting climb until mile 3.0, where it levels upon reaching a pair of lovely beaver ponds. Gazing up the Vestal Creek drainage, one enjoys an outstanding view of the Grenadiers, including the spires of Arrow and Vestal Peaks. An unmaintained climber's path provides access into this spectacular valley, offering the first of many daylong diversions on this circuit. After climbing through a rockslide area, the trail enters a broad meadow at about mile 4.0. Because of the short day necessitated by the train's schedule, most people camp in this vicinity, where numerous sites may be located. Be sure to select a previously impacted site.

The trail remains gentle for the next mile, passing first through the open meadow, then dense subalpine timber before intersecting an unnamed stream, which until midsummer will probably require wading. The valley soon narrows, and the following mile adds colorful wildflowers and several waterfalls to the forest scenery. At mile 6.0, the trail steepens considerably, ascending 1,500 feet within the next 1.5 miles. Impressive vistas of the surrounding peaks, expansive wildflower gardens, and a handful of cataracts make this tiring stretch surprisingly enjoyable. The trail crosses the eversmaller Elk Creek twice within this ascent, though neither ford is challenging, usually. After tracing an old fault through a narrow gap, the ascent eases as the trail reaches timberline, 7.5 miles from the Animas River. Be prepared for snowfields, which often remain in the canyon through mid-July.

Though less dramatic than the cliff-bound peaks guarding the canyon below, the rolling green ridge behind this gentle basin carries the Continental Divide. The trail traverses beautiful meadows as it approaches, then begins its switchback ascent toward the crest of this ridge. If time and weather allow, wander these verdant slopes a bit and enjoy a brief respite from a destination-oriented journey. There are several alpine tarns in the area, and the wildflower display is among the San Juans' finest. The Elk Creek Trail is a segment of the Denver-to-Durango Colorado Trail, a 470-mile walk that many feel reaches its scenic climax right here. Reconstruction has resulted in an easily climbed path onto the 12,700-foot crest of the Divide, which exceeds scenic expectations no matter how high they may be set.

A 0.25-mile walk south, along the crest of the Divide, leads to a beautiful overlook of Eldorado Lake and the beginning of a steep but scenic descent to Kite Lake, which sits about 800 feet below the ridge at the headwaters of Bear Creek (a Rio Grande tributary). Though this is the route of both the Colorado Trail (CT) and the Continental Divide Trail (CDT), an increasingly popular alternate route continues along the crest of the Divide, rising up and over the summit of 13,136-foot Hunchback Mountain before intersecting the primary trail at the crest of Hunchback Pass. This more difficult option requires a bit of scrambling; however, the summit offers some of the most superb vistas found along the circuit. If you prefer the Kite Lake route, you'll briefly exit the wilderness and even follow a very rough four-wheel-drive road for 0.5 mile below the lake. There are several old mines in the area, but despite the presence of the road, usually very few people. The trail to Hunchback Pass diverges from the four-wheel-drive road at a signed trailhead before ascending 800 feet in just under a mile to recross the Continental Divide.

At Hunchback Pass, the trail reenters the Weminuche, descending through a rugged, alpine gulch before intersecting Nebo Creek just below treeline, 1.5 miles below the pass. The trail then turns west, making a timbered descent alongside Nebo Creek before bearing southward and into the

Vallecito Creek valley. Three miles below Hunchback Pass, the trail passes beneath the mouth of Stormy Gulch and skirts the first of a series of meadows to be enjoyed on the walk ahead. A rough path leads up Stormy Gulch and on to cliff-sheltered Trinity Lake, providing another potential daylong diversion.

The circuit continues down the Vallecito Creek valley, descending only 1,300 feet in the next 7 miles to reach the mouth of Johnson Creek. There are a number of tributary streams to be forded, including Rock Creek, which is 1.5 miles below Stormy Gulch (the Rock Creek Trail ascends this valley); and Roell Creek, which is about 2.5 miles farther. Despite its depiction on the USGS map, the trail never crosses Vallecito Creek itself, though a pair of drainages leading into the heart of the Needles beckon adventurous hikers across the stream and up their rugged corridors. Both Leviathan and Sunlight Creeks have faint usage paths that ascend to spectacular, barren headwaters basins, where alpine lakes lie tucked beneath towering spires of granite. Hikers who are content to stay with the Vallecito Creek Trail, however, will enjoy plenty of gorgeous scenery as well. Good camping sites are plentiful.

At the mouth of Johnson Creek, the circuit turns westward onto the Johnson Creek Trail, which immediately crosses Vallecito Creek on a sturdy bridge and begins a moderate to steep ascent of Columbine Pass, 6.25 miles away. Wading Johnson Creek will be necessary 0.5 mile beyond the Vallecito Creek bridge, with a possible wade of Grizzly Creek 0.75 mile beyond that. The Johnson Creek drainage is quite spectacular, especially once timberline is reached some 4.25 miles up the valley. The steep, switchback climb to this point is rewarded with views of Organ and Amherst Mountains as well as a multitude of wildflowers. Johnson Creek's best camping is in this area.

After an enjoyable stretch of relatively level walking, the trail steepens once again as it climbs towards Columbine Lake, just 0.25 mile below the pass. A pair of footpaths diverge from the main trail just above the lake. The southbound route traverses beneath Bullion Mountain to attain the narrow gap of Trimble Pass, 1.6 miles away, while the northbound path leads a mile to Hazel Lake, which is set at the foot of Jupiter Mountain and Grizzly Peak. Columbine Pass (12,700 feet) itself offers an outstanding panorama of the peaks encircling both Johnson Creek and Chicago Basin and is one of the highlights of the circuit.

Chicago Basin is perhaps the most popular backpacking destination in the San Juans, and from this point forward, any amount of solitude is very difficult to find. The trail descends about 1,500 feet in 2 miles to reach the floor of the basin, with two potential routes diverging about halfway down. The left branch is the express route to the lower end of the basin, while the right branch makes a broader loop of the basin and provides access to various climbing routes, which lead to the ring of 14,000-foot peaks that make the area so popular. Chicago Basin truly requires some extra time for exploration. There are several old mines and a handful of waterfalls to enjoy, while the tarns of Twin Lakes Basin are perfect for quiet contemplation (and home to some truly magnificent light at the edges of the day). Many hikers will be unable to resist the urge to climb one or more of the high peaks found here, including the "14'ers": Mount Eolus, Sunlight Peak, and Windom Peak. None of these peaks are technical ascents; however, each have their difficulties. Consult one of the numerous climbing guides to Colorado's 14'ers for detailed route information. Please remember that camping in Twin Lakes Basin, as well as campfires anywhere in the Needle Creek drainage, are prohibited at all times.

The whistle-stop at Needleton is on the bank of the Animas River, about 5 miles below the lower end of Chicago Basin. The descent is continuous, with several stretches of steep trail. The bridge at New York Creek, about 2 timbered miles down the trail, is a good place to stop and rest. From here, it is another 2 miles to the mouth of Needle Creek, the wilderness boundary, and the junction of the Purgatory Trail. Keep right, and enjoy a level mile of walking to reach the Animas River, which is crossed on a long suspension bridge. The train stops on the west bank of the river—consult the conductor on your inbound journey for instructions on how to flag the outbound train.

Crater Lake

Tucked beneath the rugged cliffs of North Twilight Peak, Crater Lake is a pretty alpine pool whose grassy shores and cloak of lush, subalpine forest seemingly contradict its dramatic setting. Further at odds with its location at the base of a massive rock face, the trail leading to the lake traverses gently rolling benches, with only short stretches that could be called steep. The length of the trail lends itself to an invigorating but not exhausting day hike, while the bountiful number of nice campsites near the lake invite backpackers seeking a longer stay. Indeed, the opportunity to watch the alpenglow of a clear summer morning paint the towering walls above the lake in shades of pink, orange, and gold makes an overnight excursion to this Weminuche Wilderness setting especially worthwhile.

The hike begins from the recently renovated trailhead facilities at Andrews Lake. Follow the paved path to the south side of the lake, then pick up the trail continuing south from this point. The recently rerouted tread climbs in a series of long switchbacks to the top of a ridge 500 feet above and 1 mile from the lake. The open nature of the forest on this ridge and in much of the Molas Pass area is due to a massive fire that burned the area in 1879. The harsh weather at this altitude has stunted regeneration of the forest, and even the reforestation efforts of the Forest Service have met with only limited success. The resultant meadows display a beautiful variety of wildflowers and allow views to the high peaks that surround the area.

CRATER LAKE

DISTANCE: 11 miles round-trip

ELEVATION RANGE: 10,750 to 11,700 feet

TOTAL ELEVATION GAIN: 1,900 feet

TRAIL CONDITIONS: Good tread; gentle to moderate grades; muddy during early summer

SEASON: July until mid-October

USGS MAP: Snowdon Peak (1972)

ADMINISTRATION: San Juan NF; Columbine RD

TRAILHEAD: Drive on US 550 for 7 miles south from Silverton, or for 43 miles north from Durango to a road signed ANDREWS LAKE, just south of the summit of Molas Pass. Drive a short distance on this road, following signs to hikers' trailhead.

The trail now begins a gentle descent for about 0.75 mile, passing through a set of marshy meadows before commencing on a somewhat steep climb that lasts another 0.5 mile. There are several interesting limestone outcroppings en route as well as good views across the upper headwaters of Lime Creek. As the trail begins to lose elevation once again, it drops into a shady forest that features an assortment of subalpine wildflowers. After crossing Three Lakes Creek, the trail levels off and returns to a more open environment.

Now, 3 miles from Andrews Lake, the trail begins climbing once again and will continue to do so until reaching Crater Lake, 2.25 miles distant. The grade is rarely steep anywhere in these final miles, and the steady alternation of cool forest and blossom-filled meadows makes for very scenic hiking. The meadows often permit striking vistas of distant peaks, including the prominent horn of Engineer Mountain to the west and the beautiful La Plata Range peaks farther southwest. Snow may linger in forested areas into July, and muddy sections are likely until late in the summer. As you near the lake, the imposing cliffs of North Twilight Peak increasingly dwarf the surrounding landscape.

Crater Lake sits in a small bowl, separated from the walls of North Twilight by a small cloak of forest that encircles the south shore. Small meadows abut the north and west shores of the lake, while to the east, a grassy slope climbs to a broad saddle. During calm weather, the lake perfectly mirrors the rocky cliffs and scattered trees that tower high above, with the only imperfections being those caused by trout biting at the often-abundant insect population. The best camping sites are found on the small benches on the lake's north and west sides. Try to make camp in existing sites, thus limiting the drainage to fragile ground. If time and energy allow, climb the saddle east of the lake. Less than 200 feet of climbing will reward you with awe-inspiring views across the deep chasm of the Animas River into the castellated heart of the Needles Range. Listen carefully, and you may hear the distant whistle of the Durango & Silverton Railroad, whose tracks hug the river bank more than 3,000 feet below.

**COLORADO
TRAIL–MOLAS
HIGHLANDS**

To Lime Creek
Distance: 9 miles round-trip
Elevation Range: 10,900 to 11,600 feet
Total Elevation Gain: 1,000 feet
Trail Conditions: Good tread; gentle to moderate grades; occasionally muddy; no shelter from potentially poor weather
Season: July through September
USGS Maps: Snowdon Peak (1972); Silverton (1955); Ophir (1955). (Note: These maps often do not accurately depict the trail.)

Colorado Trail–Molas Highlands

For almost 470 beautiful miles, the Denver-to-Durango Colorado Trail (CT) traverses some of the state's most impressive mountain scenery, earning a reputation as one of the best long-distance trails in the country. People fortunate enough to experience the entire trail typically agree that the most consistently spectacular of these miles are found in the San Juans, with the section west of Molas

Pass being among the most exquisite. Almost entirely above treeline, this portion of the CT features an endless panorama of ragged peaks, acres upon acres of wildflower meadows, glassy tarns, and ribbonlike waterfalls. If you have only a single day in which to a glimpse the CT's splendor, a simple out-and-back journey through this alpine Valhalla takes you to Lime Creek. If you are able to devote two days, combining an 8-mile segment of the CT with the Engineer Mountain Trail can make an outstanding one-way trip. A quick and simple car-shuttle arrangement will need to be made between the backpack's two trailheads.

Unfortunately, the dated USGS maps that cover this area do not accurately depict the trails used on either the hike or the backpack. The Colorado Trail Map series produced by the Colorado Trail Foundation is a good source; however, it does not depict the Engineer Mountain Trail. The Trails Illustrated *Weminuche Wilderness* map has the same problem. In practical terms, this trail is easily followed, as the only faint portions of tread occur where the correct route is topographically obvious. However, if you require a map to guide you every step of the way, beware.

Whether hiking only to Lime Creek or all the way to Engineer Mountain, you should begin your journey from the aforementioned

ADMINISTRATION: San Juan NF; Columbine RD

TO ENGINEER MOUNTAIN

DISTANCE: Approximately 15 miles one-way

ELEVATION RANGE: 10,700 to 12,100 feet

TOTAL ELEVATION GAIN: 2,300 feet

TRAIL CONDITIONS: Generally good trail, though faint in a few places; gentle to moderate grades, except a few short, steep descents; muddy at times; long-term exposure to poor weather

SEASON: July through September

USGS MAPS: Snowdon Peak (1972); Silverton (1955); Ophir (1955); Engineer Mountain (1975). (Note: These maps often do not accurately depict the trail.)

ADMINISTRATION: San Juan NF; Columbine RD

LITTLE MOLAS LAKE ACCESS: From US 550, 0.4 mile north of the Molas Pass summit, turn onto a dirt road signed LITTLE MOLAS LAKE. Follow this road into an informal campground, bear right at mile 0.8, right again at mile 1.0 (down a short hill), and then immediately right once more. Proceed an additional 0.1 mile, until the Colorado Trail is visible bearing to the northwest (marked by a post with the CT symbol). Park in this area.

COAL BANK PASS TRAILHEAD: Drive US 550 to the summit of Coal Bank Pass, 7.4 miles south of Molas Pass. Turn onto a small dirt road at the pass summit and drive a short distance to the trailhead parking area.

❦ ❦ ❦

Little Molas Trailhead. The trail climbs gradually in a northwesterly heading, winding through open meadows and past a pair of brooks. After about a mile, the trail turns sharply back to the east and ascends gradually along a small, sloping bench. This turn can be easily missed since an old four-wheel-drive track continues ahead—look for a post with the CT emblem. The trail continues up this bench for another 0.5 mile, providing the first of many memorable mountain vistas. The lack of trees throughout this area (and much of the hike) is the result of a massive forest fire during the summer of 1879. Scorching almost the entire headwaters basin of Lime Creek (including its east, north, and west forks), this burn has yet to regenerate, despite the efforts of the Forest Service, which planted trees in the scraggly rows that remain evident even today. A number of burnt snags remain standing in the area, though the true legacy of the fire is the resulting wildflower gardens that blanket the rolling slopes.

The CT soon bears to the north and begins a long, gentle traverse across the head of Lime Creek's north fork. A divergent trail (visible where the CT turns north) drops straight back down to Little Molas Lake; however, it has been officially abandoned, and out-and-back hikers should use care to avoid it upon their return. The trail ahead continues its easy traverse until reaching a saddle dividing the headwaters of North Lime Creek from those of Bear Creek, about 3 miles into the hike. The variety and density of wildflowers are notable, while the grand panorama includes the La Plata Range, the West Needles, Engineer Mountain, and many of the peaks to the west of Silverton. The hornlike peaks that surround these rolling highlands are known geologically as *nunataks* and were all that stood above the vast icefields that covered much of the San Juans at the height of the Ice Age. The frozen sheet that once existed here was as thick as 1,000 feet and was many miles across in length. Some of the southern Rockies's greatest Ice Age glaciers flowed from this icefield, including the Animas Glacier, which descended more than 40 miles before terminating within the present-day city limits of Durango.

Beyond the saddle, the trail continues a fairly level traverse, passing pockets of subalpine forest interspersed by more flower-filled meadows. Several small creeks are crossed, with impressive cascades both above and below the trail, as well as a series of small tarns whose location a short distance below the trail makes a fine place to rest and picnic. Of geological interest in this area are the beautiful red sandstones of the Cutler Formation, which were deposited by streams draining the Ancestral Rockies some 250 million years ago. Hikers familiar with the red-rock country of the Colorado Plateau will recognize the Cutler Formation as the same rock that has been eroded into the sharp spires and brooding monoliths of Monument Valley.

The trail makes several short switchbacks before crossing Lime Creek about 4.5 miles from the trailhead. This lovely little basin, with its dark cliffs and rushing stream, is also a good place to rest, both for day-hikers returning to the trailhead and for backpackers continuing farther along the CT. The trail climbs steadily out of the Lime Creek drainage, then continues a more level traverse beneath a long, rugged cliff. Subalpine forest is more prevalent in this stretch, but a handful of avalanche gullies are traversed by the trail, and it is here that some of the richest flower displays are enjoyed. As the snow melts from the slopes above the trail through midsummer, small rivulets pour from the cliffs above, creating a lovely collection of veil-like cascades. The trail is in excellent condition thanks to regular maintenance by volunteers of the Colorado Trail Foundation. These volunteers devote anywhere from a single weekend to many weeks each season to keep the trail well marked and in good condition throughout its statewide traverse. Volunteering is a very rewarding experience; if you have time and energy to donate, contact the foundation at (303) 384-3729.

After descending slightly to cross West Lime Creek, the trail climbs more steeply, passes treeline and several alpine tarns, and arrives at a signed junction approximately 3.5 miles beyond Lime Creek. Our route turns off the CT here, climbing gently on the left-forking trail to cross a broad, willow-dotted saddle. This saddle is the scenic climax of the journey, with a 360-degree panorama of rock- and tundra-bound peaks, including high summits of Rolling Mountain and the Twin Sisters to the north and the emerald-and rust-colored bulk of Jura Knob to the south. A large tarn is located just above the trail junction, while wildflowers are profuse in the pockets between the willows. Weather permitting, this is an ideal place to set up camp.

The Engineer Mountain Trail continues beyond the saddle, dropping gently into the lonely, beautiful basin at the head of Engine Creek. The basin is quickly exited, and the trail steepens considerably as it switchbacks down a series of ramps created by the sedimentary rock strata in the area. Engine Creek forms several nice cascades as it drops off the exposed rock ledges at the edge of these ramps. The trail levels briefly at treeline, reaching a junction with the faint White Creek Trail about 1.5 miles from the CT.

Avoid this right fork and continue ahead to commence an ascent—steep at times—onto the slopes below Jura Knob's south ridge. Reaching treeline, the trail turns southward and begins a gentler traverse below the ridge, passing through yet more wildflower gardens and offering views of the deep Cascade Creek valley and the rugged peaks to its west.

The trail crests a small ridge about a mile beyond the White Creek Trail, and as you continue southward, you'll be confronted by a splendid view of Engineer Mountain's steep north face as well as the rock glacier at its foot. Another 0.5 mile of up-and-down hiking brings you to the junction of the Coal Creek Trail. Continue to the right, pass a marshy saddle, and climb slightly into the colorful flower fields at the foot of Engineer Mountain, whose layer-cake summit is especially distinctive. Enjoy the easy stroll through this heavenly place, reaching the junction of the Pass Creek Trail some 4 miles from the CT.

Turn down the Pass Creek Trail and begin a steady descent to the trailhead at Coal Bank Pass. The first mile traverses more beautiful alpine meadows before dropping below treeline, where the final 2 miles of the hike wind through fragrant forest. The trail is easy to follow, though it can be brutally muddy if it has been rainy. The sound of traffic and a final flower-filled avalanche path herald arrival at the trailhead and the end of a fantastic walk.

Arrastra Basin

In the heart of the "Silvery San Juan" there remains a veritable museum preserving memories of the bygone mining boom: Arrastra Basin. Situated high among the austere meadows of the basin, the heavily mined shores of Silver Lake are littered with remnants of the frantic effort to pry gold and silver from these mountains. Long protected from souvenir hunters by an arduous and challenging trail, hikers will still find broken bottles, dinnerware, rotting boots, rusting pieces of mining equipment, and other artifacts scattered amongst the abandoned buildings. It is fitting that this amazing display of the past is found in such a beautiful setting, for it perfectly illustrates the marriage of history and scenery that makes the San Juans such an enchanting place.

As attractive a hiking destination as Arrastra Basin is, it is not for the neophyte hiker or small children. The route follows the trail originally built

42

by the miners in order to access the basin—a trail that has not been maintained since the boom ended many decades ago. The trail climbs steadily while traversing steep slopes; the tread, due to erosion, is extremely narrow in numerous places; and many loose rocks clutter the way. Additionally, the thousands of pieces of broken glass, chunks of rusting metal, and exposed nails lying about at the lake make injury a serious risk for the unwary.

Hikers should also be aware that most of the basin—including all structures and relics—is privately owned. The present owners currently allow public visitation, though this could change if theft or vandalism becomes a problem. Please respect their rights by leaving everything as you find it. Furthermore, respect the historical importance of the area. This is quite possibly the last place in Colorado where such a wealth of artifacts from our mining heritage can be examined just as they were abandoned. If enough people take even one small item home with them, there will soon be nothing left to enjoy.

The hike begins where the road to the old Mayflower Mine switch-

ARRASTRA BASIN

DISTANCE: 4 miles round-trip
ELEVATION RANGE: 10,600 to 12,200 feet
TOTAL ELEVATION GAIN: 1,600 feet
TRAIL CONDITIONS: Unmaintained; poor tread in places, with narrow sections and loose rock; tricky footing in several places; moderate to steep grades; snowfield often blocks trail until mid-July
SEASON: Mid-July through September
USGS MAP: Howardsville (1955)
ADMINISTRATION: Private land

TRAILHEAD: Drive east from Silverton on CO 110 for 2 miles, then turn right onto a dirt road just prior to reaching the Mayflower Mill. Cross the Animas River and pass a right-branching road. Take a left fork 0.5 mile beyond the river, then a right fork 0.4 mile farther. From this last junction, the road becomes very rocky and may not be passable for low-clearance vehicles. The trailhead is 0.6 mile farther, where the road makes a sharp switchback to the left, directly below the Mayflower Mine. Parking is available for three or four cars.

backs up the east wall of Arrastra Gulch. Now blocked to vehicles by rockslides, the road makes a generally good trail, climbing about 500 feet in 0.5 mile to arrive at the mine. Numerous relics remain at the Mayflower, including the upper terminal of a spectacular aerial tram that delivered ore from the mine to the Mayflower Mill, which can be seen far below. While the uppermost tower, which is protected by a rock avalanche–abatement structure, still stands, the next two have been demolished by slides and lay in rusting heaps at the bottom of the canyon. The remaining towers built along the 2-mile length of this tram are intact, and ore buckets still dangle from the steel cables in places. The mine portals were cemented shut in 1993 to prevent explorers from entering and injuring themselves. Piles of rusting metal are scattered around the site, and it is necessary to scramble over some of it to continue on the path to the basin—use extreme caution.

A large snowfield adjacent to the Mayflower Mine usually prohibits further travel until mid-July. Passage becomes safe when the snow melts away from the rock wall at the back of the snowfield, forming a tunnel that hikers use today as miners did in the past. If the "tunnel" has not formed, do not attempt passage across the snowfield—it is very steep, and one slip would most likely result in death on the rocks adjacent to the trailhead. Beyond this obstacle, the old footpath to the basin continues along the east wall of the gulch. The hike becomes more difficult as the tread becomes much poorer in quality. While concentrating on the path is necessary in order to avoid the loose rocks and slippery gravel on the narrow tread, be sure to stop and admire the dramatic scenery encircling you. Peaks soar into the sky in all directions, while wispy waterfalls tumble off the sheer rock faces. Mine portals and prospect holes dot the surrounding walls, as do a number of wooden avalanche-control structures and the remains of a wooden aerial tram that once transported ore from the mines at Silver Lake. The feat of engineering that allowed this tram to be constructed in such difficult terrain is amazing even today—just imagine traveling in one of the ore buckets, as miners often did, as it rode the cable down the steep headwall of the gulch.

A bit less than a mile above the Mayflower Mine, the trail nears the mouth of Arrastra Basin—a textbook example of a hanging valley. One last difficult obstacle must be negotiated: a washed-out section of trail that traverses a steep rock outcropping. While most people, at first glance, will shy away from continuing, passage is fairly easy if caution is used. Once in the basin, the trail becomes much easier as it climbs gently through flower-speckled tundra, reaching the lake in another 0.5 mile.

Silver Lake is set beneath a ring of mountains, its lovely bluish green color seemingly mixing the hue of the sky with that of the tundra. Mines are found throughout the basin, the largest being the Royal Tiger, the Iowa, and the Silver Lake Mine complex, which is where you now stand. With all of the debris strewn about the sandy lakeshore, it is not difficult to imagine a busy mining camp once operating here. Several buildings—some still standing—can be viewed, as can the foundation of a stamp mill that clings to the mountainside behind the complex. Colorful pieces of glass are scattered around the area, as are pieces of porcelain, rusting cans, and other discarded fragments of the miners' lives. Particularly eerie are the scores of boots that lie rotting in the sand. An exploration of the area could take hours, with new and interesting discoveries filling every minute. Again, take care to avoid cuts and other injuries, and please leave everything for the next hiker to enjoy. Once you return to the trailhead, a great way to end the day's explorations would be to tour both the Mayflower Mill and the Old Hundred Mine, both of which are near Silverton. Doing so will shed more light on the history of Arrastra Basin and will make you feel like you have experienced the mining boom firsthand.

Ice Lake Basin

If the San Juans have a single signature hike, it is Ice Lake Basin. Weaving together fierce-looking peaks, brilliant meadows, an array of waterfalls, and a lovely set of alpine tarns, this trail is to San Juan hiking what the Bright Angel Trail is to the Grand Canyon: an absolute must for people who want to experience the quintessential features of a classic landscape. A longtime local favorite, this trail's easy access and good tread, in addition to the superlative-inducing scenery, have resulted in its rapidly increasing popularity with visiting hikers.

Beginning adjacent to the South Mineral Creek Campground, this one-time prospectors' path has been reengineered in recent years so that the rate of ascent—at least at the hike's

---

ICE LAKE BASIN

DISTANCE: 8 miles round-trip

ELEVATION RANGE: 9,900 to 12,250 feet

TOTAL ELEVATION GAIN: 2,350 feet

TRAIL CONDITIONS: Steady, moderate to steep ascent; unbridged stream crossings

SEASON: July through September

USGS MAP: Ophir (1955)

ADMINISTRATION: San Juan NF; Columbine RD

TRAILHEAD: From Silverton, drive north on US 550 for 2.2 miles, turning west onto FR 585 (South Mineral Creek Road). Follow this dirt road for 4.9 miles, parking at the trailhead just prior to the South Mineral Creek Campground.

Winter releases its grip slowly from Ice Lake Basin.

beginning—has been eased. Several long switchbacks in the initial 0.5 mile bring the trail to the forested bank of Clear Creek, which is crossed via a wooden plank. Just upstream is the first of several splendid waterfalls spilling over ledges of red, Cutler Formation sandstones. Another 0.5 mile of steady switchbacking carries the trail through both meadow and forest settings, often quite near the creek's cataracts. When the trail intersects an old road, bear left—but only after strolling to the right a few feet in order to enjoy another impressive waterfall.

The trail continues its steady ascent, quickly passing the remains of an old mine and mill operation. The subalpine forest soon thins, and the trail enters the vast meadows of several large avalanche swaths. These gullies, cleared of encroaching forest each winter, have the right combination of insolation, copious moisture, and fertile soil to produce some amazing wildflower displays. The ascent steepens even further as it reenters the timber beneath the lip of Lower Ice Lake Basin. Hikers gasping their way up the grade will appreciate the handful of prospects that offer inspiring vistas down the valley of South Mineral Creek and an opportunity for a few moments of rest.

The ascent eases as the trail breaks into Lower Ice Lake Basin, a bit more than 2 miles from the trailhead. Though only a preview of the upper basin's scenery, this initial glimpse is nonetheless one of striking beauty. The wildflowers growing here are a dense, aromatic spectrum of color. Once you walk into this garden, your eyes will quickly be drawn toward the great peaks guarding the upper basin, but the panorama is only visible for a few moments before it fades behind the nearer wall of emerald green encircling the lower basin. These walls are streaked by a handful of magnificent, frothing waterfalls. For the next mile, the trail continues easily along the floor of the lower basin, passing within sight of a small lake about halfway across. Good camping can be found in several places; however, the recent explosion of this basin's popularity has made competition for sites more stiff while increasing the visible impact on the environment. Leaving the backpacks at home might help keep this basin in relatively pristine condition.

Toward the rear of the lower basin, the trail makes its way across several converging streams, with each ford potentially requiring a calf- to knee-deep wade when snowmelt flows from the upper basin. The waterfalls of each of these streams are unique, with one roaring behind a house-size boulder, another cascading through a lateral cliff-face fracture, and a third spilling over a high set of ledges. A more spectacular collection of cataracts could scarcely be imagined. The trail soon begins its ascent of the headwall separating the lower and upper basins. The 0.5-mile climb is steep, rocky, filled with flowers, and visually stunning.

Entering the upper basin, you'll find yourself immersed in a landscape of rolling tundra shadowed by rockbound slopes, ragged cliffs, and precipitous summits. A few more minutes' worth of walking brings you to the shore of Ice Lake. Its dark, greenish waters reflect the meadows and mountains that surround you to perfection—at least during the brief period in which the lake has thawed. Lichen-decorated boulders invite rest and contemplation, and the gentle lapping of the lake upon its bank is like a soothing lullaby.

Satisfying as it may be to while away a few hours at the edge of Ice Lake, the surrounding basin demands exploration. A series of smaller tarns may be found in the immediate vicinity, each offering its own unique reflection of the surrounding scenes. A bit farther afield is Fuller Lake, which is located a mile to the south, or Island Lake, which is set in a small, neighboring basin less than a mile to the north. There are a number of old

COLUMBINE LAKE

Distance: 7.5 miles round-trip

Elevation Range: 10,400 to 12,700 feet

Total Elevation Gain: 2,500 feet

Trail Conditions: Very steep in many places, with narrow, sometimes slippery tread; off-trail travel required in order to reach the lake; snowfields usually encountered through July

Season: Early July through September

USGS Maps: Ophir (1955); Silverton (1955)

Administration: San Juan NF; Columbine RD

Trailhead: Drive on US 550 for either 5 miles north from Silverton or 5.1 miles south from Red Mountain Pass until reaching Ophir Pass Road. Drive this dirt road for 0.4 mile and make a hard right onto FR 820 D, which is located a brief distance beyond the concrete bridge. Follow this road for 0.7 mile, until an easily discerned footpath climbing into the forest on the road's left side comes into view. A small, two-car pullout just to the south is the "trailhead." There are no signs for this trail, so pay close attention. FR 820 D is a fairly rough road, but most two-wheel-drive vehicles should be able to traverse it. If in doubt, park along Ophir Pass Road and walk to the trailhead.

prospect pits and mine dumps to explore, and the dazzling display of tundra wildflowers is the perfect backdrop for aimless strolling. Mountaineers of any mettle will find enjoyable destinations. Novices will be rewarded at the summit of 13,894-foot Vermillion Peak, while experts will be challenged by the rotten face of 13,738-foot Pilot Knob. U.S. Grant Peak, the Golden Horn, and Fuller Peak also offer variably difficult ascents for those so inclined.

Columbine Lake

Nestled high in another of the San Juans' many stunning alpine basins, Columbine Lake is the dramatic destination of a challenging and relatively unknown hike. The subalpine forest encountered en route is lush and inviting, the alpine slopes above are often cloaked in a vibrant display of summer wildflowers, and the panorama of rugged peaks and splashing cascades rivals that of any hike in the region. Especially appealing is the fact that people who find their way onto this unmarked trail are often rewarded by having the entire beautiful hike to themselves. The payoff is not without price, however: The relentlessly switchbacking trail provides a real workout.

Good hiking boots are strongly recommended for this hike. The trail switchbacks numerous times, and the tread is often composed of slippery gravel on steep slopes. Once above treeline, the trail degrades into an often muddy and rocky path, and the hike to the shore of Columbine Lake requires off-trail travel across loose talus and open tundra. Despite these obstacles and the apparent lack of "official" attention given to the trail, it is in good condition and seems to have been cleared within recent years. Because the Columbine Lake basin appears to relinquish its winter snowpack more slowly than most others, this hike should probably not be attempted until mid- to late summer unless the previous winter was drier than normal. Should snowfields remain, the final approach to the lake may be impassable without crampons and an ice ax. Case in point: After the harsh winter of 1996–97, this author found the basin surrounding the lake to be completely snowbound—even on the 15th of July. Finally, because the lake is infrequently visited, its shore and the surrounding tundra remain pristine— please be especially certain to "leave no trace" of your journey here.

After locating the trail, immediately commence a steep, switchbacking climb up the forested mountainside. Most likely constructed by miners seeking the most direct route to their prospects, this trail spares no time in its ascent. The average hiker will be huffing and puffing in no time, but it is the return descent that can be the greatest challenge. Fortunately, the grade eases somewhat after the eleventh switchback, and the remaining climb becomes more tolerable. The saving grace of this part of the hike is that the subalpine forest on this slope is especially beautiful, with an emerald understory located beneath a shade-producing, aromatic canopy.

After climbing for about 1.5 miles, the ascent briefly relents as the trail traverses a narrow bench just below treeline. This is an ideal place to rest since there is a rushing brook, a scattering of wildflowers, and stately trees that provide both shade and shelter from the alpine breezes. Climbing beyond the bench, the trail enters a smallish alpine basin and continues climbing along its floor toward a high saddle on its far wall. Though not the San Juans' most spectacular, the basin is scenic, and the vista of the distant Grenadier Range is appealing. The saddle is gained about 2.5 miles from the trailhead after conquering a steep talus slope and—depending on the presence of snowfields—scrambling over a small set of rock ledges.

Beyond the saddle, the trail descends gradually across a steep slope and into the basin at the headwaters of Mill Creek. This north-facing traverse provides the greatest potential for snowfield obstacles and should not be attempted without the appropriate gear until it has melted out. If you are unable to continue on the trail, the tundra-covered hillside north of the saddle is an excellent alternative. An easy climb, this aerie has outstanding panoramas in all directions. Assuming the trail is open and the lake is your destination, follow the path until nearly reaching Mill Creek, then diverge from the trail and climb along the path of least resistance to the lake, which is located at 12,700 feet, directly beneath the basin's headwall. The lake—when it's free of ice—is reputed to have decent fishing. Alternately, it is possible to continue on the trail, which gains a moderately steep 700 feet, to reach a pass high above Bridal Veil Basin.

Indian Trail Ridge

The hike onto Indian Trail Ridge is an unsurpassed sublime experience. Situated near the heart of the La Plata Range, Indian Trail Ridge affords magnificent views of not only nearby peaks, but also of the saw-toothed line of peaks that stretch across the breadth of the San Juans. As if the grand vistas were not enough, the ridge also boasts one of the most profuse and colorful wildflower gardens in the Rocky Mountains. A segment of the famous Colorado Trail (which runs from Durango to Denver), the route is well maintained and is not difficult. Once atop the ridge, those seeking a longer journey will enjoy miles of some of the best ridge-top hiking imaginable.

Tearing yourself away from the vista at the trailhead may be difficult. Isolated as they are from the rest of the San Juans, the La Platas offer an

---

INDIAN TRAIL RIDGE

DISTANCE: 4 miles round-trip
ELEVATION RANGE: 11,500 to 12,100 feet
TOTAL ELEVATION GAIN: 600 feet
TRAIL CONDITIONS: Tread is usually in good condition; the grade of the final 0.5 mile is moderate to steep
SEASON: July through September
USGS MAP: La Plata (1963)
ADMINISTRATION: San Juan NF; Columbine RD

TRAILHEAD: From Durango, drive west on US 160 for 11.4 miles, turning right onto La Plata Canyon Road (CR 124). Drive this road, which turns to dirt at Mayday, and continue up La Plata Canyon. At a Y intersection, 12.1 miles from US 160, bear to the left. The road becomes much rougher, and high-clearance, four-wheel-drive vehicles are required for the remaining 2 miles to the trailhead, which sits atop a saddle at the head of the canyon. If you do not have a four-wheel drive, hike the final 2 miles, which gain 1,100 feet of elevation.

unobstructed view of much of the remainder of these vast mountains. That the trailhead vista is only a sample of what lies ahead is a strong motivator, though. When you do finally begin the hike, the trail heads west, drops slightly, and then traverses a flat grade across the meadowy slopes of Cumberland Basin, which forms the headwaters of the La Plata River. Even here the views and flowers are gorgeous, and the hiking is very enjoyable.

About a mile from the trailhead is Taylor Lake, which is tucked directly beneath the rocky slopes of the ridge. The small lake is quite pretty and makes a great destination for people interested only in the easiest of hikes. A footpath branches left at the lake, leading to a number of very nice campsites. A short distance farther along the main trail is a signed junction, which is the beginning of the Highline Loop National Recreation Trail, a 17-mile circuit that climbs onto Indian Trail Ridge, drops into the Bear Creek drainage, wraps around its headwaters, then returns across the ridge. It is an excellent backpack that showcases the scenery of the La Platas. Keep to the right at this junction and commence a steadier climb. Within 0.25 mile, the trail switchbacks twice and steepens as it traverses a slope decorated with a stunning variety of wildflowers. A second, shorter set of switchbacks is near the top, where a snowfield may remain until the end of July. Passage shouldn't be too difficult, however, and with a few more steps the ridge top is gained, 2 miles from the trailhead.

The crest of Indian Trail Ridge is a mountaintop nirvana of flowers and vistas that no written account can adequately describe. To the south, the imposing line of peaks that form the heart of the La Platas burst into view as you take your last steps onto the ridge. Built of colorful rock striations, these peaks tower above patches of snow, rock, and tundra, which descend into the valley below. The more distant main body of the San Juans stands like a blue picket fence to the north, west, and east, running for nearly 100 miles from the west end of the San Miguel Range, across the Needles Range, and down the length of the South San Juans. With a good map and a familiarity with the local geography, you should be able to identify any number of peaks that you may have explored on other San Juan adventures.

Walk northward on the trail for as long as you wish. Meadows mingle in and around clumps of willow and create a mosaic of greens that are speckled by the pinks, yellows, whites, and blues of innumerable blossoms. Named for the Native Americans who traversed this ridge for thousands of years in their quest for game, Indian Trail Ridge remains a viaduct across the sky, beckoning you onward as it slopes gently northward into the vastness ahead. When you have traveled as long or as short as you like, stop, sit, stare, and soak in the magnificent scenery.

San Miguel Traverse

Among the most rugged and colorful summits in the region, the great mountains of the San Miguel Range stand as the San Juans' western-most battlements. Crowned by three peaks that exceed the magical (if not arbitrary) 14,000-foot contour, the San Miguels have long drawn mountaineers and other wilderness explorers. As early as 1932, the heart of the range was protected as the Wilson Mountains Primitive Area, and the accompanying emphasis on foot-bound recreation has resulted in a diverse trail system that crisscrosses the heart of the range, which is now preserved as the Lizard Head Wilderness. The classic traverse of the San Miguel Range starts at its southern foot, follows the west fork of the Dolores River past the chilly waters of Navajo Lake, and plunges deep into the confines of Navajo Basin. The path then continues beneath the shadows of three "14'ers" before cresting a 13,000-foot pass and descending through the dramatically austere Silver Pick Basin to terminate on the range's north flank.

Though not great in distance, the "San Miguel Traverse" is best suited as a backpack due to the lengthy car shuttle that must be arranged. If you are unable to overcome these logistical challenges, an out-and-back hike or backpack is still a rewarding option, with Navajo Lake the ideal destination. The lake itself is a beautiful alpine pool, and the peaks surrounding Navajo Basin are an attractive mountaineering diversion. Of course, as is the case throughout Colorado, the presence of "14'ers" draws a steady stream of wilderness visitors. Though few people actually attempt the traverse described here, expect to see other hikers—at least on weekends—throughout your travels. As always, the same low-impact techniques encouraged at other popular backcountry destinations should be practiced here, and backpackers should honor the permanent ban on campfires in Navajo Basin.

Departing the Navajo Lake Trailhead, our route stays close to the bank of the west fork, quickly passes the left-branching Groundhog Stock Driveway and enters the Lizard Head Wilderness. A sign at this junction notes a lack of footbridges on the trail ahead, and the warning comes to fruition after a

and pass through the community of Dunton after 22 miles. Turn left into the signed trailhead about 3 miles above Dunton. Alternately, coming from Lizard Head Pass, drive south on CO 145 for 5.5 miles and turn right onto FR 535. Drive this gravel road for 7.4 miles until you reach the signed trailhead.

SILVER PICK TRAILHEAD: From the junction of CO 145 and CO 145 Spur just west of Telluride, drive north on CO 145 toward Placerville. Turn left onto Silver Pick Road after 5.9 miles. Drive this gravel road, which bears left at 3.2 miles, and you will arrive at a somewhat tricky four-way intersection 0.7 mile farther. Make a soft right turn, avoiding the left-bending main road as well as a private road on the hard right (a sign directing traffic towards Silver Pick Basin should be visible here). This road climbs steadily, passes the West Wilson Mesa Trailhead after 2.2 miles, then becomes rougher as it continues onto the Silver Pick Trailhead 0.7 mile farther. Passenger cars may be unable to negotiate the final 0.2 mile of this road—if so, park back at the West Wilson Mesa Trailhead.

pleasant, 0.75-mile stroll through the open forest and grassy meadows of the streamside environment. Here the trail makes its way to the far bank of the west fork and to a wade that can be daunting at anytime and that can be downright impossible before the end of spring runoff in mid-July. Once safely across, the hike follows the trail onto a bench above the river. Angling away from the water, the trail soon enters a large meadow, which is traversed for more than a mile. Dense with false hellebore and surrounded by aspen, the meadow provides excellent vistas of 14,159-foot El Diente—an apt moniker whose English translation is "the tooth."

The faint Kilpacker Creek Trail is intercepted about 2.25 miles above the trailhead, after which the trail steepens as it enters subalpine forest. The steady climb continues as the trail breaks into steep meadows thriving in the run-out zones of a series of avalanche paths. These meadows are home to the hike's best array of wildflowers, and as the trail climbs through a rather large avalanche path at about mile 3.5, there is a clear view of a rather impressive waterfall. For the next 0.75 mile the trail continues its unrelenting ascent and finally reaches an apex, where it intersects the Woods Lake Trail. Another 0.25 mile of downhill walking brings you to the shore of Navajo Lake.

Navajo Lake sits at the lower end of Navajo Basin, which is a deep glacial bowl tucked into the midst of the San Miguels' highest peaks. Willows and ground-hugging spruce fringe the lake, and decent campsites can be located throughout the area. Pockets of wildflowers lend a measure of softness to the scene, but it is the surrounding mass of gray rock that creates the somber air that permeates the place. Both El Diente and 14,246-foot Mount Wilson form the highest ramparts on the basin's south rim, though both summits are hidden behind the lower, rock-strewn slopes. Gladstone Peak is slightly lower but no less imposing, as its sculpted summit and snow-streaked west face form a dramatic—and often reflected—skyline directly up-basin. The north wall of the basin is equally rugged, though its culmination at the 14,017-foot summit of Wilson Peak is also hidden from this vantage. That two separate 14'ers located adjacent to one another each carry the name Wilson is an interesting quirk. Named for A. D. Wilson, a member of the 1874 Hayden Survey, the designation of both peaks as Wilson appears to be a cartographic error and not an example of gross egocentrism.

The trail continues above the lake and climbs the barren floor of the basin in a stair-step fashion for another 2 miles. The point where the trail turns to the north and begins a steep ascent of the basin's wall marks the departure point for mountaineers seeking the summit of Mount Wilson and/or El Diente. An ascent of either is physically demanding, and while both can be accomplished without technical equipment, the respective routes feature a significant amount of scrambling and some exposure. The knife-edge ridge between the two summits is considered a Colorado classic. The rock is stable, but the pinnacles and gaps are beyond the abilities of casual hikers and novice mountaineers. Consult a guide to Colorado's 14'ers for specific details.

The ascent of the basin's north wall can be challenging in itself, especially if you are carrying a large backpack. The trail winds back and forth across steep, sometimes unstable talus slopes, and snowfields may linger well into summer. Gaining nearly 1,000 feet in a single mile, the unrelenting grade and lofty elevation sucks the breath from you. Among the numerous places you'll likely stop and rest is the Rock of Ages Mine, which is just below the 13,000-foot apex of the trail. The relatively straightforward route to the top of Wilson Peak continues eastward from this saddle, and its successful ascent is a satisfying bonus. The 0.5-mile route to the summit follows a faint climber's path just below the crest of the ridge. Other than a bit of scrambling near the summit, the climb is moderate.

The traverse continues onto the north side of the San Miguels by dropping into Silver Pick Basin, which lies outside the boundaries of the Lizard Head Wilderness. The descent off the saddle is rough and is often complicated by snowfields, which sometimes last into August. About 500 feet below the saddle, the trail reaches the sloping floor of the basin, which is a picture of austerity. Unlike many other San Juan basins, which are softened by a lush expanse of tundra, Silver Pick is composed almost entirely of bare rock, with the expanse of gray and tan tempered only by the faint greens, oranges, and blacks of lichen. Even the streams here run counter to the idyllic alpine setting, as they often sink beneath the great jumbles of rock and leave only a haunting, subterranean gurgle to mark their course.

There are two possible routes through the basin. The easier, more expedient of the two follows an old mining road across the floor of the basin to the site of the Silver Pick Mill. The more scenic alternative continues on a rough footpath, which descends on a moderate to steep grade on the east side of the basin and intersects the mining road just above the Silver Pick Mill. Rebuilt as a privately owned summer cabin, the mill once served the Silver Pick Mine, which was located higher in the basin. A wooden aerial tram connected the two structures, traces of which remain visible. Please respect the owner's privacy by remaining on the road until exiting the basin.

From the mill site, it is less than a mile of steady downhill walking to the Silver Pick Trailhead. Except for property owners, the road you will

LIZARD HEAD TRAIL

VIA CROSS MOUNTAIN

DISTANCE: 9 miles one-way

ELEVATION RANGE: 10,100 to 12,200 feet

TOTAL ELEVATION GAIN: 2,500 feet

TRAIL CONDITIONS: Well-defined tread; some steep grades; steep snowfields likely through July; extensive sections exposed to potentially poor weather

SEASON: July through September

USGS MAP: Mount Wilson (1953)

ADMINISTRATION: San Juan NF; Dolores RD

VIA BILK BASIN

DISTANCE: 11.5 miles one-way

ELEVATION RANGE: 9,700 to 12,200 feet

TOTAL ELEVATION GAIN: 2500 ft.

TRAIL CONDITIONS: Moderate to steep grades; sometimes rough; several un-bridged stream crossings; extensive sections exposed to potentially poor weather

SEASON: July through September.

USGS MAPS: Mount Wilson (1953); Gray Head (1953)

ADMINISTRATION: San Juan NF; Dolores RD; Uncompahgre NF; Norwood RD

LIZARD HEAD PASS TRAILHEAD: Located at the summit of Lizard Head Pass on CO 145, about 12 miles south of Telluride.

CROSS MOUNTAIN TRAILHEAD: Located just west of CO 145, 2.2 miles south of Lizard Head Pass.

SUNSHINE MESA TRAILHEAD: From the intersection of CO 145 and CO 145 Spur near Telluride, drive west on

follow for the remainder of the walk is closed to vehicles. Leaving the basin, the trail contours above the rapidly descending course of Big Bear Creek. You'll enjoy open vistas of aspen- and spruce-cloaked slopes below as well as panoramas of the distant Sneffels Range. Before dropping completely into the forest, pause to enjoy a final peek at the San Miguels' great ridges and peaks, which tower high overhead.

Lizard Head Trail

Many people find alpine ridge walking to be among the most enjoyable aspects of hiking in the Rocky Mountains. On these airy promontories, even the highest peaks seem to be within arm's reach. Meadows unfold in all directions, broken not by forest, but by bare rock, snow, and sky. This is nature at its rawest—where biting winds, thin air, and violent storms challenge the hiker before rewarding him or her with glimpses of stunning scenery. As might be expected, the San Juans suffer no shortage of such places; however, few are as easily accessible and beautiful as the Lizard Head Trail.

The Lizard Head Trail loops through the eastern edge of the Lizard Head Wilderness, whose 41,000 acres preserve the heart of the San Miguel Range in its primeval condition. Starting at Lizard Head Pass, the trail ascends the steep shoulder of Black Face Mountain, traverses atop its long summit ridge, and continues directly beneath the imposing rock spire that gives the trail, the pass, and the wilderness its name. Turning northward, the trail then descends through the magnificent Bilk Creek drainage and exits the wilderness at Sunshine Mesa. Hiking the entire Lizard Head Trail requires a lengthy car-shuttle arrangement, so many people hike southward via the Cross Mountain Trail instead of via Bilk Basin. The Cross Mountain Trailhead is 2.2 miles south of Lizard Head Pass, so some sort of shuttle arrangements will have to be made (a stashed bike works well) unless you are willing to walk back to your car at Lizard Head Pass.

CO 145 toward Placerville. After 2.6 miles, turn left onto South Fork Road (FR 623). Drive on this road, which quickly turns to gravel, for 2.1 miles, turning right onto Sunshine Mesa Road (still FR 623). Continue for 3.7 miles, bear left at the junction, and then go another 1.8 miles and park at the trailhead where the road is gated. This final 1.8 miles is rough but should be passable by all vehicles.

From Lizard Head Pass, the trail heads northward and traverses a meadow before entering a lush aspen grove. The initial 1.5 miles are gentle and pleasant, with numerous wildflowers. After passing the wilderness boundary, the trail steepens and commences a long series of switchbacks. Gaining more than 500 feet in little more than 0.5 mile, the trail ascends through a bushy avalanche path, which opens to views of the striking peaks that rise above Trout Lake. Finally easing into a small meadow that is 2.25 miles from the pass, the trail splits. The Wilson Meadows Trail continues ahead and reaches the namesake glade in an additional mile, while the Lizard Head Trail forks left and continues its upward tack.

Climbing steadily, the trail mainly remains within a shady spruce/fir forest as it ascends the north flank of Black Face Mountain. Breaks in the forest allow glimpses northward toward the Sneffels Range. After about a mile of such hiking, the trail finally gains the top of the ridge at the upper fringe of the subalpine zone, where it turns westward to ascend gently sloping meadows. Vistas are exemplary, with rugged peaks visible in all directions. When the spectacular heart of the San Miguel Range comes into view, the tower of rock known as the Lizard Head stands most prominently, while the often snow-speckled summits of Gladstone Peak and Wilson Peak form a striking backdrop.

The 12,147-foot summit of Black Face is reached after 0.75 mile of ridge-top walking. The expansive view is enhanced by the spread of wildflowers that carpet the tundra-covered slopes. Look carefully for alpine columbine, a miniature version of Colorado's beautiful state flower. Here, where the winds howl and the temperature hovers far below freezing for all but a few summer months, flowers adapt by growing tiny blooms that hug the ground. The effectiveness of this strategy is easily understood on a windy day: Allow the breeze to buffet you while you stand straight up, then lie flat on the ground. The 30 mph gusts you feel at eye level often diminish to less than 5 mph at ankle level. While lying prone, take a moment to look across the open slopes for a possible glimpse of elk, and listen for the ubiquitous squeaks of marmot and pika.

Continue beyond the summit and descend gradually through scattered tundra and clumps of willow until you have returned below timberline and reached a broad, grassy saddle at 11,500 feet, 5 miles from the trailhead. A short distance farther, the ascent begins once again, this time directly toward the Lizard Head. Shortly beyond the saddle, the trail traverses a slope where a steep snowfield usually remains until at least late July. Use extreme caution in attempting a crossing, or scout for a suitable detour. Once past the snowfield, the trail winds upward to crest a 12,100-foot ridge that is 0.5 mile beyond the saddle. A most dramatic view of the Lizard Head is enjoyed from here. Rising more than 400 feet above its base to a peak of 13,113 feet, this vertical spire of rotten rock is considered to be Colorado's most difficult ascent.

The next 0.5 mile traverses a steep gully, where another treacherous snowfield may exist. At mile 6.0, the Cross Mountain Trail branches left. Even if you plan on diverging from the Lizard Head Trail at this point, stroll 0.25 mile farther to the saddle above Bilk Basin for a final close-up view of the many flowers and gorgeous peaks of the San Miguels. The Cross Mountain Trail descends moderately and returns below timberline a final time after the initial 0.5 mile. The remaining 2.5 miles of trail continue through the forest and use an abandoned logging road once outside of the wilderness boundary. Remember that the Cross Mountain Trailhead is 2.2 miles from Lizard Head Pass, so if you do not have return transportation, you'll have to walk along CO 145 to complete the loop.

From the saddle overlooking Bilk Basin, the Lizard Head Trail descends into the Bilk Creek drainage on a steep and rough track. The scenery remains first-rate, with an impressive collection of peaks towering above

The delicate backlit blossoms of Indian paintbrush contrast strikingly with the daunting peaks above Black Face Mountain.

verdant, flower-dotted tundra; shimmering cascades; and gleaming snow-fields. Once you've descended into the lower reaches of the basin, cross a small brook near a long cascade (a possible wade during July), then wind down through willow thickets and past a marshy meadow.

Timberline is reached about 2 miles from the Cross Mountain Trail junction, though timber along the trail itself is sparse as it switchbacks down a large, lush avalanche path that is home to some noteworthy flower gardens. The trail hasn't been brushed out in recent years, so the thick shrubbery can soak a hiker if it has rained recently. The grade is rarely very steep, but the rocky and often wet trail requires caution. At the bottom of the last switch-back, the trail enters a small bowl cleared of forest by powerful snowslides, which roar down five converging gullies. Long cascades pour down each of these gullies, but it is the tremendous falls on the main stem of Bilk Creek that command attention. Plunging straight off a 100-foot-high cliff, the creek washes down a face of bedrock before crashing through a series of stair-step cataracts. Though this is perhaps the most spectacular single waterfall of any hike in this guide, a single unobstructed view of its entire length is hard to come by, owing to a stand of spruce surrounding the cliff.

Below the falls, the trail ducks back into the forest alongside the rushing creek. Just past the wilderness boundary is the long-abandoned Morningstar Mine, which is 2.25 miles from the Sunshine Mesa Trailhead. Resist any urge to explore this junk-strewn prospect, as it remains private property. A short distance below the mine, the Bilk Creek Trail branches to the left. Stay to the right and immediately cross Bilk Creek. While there is no bridge here, a small logjam should keep your feet dry. If this jam is not present (or not safe), you may wish to walk a short distance upstream in search of an easier ford.

Once across, the footpath becomes an abandoned road that traverses several steep and rocky avalanche slopes. Bilk Creek falls away quite rapidly, and some impressive views of Wilson Peak and the aspen groves down the valley open up by the time the road swings away from the drainage. The old road soon enters a damp, shady forest of spruce, fir, and aspen, where during early morning hours, herds of deer and elk can often be seen. About a mile from the Sunshine Mesa Trailhead, the Wilson Mesa Trail joins from the right. This is a popular mountain-bike route, so keep an eye out for passing cyclists. Otherwise, enjoy a pleasant end to this beautiful walk.

Wasatch Trail

A century ago, the handful of miners who staked their claims in the Bear Creek drainage south of Telluride made their commute via a steep and narrow path known today as the Wasatch Trail. Perhaps the miners, in their rush to the riches, failed to notice the spectacular scenery that opened before them as they under-

---

WASATCH TRAIL

BEAR CREEK FALLS

DISTANCE: 4.4 miles round-trip

ELEVATION RANGE: 8,750 to 9,800 feet

TOTAL ELEVATION GAIN: 1,050 feet

TRAIL CONDITIONS: Route follows a closed four-wheel-drive road with generally gentle grades

SEASON: May through October

USGS MAP: Telluride (1955)

ADMINISTRATION: Uncompahgre NF; Norwood RD

WASATCH TRAIL

DISTANCE: 10 miles round-trip

ELEVATION RANGE: 8,750 to 13,050 feet

TOTAL ELEVATION GAIN: 4,300 feet

TRAIL CONDITIONS: The initial 2 miles follow a closed four-wheel-drive road; however, the reminder of the hike is on a steep, often rocky, and sometimes brushy path

took the arduous climb to their prospects. However, it is somehow satisfying to think that the beautiful scenery that stops us in our tracks had the same arresting affect on these men of the past. Surely they were entranced by the many sparkling waterfalls, the vast fields of wildflowers that blossom each summer, and the inspiring panorama of jagged peaks. Those hardy men of history made this journey not for pleasure, but for duty, yet it seems unreasonable to think that their impressions of this alpine landscape are different than those of the scenery-sated hikers of the present.

SEASON: Mid-July through September
USGS MAP: Telluride (1955)
ADMINISTRATION: Uncompahgre NF; Norwood RD
TRAILHEAD: In the town of Telluride, drive to the south end of South Pine Street, which terminates just after crossing the San Miguel River. The hike begins on the gated road that continues directly ahead. Do not park in the private lots adjacent to the trailhead—utilize legal parking alongside South Pine Street or on another nearby block.

That such a beautiful hike is so easily accessible is one of the Wasatch Trail's primary attractions (the trailhead is a short walk from anywhere in town). There is, however, a steep price to be paid for the rewards of the hike—steep as in 4,300 vertical feet ascended within 5 miles. While it may be tempting for many out-of-state visitors to tackle this hike during their stay in Telluride, this trail demands mountain fitness and altitude acclimation. The shorter hike to Bear Creek Falls is a wonderful alternative for those who doubt their stamina.

The first 2 miles of the hike follow the now-closed Bear Creek Road. In 1995, the town of Telluride and the San Miguel Conservation Foundation joined forces to procure the lower end of the Bear Creek drainage as an open-space reserve. The Bear Creek Preserve ensures that this beautiful canyon will remain a sanctuary, untouched by Telluride's sprawling growth. The road is now accessible only to hikers and mountain bikers, and its cool, forest-shrouded route up the canyon is in itself a very satisfying hike. An excellent interpretive brochure has been created for this portion of the route; pick one up for a nominal fee at the Telluride Parks and Recreation office in Town Park.

The actual Wasatch Trail veers to the right about 0.25 mile below Bear Creek Falls. Those making a destination of the falls (and those willing to make the short side trip before proceeding farther up the canyon) should continue on the roadbed until it nears the creek and the aptly named Big Rock. From here, follow the winding footpath a few hundred feet to the base of the falls. Spilling over a reddish cliff, Bear Creek dances down a series of ledges in one of the San Juans' most graceful water displays. With plenty of flat rocks on which to sprawl, the falls are both literally and figuratively a very cool place to relax on a hot summer afternoon.

The Wasatch Trail gets right down to business as it begins a switchbacking ascent up the west canyon wall before traversing across a series of flower-decorated avalanche paths and through a tight notch in the steeply rising drainage. Gaining 1,000 feet within a mile, this section is hot and tiring anyway, but especially so on sunny afternoons when the thick brush adds humidity to the heat. Avoid this with an early start—fortunately, the towering east wall of the canyon shades the trail for a good two hours after true sunrise. Be careful on the steep and slippery tread as the trail climbs through the aforementioned notch, where the Forest Service has had to bridge a crevasse in the canyon wall.

After working through the notch, the trail eases onto the floor of a small, pretty basin, where it arrives at the shattered remnants of the Nellie Mine. The small stamp mill associated with the mine is just off the trail, with quite a bit of rusting machinery available for casual inspection. It seems the Nellie suffered from a poor location, as the mill has obviously been demolished by the massive avalanches that roar down the opposite mountain wall. It's hard to imagine that the mill could have survived even one winter in this shooting gallery.

Just above the Nellie is a faint, unsigned trail junction. The left branch is the East Fork Bear Creek Trail, which reconnects with the Wasatch Trail about 1.5 miles farther ahead. This trail can be used as an alternate return route, though it is in relatively poor condition and is not recommended. Our route continues to the right, where it soon begins another steep, switchbacking ascent of the west drainage wall. After gaining another 500 feet, the trail traverses into a second small basin, this one even more scenic than the last. Another junction presents itself here; bear left this time, rock-hop the west fork of Bear Creek, and begin another steep climb. The scenery from here forward truly outdoes itself, as the waving fields of flowers and surrounding peaks are especially magnificent. The small bowl of Lena Basin is visible to the south, while the steep slopes and cliffs of Gold Hill, Palmyra Peak, Silver Mountain, and San Joaquin Ridge rise toward the clouds. Look for the many small mines and prospect pits that dot these mountainsides.

Once you make your way another 500 feet closer to heaven, you'll find that the trail crosses a small flat, where several large rocks and an outstanding northward vista of the Sneffels Range invite a prolonged rest stop. Beyond this, the trail drops slightly to cross the east fork of Bear Creek, rejoins the East Fork Trail, and climbs another set of switchbacks in order to gain the lower edge of the east fork's broad headwaters basin. The hike's final mile makes its way through this austere alpine setting and gains 800 more feet before arriving at the 13,050-foot pass that overlooks the expansive Bridal Veil Basin. While most hikers will wish to backtrack from here, an alternate return is possible by dropping into Bridal Veil Basin, following the old jeep road past Bridal Veil Falls (Colorado's highest), and continuing on to the Pandora Mill, about 2 miles east of Telluride.

Sneffels Highline

As the northernmost rampart of the San Juans, the Sneffels Range rears skyward in a dramatic arc of rock that towers high above the gently rolling country below. Justly famous as one of America's most spectacular mountain scenes, these peaks have appeared in countless advertisements, postcards, and calendars. A network of excellent trails traverses the Sneffels Range, the newest and arguably most scenic addition being the Sneffels Highline. The Sneffels Highline loops through a portion of the Mount Sneffels Wilderness to connect with a set of trails on the lower mountain flanks,

SNEFFELS HIGHLINE

DISTANCE: 13 miles round-trip

ELEVATION RANGE: 9,450 to 12,250 feet

TOTAL ELEVATION GAIN: 3,000 feet

TRAIL CONDITIONS: Well constructed, but frequently steep, with some rocky sections

SEASON: Mid-July through September

USGS MAP: Telluride (1955) (trail not shown)

ADMINISTRATION: Uncompahgre NF; Norwood RD

TRAILHEAD: From the junction of CO 145 and the CO 145 Spur just west of Telluride, drive east on the CO 145 Spur toward town. After 1.9 miles, turn left onto an unmarked dirt road. Drive up this road, switchback to the right after 0.6 mile, and continue an additional mile to the Deep Creek Trailhead, which is adjacent to Telluride's water-treatment facility.

and the resulting circuit climbs through a wide variety of environments, which range from extensive aspen groves to alpine wildflower meadows. Vistas are superb throughout, with an encircling ring of peaks that can easily be inspected nearly every step of the way. The only price of "admission" is the rarely relenting grades that carry the trail through this precipitous setting.

The hike begins from the Telluride water-treatment facility and follows the Deep Creek Trail above the left bank of rushing Mill Creek. The trail climbs gently along the base of the aspen-cloaked canyon wall for roughly 0.25 mile before it reaches a trail junction. Bear left, and begin ascending the 0.5-mile set of switchbacks that carry the trail into flatter terrain above the lip of the canyon. Luxuriant aspen groves such as those along this portion of the trail are common on the moist subalpine slopes of the San Juans. Bright green in summer and richly gold in autumn, aspen lend a swath of light color to the monotonous deep greens of the otherwise coniferous forests. The quiet rustle of quaking leaves and the sweet aroma of aspen bark, together with the promise of numerous wildflowers and random berry patches, make an aspen grove a place worth lingering.

As the climb eases, the trail winds through a series of open glades, allowing the first glimpses of the rugged peaks nearby. Tucked beneath the slopes of Dallas Peak, Mill Creek Basin may be seen to the north. An eventual destination of the trail, the basin hangs more than 1,000 feet above the meadows at your feet. Soon the forest closes in once again, with spruce and fir gradually outnumbering the aspen. The grade steepens, and after a long switchback the trail gains the crest of a ridge separating the Mill Creek and Eider Creek drainages, 1.75 miles from Mill Creek.

The Sneffels Highline diverges from the Deep Creek Trail here; bear right and continue along the crest of this ridge. Recently constructed, the Sneffels Highline does not appear on the outdated USGS map for Telluride and vicinity. Fortunately, the trail has been built according to high standards, and the entire route is easily followed. Initially, the ridge is nearly flat as it winds through another small aspen grove and into a clearing. Pause a moment to admire the panorama, for as the trail crosses into the Mount Sneffels Wilderness, the ascent begins in earnest. Winding through a long series of switchbacks, the trail climbs through a final grove of aspen, which, at more than 11,000 feet, is a rather high elevation for the species. Upon completing the final switchback, the trail turns eastward and begins a 2-mile traverse beneath the flanks of Dallas Peak. With modest grades, brilliant wild-flowers, long cascades, and outstanding views of the peaks ringing the upper San Miguel River drainage, these miles are among the most enjoyable of the hike.

The trail exits the wilderness area just before it begins a short climb into Mill Creek Basin. Guarded by the rocky summits of Gilpin Peak and Mount Emma, the basin is a garden of wildflowers all summer long. From the banks of ice-cold rivulets on the basin floor, columbine, paintbrush, bluebell, and snow buttercup grow high up the mountain walls before they finally disappear into the bare rock and scattered snowfields that reach towards the sky. After climbing gently along the basin floor, the trail once again commences a steeper climb. Switchbacking up bare rock slopes, the trail gains its apex on a ridge running west from the summit of Mount Emma. The vista from this airy promontory is the most dramatic of any on this hike—the towering summits of numerous peaks seem to be within arm's reach.

Descending the south side of the ridge, the trail drops into Pack Basin, a smaller but equally scenic version of Mill Creek Basin. Passing a long-abandoned cabin at the lower edge of the basin, the trail once again enters dense subalpine forest. Traversing away from the sloping gully floor, the trail gains the edge of a long ridge, then begins a steep descent down its eastern side. After winding back to the edge of this ridge, which offers a view deep into Mill Creek's canyon, the trail plummets into the Butcher Creek drainage and passes scattered meadows before it reenters a vast aspen grove. Upon reaching the floor of the gulch, the trail parallels the creek for nearly a mile until it eases into Epees Park, where there is a third trail junction.

After 8.5 miles of steep grades along Sneffels Highline, your knees will likely be grateful as the hike turns westward onto the newly reconstructed Waterline section of the Deep Creek Trail. (The Jud Weibe Trail splits from the Deep Creek Trail on the other side of Butcher Creek and arrives in Telluride after about a mile.) The final 2.25 miles of hiking are fairly level as the trail traces the path of Telluride's water pipeline en route to Mill Creek. Just beyond the bridge over Mill Creek, the path to the Mill Creek Trailhead splits to the left. Leave the Deep Creek Trail here and walk the 0.25 mile downstream to the trailhead.

BLAINE BASIN

DISTANCE: 6.5 miles round-trip

ELEVATION RANGE: 9,400 to 11,200 feet

TOTAL ELEVATION GAIN: 1,800 feet

TRAIL CONDITIONS: Generally moderate grade with good tread though steep and rocky at times; several stream crossings

SEASON: Late June until mid-October

USGS MAP: Mount Sneffels (1983)

ADMINISTRATION: Uncompahgre NF; Ouray RD

TRAILHEAD: From Ridgway, drive west on CO 62 and turn left onto CR 7 (marked East Dallas Creek) after 4.9 miles. Follow this dirt road and stay on the main road (which is usually signed Uncompahgre NF Access) until you arrive at the Blue Lakes Trailhead, which is 9.1 miles from the highway.

Blaine Basin

Well watered and verdant, Blaine Basin typifies the spectacular scenery of the Sneffels Range: a massive wall of peaks famous for its dramatic skyline; particularly expansive wildflower meadows; waterfalls; and historic mining relics. Though the trailhead is often crowded, the vast majority hike the well-known Blue Lakes Trail and leave Blaine Basin hikers in solitude. Because of past logging on nearby slopes, the basin was left outside the boundaries of the Mount Sneffels Wilderness. However, do not let this administrative decision diminish your expectations.

From the trailhead, hike past the gate, and you will quickly reach a signboard and registration box. The trail forks here, and the Blaine Basin route stays to the left and soon crosses East Dallas Creek. The trail—actually an old logging road—climbs back up the valley wall, switchbacking once before it turns into the Wilson Creek drainage. Before making the turn, steal a look over your shoulder for inspiring views of Dallas Peak. Once around the corner, the trail levels off and passes through scattered aspen and meadow before it reaches Wilson Creek, which is about a mile from the trailhead. Just before you reach the creek, look for a footpath that branches off the old road to the right—this leads to a plank crossing of the creek and a temporary postponement of wet feet.

Once across the bridge, climb away from the creek and you will soon reach a junction. Turn sharply to the right and continue following Wilson Creek upstream. The trail continues through both aspen and spruce forest, as well as grassy meadows, and remains quite gentle in grade for an additional 0.5 mile. Then it returns to the creek and crosses without benefit of a bridge, which can present problems during early-summer runoff. While a footpath leads upstream along the near bank, enticing you to search for alternate crossings, the ford before you is indeed the least difficult. Once across, the path leads through a sea of bluebells and other flowers before it reaches another unbridged creek crossing.

The real work of the hike commences from this point. After following the stream for a short distance and allowing a glance at the cataract pouring out of Blaine Basin, the trail bears to the left and begins to climb rather steeply up a rocky slope before it turns back to the right to ascend into the lower basin, 1 mile past and about 800 feet above the third creek crossing. This stretch can be narrow, and recent flooding has created erosion problems—use caution.

The lower basin offers an introduction to the wonders of the area. A sizable meadow, surrounded by steep mountain walls and several pretty cascades, invites rest and contemplation. Mount Sneffels—at 14,150 feet, the crown of the Sneffels Range—stands guard at the basin's rear, while innumerable wildflowers grace the open slopes. Backpackers will find several excellent campsites in the forest surrounding the meadow. The trail continues through the meadow, where it is obscure in places, then climbs up the avalanche-cleared slope below the upper basin, where the flowers are even more profuse and the peaks even more imposing. Though the trail soon disappears, wanderers will enjoy exploring a pair of abandoned mines and perhaps climbing to one of the high saddles at the back of the basin. The steep and ice-cloaked couloirs that lead to Mount Sneffels's lofty summit are the exclusive domain of technical climbers.

Bear Creek–American Flats

The Bear Creek drainage and the adjacent alpine plateau known as American Flats epitomize the spectacular scenery for which the San Juans are famous. Bear Creek rushes through a world of deep gorges, steep mountain walls, cool forests, and numerous mining relics. American Flats is a vast flower-bespeckled meadow that stretches to a panorama of sky-scraping peaks. The trail system through this slice of America's Alps provides opportunities for excellent hikes lasting anywhere from a few hours to several days. However you choose to explore the area's scenery and history, it is likely to become a favorite for years to come.

BEAR CREEK–AMERICAN FLATS

GRIZZLY BEAR MINE

DISTANCE: 4.5 miles round-trip

ELEVATION RANGE: 8,500 to 10,000 feet

TOTAL ELEVATION GAIN: 1,500 feet

TRAIL CONDITIONS: Moderate grades; steep drop-offs below trail; trail is narrow in places

SEASON: Mid-May through October

USGS MAPS: Ouray (1955); Ironton (1955)

ADMINISTRATION: Uncompahgre NF; Ouray RD

YELLOW JACKET MINE

DISTANCE: 8.5 miles round-trip

ELEVATION RANGE: 8,500 to 11,100 feet

TOTAL ELEVATION GAIN: 2,600 feet

TRAIL CONDITIONS: Moderate grades; steep drop-offs below trail; trail is narrow in places

SEASON: Mid-June through September

USGS MAPS: Ouray (1955); Ironton (1955); Handies Peak (1955)

ADMINISTRATION: Uncompahgre NF; Ouray RD

AMERICAN FLATS

DISTANCE: 7 miles round-trip

ELEVATION RANGE: 11,200 to 12,800 feet

TOTAL ELEVATION GAIN: 1,800 feet

TRAIL CONDITIONS: Tread faint in places; majority of hike above treeline and exposed to poor weather; moderate grades

SEASON: Late July through September

USGS MAPS: Handies Peak (1955); Wetterhorn Peak (1963)

ADMINISTRATION: Uncompahgre NF; Ouray RD, BLM; Gunnison RA

As described here, the entire hike is a multiday "dumbbell" circuit; however, this can be split into several smaller day hikes in order to sample smaller portions of the trail system. The most popular options are to hike to either the Grizzly Bear Mine or the Yellow Jacket Mine, beginning from the lower trailhead on US 550. Both destinations offer very scenic hiking and numerous mining relics. If a high-clearance, four-wheel-drive vehicle is at your disposal, a high-altitude option is to make a loop across American Flats and the headwaters basin of Bear Creek. This segment features some of the most beautiful alpine scenery around.

Though generally safe, the trail along the lower 2 miles of Bear Creek is not for the faint of heart, nor for small children. Originally built by miners to access the canyon, the trail is carved directly from sheer cliffs in places, and a slip could spell a disastrous descent into the gorge below. However, despite its vertiginous nature, the trail is fairly wide, and except in a few locations where washouts and rock slides have damaged the tread, there is little in the way of tricky footing. The remainder of the Bear Creek Trail is straightforward and is traversed with little difficulty. Because the trail across American Flats is faint and possibly confusing in places, good navigation skills are required for this segment. Additionally, hikers on the Flats are completely exposed to potentially dangerous weather, so an early start and a keen eye for the weather are highly recommended.

The Bear Creek Trail begins across US 550 from the parking area at the south end of the highway tunnel. The trail climbs atop the tunnel and begins a somewhat steep ascent. After switchbacking for nearly a mile, the trail turns and enters the Bear Creek canyon, which is nearly 1,000 feet above the highway. The unique geology of the area is readily apparent throughout this portion of the hike, which traverses some of the oldest and most tortured rocks in the San Juans. At first the trail winds through a barren slope of slate, then after a brief area of quartzite, it enters a thick layer of tuff. Slate and quartzite are metamorphic rocks, altered from their original sedimentary state by intense heat and pressure. Tuff is composed of compressed and hardened volcanic ash, and the fact that this layer of rock is thousands of feet thick in this area illustrates the massive scale of the volcanic eruptions that raked the San Juans millions of years ago.

BEAR CREEK–AMERICAN FLATS CIRCUIT
DISTANCE: 16 miles round-trip
ELEVATION RANGE: 8,500 to 12,800 feet
TOTAL ELEVATION GAIN: 4,500 feet
TRAIL CONDITIONS: See both the Grizzly Bear Mine and American Flats descriptions
SEASON: Late July through September
USGS MAPS: Ouray (1955); Ironton (1955); Handies Peak (1955); Wetterhorn Peak (1963)
ADMINISTRATION: Uncompahgre NF; Ouray RD, BLM; Gunnison RA

BEAR CREEK TRAILHEAD: Located just south of the US 550 tunnel, 2.3 miles south of Ouray.
AMERICAN FLATS ACCESS: Drive south from Ouray for 3.6 miles on US 550 and turn left on Engineer Pass Road, which requires a high-clearance, four-wheel-drive vehicle. Drive for about 10 miles on this very rough road, being sure to stay on the most heavily traveled track and follow signs to the pass. Park at the summit of the pass, near the sign. To reach the pass from Lake City, drive west on Henson Creek Road for 18 miles. The last few miles of this route also require a four-wheel-drive vehicle.

❦❦❦

Once into the deeply incised canyon of Bear Creek, the trail becomes more gentle; however, it clings to near-vertical cliffs several hundred feet above the rushing water. This section of the tread was hand hewn by prospectors using nothing more than picks, shovels, and a few sticks of dynamite. Washouts and rock slides are beginning to take their toll on this engineering feat, and extra caution should be exercised in such places.

The juxtaposition of American Flats: rolling tundra spread before rocky spires.

Rust-colored mineral veins can be seen in this area and often include small groups of quartz crystals, pyrite, and galena.

As you near the Grizzly Bear Mine, some 2 miles from the trailhead, you'll start seeing scattered pieces of rusty mine equipment, including a massive iron boiler. Considering the condition of the trail, the transport of such equipment was a herculean effort that speaks powerfully of the determination of those looking for gold. The Grizzly Bear was established in 1875 and operated with varying degrees of success for several decades. The wood structure adjacent to the trail is what remains of the boardinghouse, while the actual mine is located on the opposite side of the narrow gorge. The two were connected by a beautiful wooden bridge that has long since been demolished by floods and snowslides. The boardinghouse has recently begun to collapse at an accelerated rate, and the relics left by the dozens of people who lived and worked there are slowly melting into the earth.

Above the Grizzly Bear, the trail continues along the north side of Bear Creek, climbs moderately up the valley, and alternates between brightly colored meadows and cool subalpine forest. The quiet hiker may glimpse deer and elk, or perhaps a solitary black bear. While the trail to the Grizzly Bear Mine, with its southern exposure, usually melts free of snow by mid-May, this section does not tend to open up until mid-June.

The Yellow Jacket Mine is encountered 2 miles beyond the Grizzly Bear. Developed around 1915, there is still a large amount of detritus strewn about the vicinity. Several waterfalls are nearby, and there are ample, well-sheltered campsites available. A short distance above the Yellow Jacket the trail splits, and the loop portion of the hike begins. Keeping to the right, the trail continues upward along Bear Creek. Though neither crossing is typically challenging, the trail does ford the creek twice within the 0.5 mile above the junction. Shortly above the second crossing the trail climbs a short, steep hill, the top of which marks treeline and the lower edge of the broad basin at Bear Creek's headwaters. Hiking through the meadows of the basin is very pleasant, though the tread can be sketchy in places. An encircling ring of peaks forms the basin walls, while mines and prospect holes dot the basin's carpet of flowers and grass. Upon reaching a larger mine near the rear of the basin, the trail turns onto an abandoned road and climbs somewhat more steeply for the remaining 0.5 mile to the jeep road at Engineer Pass, 3 miles from the Yellow Jacket.

Crossing the pass, the route continues toward American Flats by contouring around the east side of the ridge that divides Bear Creek from the drainages to the east. The trail is faint and is often confused by braided paths caused by frequent sheepherding. The general idea is to stay as high on the gentle slopes below the aforementioned ridge as possible and bear directly north toward Wildhorse Peak. The desire to wander aimlessly across the tundra is strong, as the vast meadows—which are usually blanketed in a rainbow of wildflower color—that lead you toward the awesome pinnacles of Uncompahgre Peak, the Wetterhorn, the Matterhorn, and Wildhorse Peak allow some of the most scenic (and easy) alpine hiking in the Rockies. Be cautious of the weather, however, as these nearly 2.5-mile-high slopes are exposed to severe thunderstorms, blustery winds, and frigid temperatures—even in midsummer. Furthermore, the lack of trees and other landmarks makes it frighteningly easy to become disoriented, especially when visibility is reduced. A map, compass, and route-finding skills are essential for a safe traverse of American Flats.

Finding the correct trail back in toward Bear Creek—indeed, finding the correct drainage—can be tricky. No easily discerned path leads in the right direction, while visible paths that head east toward American Lake and northwest across open slopes confuse the situation. Consult your map often to locate the correct route. What may be easiest is to hike north from Engineer Pass for about 1.5 miles until you reach the wide saddle directly south of Wildhorse Peak. The Horsethief Trail, which heads northwest, diverges from the trail to American Lake at this saddle—a sign may be posted at the junction. From this junction, climb gently across open tundra at a bearing of 240 degrees (gaining some 200 feet until cresting a broad hill, where a medium-size cairn is located). The USGS map shows a trail, though none is discernible at the present time. From this hill, which divides American Flats from a tributary of Bear Creek, a faint path can be followed westward as it descends across a talus slope and into a small basin on the north side of Peak 13132. Once in the basin, the tread becomes easier to follow as it drops rapidly down the small gulch, passes the snout of a small rock glacier, and eventually joins the Bear Creek Trail just below treeline, 2.5 miles from American Flats. A right turn on the Bear Creek Trail soon leads to the Yellow Jacket Mine, and eventually to US 550. A left turn returns to Engineer Pass.

Wetterhorn Basin

Billing itself as the Switzerland of America, Ouray County does so in large part due to the dramatic sculpted peaks of the Uncompahgre Wilderness. This collection of jagged, cliff-bound giants—Uncompahgre, Precipice, Coxcomb, the Matterhorn, and the Wetterhorn, each of which rise far above an emerald carpet of tundra—resembles the European Alps more closely than just about any North American mountain range. Centered near the heart of this magnificent alpine setting is a broad, flower-filled cirque called Wetterhorn Basin, and a journey into its expansive fold is particularly satisfying.

The hike begins near the headwaters of the Cimarron River's west fork, climbs through a 12,500-foot pass at the head of that valley, and drops into Wetterhorn Basin. Though it is a worthy backpacking destination, Wetterhorn Basin is regarded as one of the best day hikes in the entire Uncompahgre Wilderness. Because the trail has recently been reengineered, the hike is suitable for anyone willing and able to tackle a bit of steep climbing and the rather high altitude. Be forewarned: Most of the hike is above timberline, and summer storms seem to strike this area with a particular ferociousness, often sneaking up very quickly from behind the wall of peaks that encircle the area.

From the end of West Fork Road, the trail climbs gently through the open meadows of the west fork's valley. From the very beginning of the hike, the panorama of mountains surrounding the valley is exceptional, and the knowledge that the trail will soon carry you high onto their shoulders is likely to spur you eagerly upward. The trail officially enters the Uncompahgre Wilderness after 0.75 mile, and after a brief interlude of subalpine forest, it breaks into the open basin at the head of the valley. The most impressive of the cirque's ring of peaks is the distinctive block of the Coxcomb. This 13,656-foot summit is a rectangular mass of volcanic rock, capped by a sheer face 500 feet high. The basin in its shadow is a verdant beauty, well decorated by wildflowers and cascades.

The first 1.5 miles of trail leading into the basin are rather easy, but the next mile to the pass at the head of the valley is a much steeper climb. Fortunately, this ascent has been made more reasonable by the realignment of the trail. Instead of climbing directly up the slope, the trail now has a series of switchbacks, which were constructed to ease the overall grade of the trail and make it a bit easier to enjoy the many wildflowers and fabulous vistas as the elevation slowly increases. A small bench located at the 12,000-foot level is an excellent place for a breather; the view down valley encompasses the spire of Chimney Rock, the adjacent bulk of Courthouse Mountain, as well as the distant silhouettes of both the West Elk Mountains and Grand Mesa—both of which are scores of miles away. Parts of this bench are reminiscent of the glacial "forefields" found in the Alps as well as other glaciated mountain ranges. Forefields are barren expanses of gravel and scoured rock that have so recently been released from glacial ice that little

WETTERHORN BASIN

DISTANCE: 9 miles round-trip

ELEVATION RANGE: 10,750 to 12,500 feet

TOTAL ELEVATION GAIN: 2,450 feet

TRAIL CONDITIONS: Good tread, though steep in a few places; occasionally rocky

SEASON: July through September

USGS MAP: Wetterhorn Peak (1983)

ADMINISTRATION: Uncompahgre NF; Ouray RD

TRAILHEAD: From the intersection of US 550 and CO 62 in Ridgway, drive north on US 550 for 1.8 miles and turn right onto CR 10 (signed Silver Jack Reservoir and Owl Creek Pass). After traveling 0.9 mile on this gravel road, bear left. Continue directly ahead at another junction 1.5 miles farther, then bear right at a third junction 1.3 miles beyond that. Finally, 5.3 miles from US 550, bear left onto CR 8, which becomes FR 858 at the Uncompahgre NF boundary. Continue for 10.4 miles on this road, and turn right onto West Fork Road (FR 860) just after cresting Owl Creek Pass (this intersection is 25.6 miles south of US 50 via FR 858). All vehicles can manage the first 2 miles of West Fork Road, but a four-wheel drive is required for the final 1.3 miles to the trailhead. If a four-wheel drive is unavailable, add 2.6 miles round-trip to your hiking distance, with about 200 feet of additional elevation gain.

or no vegetation has been able to establish a foothold there. Of course, these mountains have been without significant glaciation for the last ten thousand years; however, rock slides, avalanches, and the rapid erosion of the volcanic rock have combined to make life difficult for plants in many places.

The final 500 feet of ascent to the pass is the steepest, and this north-facing slope often remains buried beneath the previous winter's snow until July. However, even this part of the hike is not particularly difficult, and the satisfaction of reaching the pass makes the effort worthwhile. Many hikers will be tempted to make the pass their turn-around point, but the verdant expanse visible in the basin below—Wetterhorn Basin—is likely to draw you downward. The prize of the hike is the view of the great west face of Wetterhorn Peak, which, at 14,015 feet, attains an elevation equal to its massive stature. From the crest of the pass, the peak is hidden behind the shoulder of an intervening mountain, but it quickly comes into view as you descend into a small gully. The trail becomes a bit fainter, though cairns lead you on the correct route. The trail drops about 700 feet in 1.5 miles to reach the floor of the basin and the bank of Wetterhorn Creek, which lies at the center of a grandiose heaven of flowers, mountains, and sky.

Cimarron Headwaters

Backpackers who seek to immerse themselves in some version of alpine heaven need look no further than the headwaters of the Cimarron River. At the heart of the Uncompahgre Wilderness, the forks of the Cimarron flow through three magnificent glacial valleys, each of whose walls are lined by castellated ridges of volcanic rock and whose far reaches are guarded by savage peaks. These valleys—indeed, the entire Uncompah-gre Wilderness—are further distinguished by the extent and beauty of their alpine tundra, which from distant vantages appears to be uniformly green, but proves to be a true panoply of wildflowers trailside. While the west fork leads hikers into Wetterhorn Basin, looping through the east fork and middle fork valleys can create a classic shuttle hike.

A departure from the East Fork Trailhead is recommended, despite the fact that this trailhead is 800 feet lower than the Middle Fork Trailhead. A journey in this direction results in a greater sense of anticipation as progress is slowly made up valley, though hiking in the reverse direction is ultimately just as satisfying. If a car shuttle or some similar arrangement cannot be made, it is possible to complete the loop by walking an additional 6.5 road miles between the two trailheads. Note: Despite its wilderness status, the Uncompahgre—particularly these valleys—remain sheep-grazing country, and the presence of a herd may require changing the location of your camps.

Ascending the east fork, the trail climbs easily up the beautiful valley and hugs the riverbank at first before it traverses a series of grassy meadows. The walls on either side of the valley are spectacularly rugged, sufficient to inspire a moniker such as the "Devil's Picket Fence" or something equally as descriptive. Alas, the first explorers of this drainage ignored the opportunity to bestow such a name, but this oversight in no way diminishes from the sharp spires and steep cliffs that steadily rise toward the collection of peaks in the distance.

About 2 miles in, the trail enters into the subalpine forest, and shortly beyond this, crosses a small tributary brook. This drainage, like most others in the upper Cimarron valleys, has obviously been ravaged in the very recent past by some tremendous flooding. Boulders are strewn about the area, and vegetation has been stripped away from the bank of the stream. After climbing somewhat steeply out of the streambed, the trail

CIMARRON HEADWATERS

DISTANCE: 16 miles one-way

ELEVATION RANGE: 9,300 to 12,600 feet

TOTAL ELEVATION GAIN: 3,300 feet

TRAIL CONDITIONS: Good trail with gentle to moderate grades, though 1.5-mile sections on either side of the pass are steep and the tread is faint to nonexistent; trail can be muddy, particularly if sheep herds have been moved through the area; wading the Cimarron River's east fork is necessary, though it is usually only ankle- to calf-deep by midsummer

SEASON: July through September

USGS MAPS: Sheep Mountain (1963); Uncompahgre Peak (1982); Wetterhorn Peak (1983); Courthouse Mountain (1983)

ADMINISTRATION: Uncompahgre NF; Ouray RD

EAST FORK TRAILHEAD: From the junction of CO 62 and US 550 in Ridgway, drive north on US 550 for 1.8 miles and turn right onto CR 10 (signed Silver Jack Reservoir and Owl Creek Pass). After 0.9 mile on this gravel road, bear left, continue directly ahead at another junction 1.5 miles farther, then bear right at a third junction 1.3 miles beyond that. Finally, 5.3 miles from US 550, bear left onto CR 8, which becomes FR 858 at the Uncompahgre NF boundary. Continue on this road, crest Owl Creek Pass, and avoid West Fork Road, which is reached after an additional 10.4 miles. Avoid Middle Fork Road, which is 6.2 miles after this intersection, and turn right onto East Fork Road, 0.3 mile farther. (This junction is 19.1 miles north of US 50 via FR 858.) Drive 1.6 miles to the trailhead at the end of East Fork Road.

MIDDLE FORK TRAILHEAD: From the aforementioned intersection of Middle Fork Road and FR 858, drive Middle Fork Road for 1.9 miles, bear left at a fork, and continue another 2.7 miles to the trailhead at road's end. This road is rough in a few places.

levels and traverses a steep sidehill (caution: footing is tricky when it's wet) before it eases back onto the gently sloping forest floor. The hike continues in this manner for the next 4 miles: easy grades with minor ups and downs, shady subalpine forest, and numerous brooks, with the east fork usually near at hand. Good camping is available in many places.

Finally, the forest opens as the trail enters a long meadow some 6 miles above the trailhead. The magnificent north face of 14,309-foot Uncompahgre Peak towers above the valley ahead, steep mountain walls give rise to numerous cascades, and the meadow offers the first of what promises to be many outstanding flower fields. After another mile of pleasant walking, you'll arrive at the site of the old Silver Jack Mine. The Silver Jack dates from the early twentieth century, when gold, silver, zinc, and lead attracted miners to this remote setting. The historic buildings at the mine remained in reasonably good condition until the winter of 1996, when a tremendous avalanche obliterated the site and leveled the two hundred- to three hundred-year-old trees surrounding it. The trail has been rerouted through the matchstick remains of this forest, and the remnants of the old cabins are slowly crumbling into the earth.

Just beyond the Silver Jack, the trail crosses the east fork. Except during spring runoff, this ford is without difficulty, and it may be possible to leap the various channels of the braided stream. The trail then climbs moderately through open meadow, winds through another tributary stream, and breaks above treeline just prior to a faint junction, which is 1 mile above the river crossing. This junction, which is not depicted on the Uncompahgre Peak map, is marked by a post located just off the trail; our route bears right onto very faint tread and climbs along the valley's west wall. The more discernible tread continues directly ahead, soon returns to the bank of the east fork, and crosses to the other side. If you arrive at the river bank, simply backtrack and locate the junction within 0.25 mile.

Fiery light falls upon the walls of the Cimarron as an afternoon storm fades into night.

Once on the fainter path, the grade remains moderate for about 0.5 mile, then levels and returns to the open valley floor. These alpine fields are home to beautiful wildflowers and provide outstanding vistas to the peaks surrounding the valley. Uncompahgre Peak looms almost directly overhead, while Matterhorn Peak stands just beyond. Soon, the dark spire of Wetterhorn Peak comes into view, completing the trio of Swiss Alp–like summits. About 0.75 mile above the previous junction, the USGS map indicates a second junction, though this divergent path is no longer visible on the ground. A half mile beyond this point is a discernable junction (marked by another post). Keep to the right, and continue up through the basin while the left branch crosses the east fork and climbs along an old prospector's road on the slopes of the Matterhorn.

The tread on our route soon begins to peter out as it climbs toward the head of the valley. At last glance, you'll see the trail climbing steeply up the mountain slopes, just to the right of a ravine. Beyond this point, posts mark the route; however, a few random posts are in the open basin, which could potentially throw a wrench in your route-finding machinery. The visible goal is the lowest saddle on the basin's west wall: a 12,595-foot pass separating the east and middle fork drainages. In general terms, the route climbs parallel to the ravine until the 12,000-foot contour, turns west and crosses the drainage, and follows a small ridge toward the pass. The hiking— though steep in places, and potentially snowy until at least mid-July— is magnificent.

Upon cresting the pass (10.75 miles from the East Fork Trailhead), take a last look back at Uncompahgre and the Wetterhorn, then begin an equally steep descent into the grassy basin at the head of the middle fork. Again, the trail is very faint, but posts have been placed to aid in navigation. After about a mile, you'll see a trail after you reach a grassy bench. A few switchbacks farther is the floor of the basin and another unmarked trail junction. Turn to the right and proceed down valley, enjoying a mile of gentle strolling in a lovely alpine setting. Like the east fork's headwaters, this basin is a perfect mix of wildflowers, cascades, and striking peaks. Coxcomb Peak—one of the San Juan's most distinctive summits—is the prominent column of rock towering above the head of the basin.

Leaving the basin, the trail descends moderately through subalpine forest and arrives at the creek that drains Porphyry Basin in a little more than a mile. An old footbridge here is no longer safe, but logs and rocks should keep your feet dry. Below this crossing, 2 miles of trail remain, with forested descent being the general character throughout the remainder of the hike. The rushing middle fork is always nearby, and good campsites are plentiful. Occasional breaks in the forest permit excellent views of Precipice Peak, as well as of numerous other spires of gray, volcanic rock along the valley walls. Arrival at the wilderness boundary signifies that the end of the hike is near, and a few more minutes' worth of walking brings you to the Middle Fork Trailhead and journey's end.

Uncompahgre Peak

The literal culmination of the San Juans is found atop the 14,309-foot summit of Uncompahgre Peak. Its status as the sixth-tallest peak in the Rockies ensures the hike's popularity; however, many people are drawn to the mountain after simply admiring its impressive form rising far above surrounding slopes of verdant tundra. Few who embark upon the ascent are disappointed, either in terms of dramatic alpine scenery or a sense of accomplishment.

The summit of Uncompahgre falls away on three sides in broken slopes and sheer cliffs as high as 800 vertical feet. However, on the fourth side a long, ramplike ridge permits people to walk directly to the top. There is only one short section on this route that requires particular caution: a steep slope of slippery scree and loose talus that is about 100 feet in height— but even this obstacle is easily overcome by all but the most inexperienced hikers. The most dangerous aspects of the climb are two that are common to any alpine hike in the San Juans: high altitude and changeable weather. The entire hike is above timberline, so start early and plan to be back at the trailhead by noon in order to avoid afternoon thunderstorms. Stretch this deadline only if the skies show no signs of tempestuousness.

From the trailhead, a fine trail climbs gradually along Nellie Creek and into the Uncompahgre Wilderness. The trail closely follows the rushing creek for much of the first mile, winding through patches of forest and

UNCOMPAHGRE PEAK

DISTANCE: 7 miles round-trip

ELEVATION RANGE: 11,400 to 14,309 feet

TOTAL ELEVATION GAIN: 2,900 feet

TRAIL CONDITIONS: Constructed trail with moderate to steep grades, except a single portion of steep scrambling on loose talus near the summit; snowfields are usually encountered until mid-July

SEASON: July through September

USGS MAP: Uncompahgre Peak (1982)

ADMINISTRATION: Uncompahgre NF; Ouray RD

TRAILHEAD: In Lake City, drive west from CO 149 on Second Street (signed Engineer Pass) for 2 blocks, then turn left on Henson Creek Road. Drive this dirt road for 5 miles and then turn right onto Nellie Creek Road. The trailhead is at the end of this road, 4.1 miles away. The road requires high-clearance, four-wheel-drive vehicles but is not particularly difficult. If you do not have a four-wheel drive, you'll need to park at this junction, which makes the hike much more difficult.

small meadows bright with spectacular displays of bluebell, columbine, and bittercress. After a moderately steep switchback, the trail arrives at the lower end of a broad, alpine basin and a signed trail junction. Take the left fork and enjoy another mile of gentle to moderate ascent across the basin's beautiful floor. This is classic alpine scenery, complete with roaring cascades, breeze-swirled wildflowers, and rock-strewn ridges. Uncompahgre, which rises yet another 2,000 feet into the sky, overshadows all of this, as its great thrust of dull gray rock is the epitome of the archetypal mountain image.

The trail steepens and becomes rougher as its ascends to the side of the basin and onto Uncompahgre's southeast ridge. A second trail junction is located here; our route stays to right, while the fainter left fork continues into the basin farther west and eventually to the base of 14,015-foot Wetterhorn Peak. The ascent onto the ridge is also where snowfields are likely to remain longest into the summer, though none are steep enough to present a serious hazard.

Once onto the ridge, the climb becomes more arduous as the grade relents in fewer places, and the ever-thinner air takes a greater toll on the body's energy. Ample excuse to stop and rest is found in the increasingly spectacular vistas seen from the mountain's slopes. After a brief, level stretch at the 13,400-foot level, the trail ascends a series of steep switchbacks to arrive on a small saddle above a set of impressive cliffs. The "crux" of the climb is upon you now; after a brief traverse across a steep talus field, the route—marked by cairns—turns directly up a slope of broken talus and scree. While the ascent isn't very difficult, the descent can be somewhat tricky. Just above this slope is the much gentler summit ridge, upon which the final 200 feet are gained over another 0.25 mile. The trail ends on the summit of Uncompahgre, just a few steps from the brink of its great north-facing cliffs.

Befitting the crown of the San Juans, the panorama below you encompasses a sea of rock, snow, and sky. Countless peaks line the horizon, with the great pinnacles of the Uncompahgre Wilderness—among them Wetterhorn Peak, Coxcomb Peak, and Precipice Peak—and the massive shoulders of the Sneffels Range, the west Silverton group, and the La Garitas among the many identifiable mountain groups rising beyond the intervening ridges, basins, and valleys. At your feet, the glacial valleys of the Cimarron River, Big Blue Creek, El Paso Creek, and Nellie Creek radiate toward the four points of the compass, while a mosaic of emerald-green tundra and blinding white snow paint all that is not bare rock. In short, it is a most satisfying finale.

Cataract Gulch

No bubbling brook, this; it is a torrent of icy water that roars over the rocks and logs of Cataract Gulch, a steep, hanging valley that drains the Continental Divide high above the Lake Fork valley. Several small waterfalls mark its course, and both banks are lined with lush growths of bluebells, bittercress, and paintbrush. At its headwaters is a broad alpine cirque, where willows and tundra crowd the shore of a placid tarn. The hike up the gulch is not incredibly difficult, but bring some wading shoes, because with five different fords of the creek, your feet will get wet.

The first stream crossings appear immediately after you depart the trailhead, but these—across Cottonwood Creek—are made via a pair of anchored logs. The trail then enters the Handies Peak Wilderness Study Area, which is part of the greater Carson Peak Roadless Area (which hopefully will someday be added to the San Juans' collection of designated wilderness). Climbing steadily, the trail bears directly toward the mouth of the gulch before it turns and switchbacks up the mountain wall east of the gulch. Recently reconstructed, this portion of the trail does not appear on the Redcloud Peak map. However, the grade is steady, the tread is smooth, and the damp forest is refreshing.

Announced by the steady roar of the creek, the trail turns into the gulch after it completes its sixth switchback. Now on the route of the original miners' path into the gulch, the trail steepens and becomes rougher. The creek is entrancing, and brief stops to enjoy its many riffles and eddies are warranted. With progress up the gulch, the surrounding wildflower gardens become ever more impressive, and by

CATARACT GULCH

DISTANCE: 9 miles round-trip
ELEVATION RANGE: 9,600 to 12,100 feet
TOTAL ELEVATION GAIN: 2,500 feet
TRAIL CONDITIONS: Steady, moderate to steep grades; rough in places; multiple unbridged stream crossings
SEASON: July through September
USGS MAPS: Redcloud Peak (1964); Pole Creek Mountain (1964)
ADMINISTRATION: BLM; Gunnison RA

TRAILHEAD: From Lake City, drive south on CO 149 for 2.3 miles and turn right onto the road signed Lake San Cristobal and Alpine Loop Backcountry Byway. Drive this road, which turns to gravel after about 4 miles, for approximately 12 miles. Bear left at the road signed Sherman and continue another mile to the large, signed trailhead.

the time the trail climbs across a series of avalanche-cleared slopes, the display is at times quite phenomenal. A bit less than 2 miles from the trailhead, the trail crosses the overgrown remains of an old mine dump. A few steps farther—safely out of reach of winter's avalanches—is the miners' cabin. The first stream crossing is here—expect 10 to 15 yards of calf-deep water. Upon reaching the opposite bank, the trail switchbacks up the gully wall adjacent to the hike's most impressive waterfall. The trail then recrosses the stream just above the top of the cascade, where the stream races through an interesting bedrock chute. Use caution when crossing here—the rock is slippery, and the brink of the falls is just a few feet below the ford.

After a short, forested climb, the trail crosses the creek yet again. This ford, like the last two, does not appear on the USGS maps. With three fords within 0.5 mile, hikers who try to preserve dry boots by wading barefoot will find this portion of the hike slow, painful going. (As previously mentioned, wading shoes are highly recommended for this hike.) A steep, slippery climb awaits on the opposite bank, which brings the trail onto a talus bench at the lower end of Cataract Creek's headwaters basin. Though the lower gulch features scenery typical of the western San Juans—somber cliffs, waterfalls, a carpet of wildflowers—the upper basin is more representative of terrain common to the eastern San Juans: rolling, tundra-covered slopes; broad-shouldered mountain peaks; and dense willow thickets. The willows create the impression of a plush jade carpet blanketing the lower slopes of somber, gray peaks, while glistening snowfields and cascades drape the basin's walls.

A fourth ford comes a frustratingly short distance after the third. Pause here to admire both the scenic cascade just upstream as well as 14,001-foot Sunshine Peak behind you, which is perfectly framed between the lower walls of the gulch. The next 1.5 miles of hiking are easy and enjoyable as the trail ambles along the basin floor, passes a series of small ponds, and crosses the stream a fifth and final time. Cataract Lake is nestled just below the rolling crest of the Divide. The largest of several nearby tarns, it typically offers poor fishing but is a satisfying destination nonetheless. If you wish to hike farther afield, the Continental Divide Trail (CDT) is intercepted just south of the Divide itself, with many wilderness miles in either direction. The most popular extension of this hike travels cross-country along the Divide crest until it intersects the Cuba Gulch Trail a few miles to the west. Descending this scenic trail will bring you to the Cottonwood Gulch four-wheel-drive road, about 3 miles above the Cataract Gulch Trailhead.

American Basin– Handies Peak

American Basin deserves special mention, even among the seemingly endless number of outstanding San Juan hiking trails. From its expansive floor to its soaring walls, the basin is perfect for both casual wandering and determined trekking. In your quest for the beautiful, dramatic, and interesting, you may choose to roam among vast meadows; hike to an austere, cliff-sheltered lake; or even scale one of Colorado's highest mountains. Distinctive because it allows relatively easy access to such a lofty point (14,048-foot-high Handies Peak), an American Basin hike is a fun, scenic, and easy way to feel like you're on top of the world.

Before setting out, consider a pair of warnings. As with any hike above treeline, lightning is a serious hazard on many summer days. Hikers who have spent any length of time huddled beneath the onslaught of a mountain thunderstorm know what a frightening, uncomfortable, and potentially dangerous situation it can be. To avoid such unpleasantness, begin your day early, plan on returning to the trailhead by noon, and watch the weather with a careful eye and a willingness to retreat.

AMERICAN BASIN– HANDIES PEAK

SLOAN LAKE
DISTANCE: 3.5 miles round-trip
ELEVATION RANGE: 11,600 to 12,900 feet
TOTAL ELEVATION GAIN: 1,300 feet
TRAIL CONDITIONS: Rocky in places; moderate to steep grades throughout
SEASON: July until mid-October
USGS MAP: Handies Peak (1955)
ADMINISTRATION: BLM; Gunnison RA
HANDIES PEAK
DISTANCE: 5.5 miles round-trip
ELEVATION RANGE: 11,600 to 14,048 feet
TOTAL ELEVATION GAIN: 2,450 feet
TRAIL CONDITIONS: Rocky in places, with some areas of loose scree; moderate to steep grades; constant exposure to poor weather
SEASON: July through September
USGS MAP: Handies Peak (1955)
ADMINISTRATION: BLM; Gunnison RA

TRAILHEAD: From Lake City, drive south on CO 149 for 2.5 miles and turn right onto the route signed Lake San Cristobal and Alpine Loop Scenic Byway. This road passes the lake and turns to gravel after 4 miles. After an additional 8.5 miles, the road splits—take the right fork, signed Cinnamon Pass. This road becomes much rougher, but it should still be passable for most two-wheel-drive vehicles with moderate clearance. Another 8 miles brings you to a left-branching road marked American Basin. This road requires a high-clearance, four-wheel-drive vehicle and ends 0.75 mile farther, at the trailhead. If a four-wheel-drive vehicle is not available, park at this junction and walk the additional 0.75 mile, which adds 300 feet of elevation.

Equally as important—especially if the summit of Handies is your goal—be cautious of what effect the high altitude may have upon you. At nearly 3 miles above sea level, even the simple act of breathing can be a struggle. Should you begin to experience symptoms of altitude sickness, an immediate descent to lower elevations will spare you discomfort and possibly even serious illness.

From the end of the American Basin four-wheel-drive road, which is adjacent to the vestiges of the Old Gnome Mine, the trail climbs moderately along the east side of the valley floor. From the very beginning, the track is surrounded by showy wildflower meadows. Entirely above treeline, the basin's fertile volcanic soil and abundant precipitation have resulted in a particularly lush garden of alpine flora. From a carpet of emerald green, acres upon acres of blossoms explode during the short summer. As if a full palate had been spilled upon the mountain slopes, broad sweeps of blue, red, white, and yellow paint this natural canvas. A steady breeze blurs the individual flowers into one large mass of swaying color, which even the best impressionist painter could only dream of duplicating.

Forming a striking contrast with this display of nature's delicate beauty is the raw power of the basin's imposing mountain walls. The western ramparts are steeply sloped masses of rock and tundra, whose small ravines are graced by long cascades and whose high shoulders cup small ponds. The basin's southern headwall forms a brooding barricade with sheer rock faces, saw-toothed silhouettes, and shade-protected snowbanks, which form the quintessential mountain panorama. To the east looms the great bulk of Handies Peak, which in form may seem subdued compared to the southern wall, but whose elevation exceeds all others in the vicinity.

Near the back of the basin the trail splits, and our fork proceeds to the left and commences a steeper climb. In a short time this grade slackens, and the trail enters a small bowl through which pours the cascading rivulets that form the headwaters of the Lake Fork of the Gunnison River. The trail becomes confusing here—a boot-beaten path, which seems to be the obvious route, steeply ascends the scree slope to the left; however, the actual trail switchbacks up the short, steep slope to the right to arrive at the shore of

Sloan Lake. A worthy destination on its own, the lake rests beneath an encircling line of cliffs that shelter the lake from the sun for all but a few hours of the day. The result is a lake whose radiant surface is often glazed by ice, dotted with miniature icebergs, and fringed by snowfields for most of the summer.

The trail continues toward the summit of Handies Peak, losing a small amount of elevation before climbing once again around the back side of the bowl and crossing talus and (until late July) a broad snowfield. The grade steepens for a short section as it gains the flank of Handies, then eases as it begins several long switchbacks up the tundra-covered mountainside. Roughly 0.75 mile beyond the lake, the trail attains a narrow sad-

American Basin's first dusting of snow at the end of an autumn storm.

dle at the 13,500-foot level. Pause here to regain energy and admire the beautiful views down the steep-walled basin at the head of Boulder Gulch. The remaining 0.25 mile climbs rather steeply up loose scree and through rarefied air to Handies's 14,048-foot-high summit.

If time and weather permit, sit awhile atop the summit and ponder the vast panorama of peaks visible in all directions. Some mountaineers insist that the view from Handies offers the most inspiring view of the surrounding San Juans. Summits in the Grenadier, San Miguel, and Sneffels Ranges, as well as the west Silverton group, are easily identified to the south and west. Behind the 14,000-foot bulks of Sunshine and Redcloud Peaks, the La Garitas form the eastern horizon, and the unmistakable skyline created by Uncompahgre Peak, Wetterhorn Peak, and others in the Uncompahgre Wilderness dominate the view to the north. When your appetite for the vista is sated and your breath regained, retrace your steps past the lake and through American Basin en route to the trailhead.

Powderhorn Lakes

Featuring the greatest expanse of alpine tundra in the contiguous United States, the rolling country of the Powderhorn Wilderness is unique in the San Juans. Crowned by Calf Creek Plateau, this landscape is the antithesis of the Alps-like terrain common elsewhere in the region. Instead, the Powderhorn encompasses a massive, flat-topped "mountain" that rises high above the forests and sagebrush plains of the Gunnison Valley, a geography due in part to the scarcity of Ice Age glaciers in this dry corner of the San Juans. Because of this, few cirques have been carved from the plateau's flanks, and only a handful of alpine tarns decorate it. The Powderhorn Lakes are the largest of these scattered pools and are the wilderness' most popular destination. Among the highlights of this easy, satisfying trip to the lakes are pleasant scenery and a good chance of spotting wildlife. Even better is the stroll across the top of the plateau, where splendid panoramas and flowering tundra await. The 3-mile walk around the perimeter of the Powderhorn cirque is highly recommended.

Skirting an old clear-cut near the parking area, the trail ascends a forested slope on a steady, moderate grade. This subalpine forest is dense with blown-down timber, especially beyond the wilderness boundary, which is passed 0.5 mile into the walk. During the first weeks of September, the ground-hugging shrubbery that spreads across the forest floor becomes a tasty commissary, as the otherwise innocuous grouse whortleberry ripens into a small but flavorful fruit. The apex of the initial climb comes at 1.5 miles, soon after which the trail traverses a large meadow. Unlike the garish displays common of the meadows of the San Juans' windward slopes, this rain-shadowed meadow is filled not with flowers, but with grass. Elk and deer find this forage ideal, and large herds are sometimes spotted in the vicinity.

Below the meadow, the trail undulates through a series of shallow drainages and remains uneventful for the next 2 miles. The only break in the otherwise monotonous forest is a small, murky, bug-infested pond— not exactly a prime picnic spot. Shortly beyond the pond, the trail climbs more steeply as it turns into the valley of Powderhorn Creek's west fork. The scenery improves considerably at the end of this 0.5-mile ascent as the trail enters an open meadow and intersects the West Fork Trail. Continue upstream and wind around the edge of this marshy meadow to arrive at the shore of the lower Powderhorn Lake, 0.5 mile beyond the junction.

Although the lower lake is pretty, continue to the more memorable upper lake—0.5 mile farther. Sheltered by a semicircle of dark, volcanic cliffs, the lake's waters lap at great talus piles on its far shore and at a bucolic mixture of forest and meadow on its near shore. Excellent campsites are available throughout the area, and the countless concentric rings (and the general swarm of insects) that ripple across the water promise good fishing. The first light of a clear, summer morning bathes the surrounding cliffs in dramatic shades of pink and orange—a scene for which it is worth waking up early.

The windswept crest of Calf Creek Plateau beckons adventurous trekkers, and while the hike to the lakes and around the cirque can be completed in a single day, it is best enjoyed as part of an overnight excursion. Not only will this permit more time to wander and explore, but an early-morning circuit is less likely to be disrupted by stormy weather. The route recommended here traces informal paths onto and across the plateau. Because tundra is exceptionally fragile (the growing season in which trampled plants repair themselves is often less than sixty days long, which means an inch of new growth may take fifty to one hundred summers), extreme care must be taken to minimize your impact. Use any existing footpaths you

POWDERHORN LAKES

POWDERHORN LAKES
DISTANCE: 9 miles round-trip
ELEVATION RANGE: 11,000 to 11,850 feet
TOTAL ELEVATION GAIN: 1,250 feet
TRAIL CONDITIONS: Generally good tread with moderate grades; rocky and muddy in places
SEASON: Mid-June through October
USGS MAP: Powderhorn Lakes (1982)
ADMINISTRATION: BLM; Gunnison RA

CALF CREEK PLATEAU
DISTANCE: 12 miles round-trip
ELEVATION RANGE: 11,000 to 12,500 feet
TOTAL ELEVATION GAIN: 1,900 feet
TRAIL CONDITIONS: Route climbs steeply from Powderhorn Lakes on an informal path to gain plateau; informal paths or trailless tundra on plateau; steep, rocky descent back to lakes
SEASON: Late June through October
USGS MAP: Powderhorn Lakes (1982)
ADMINISTRATION: BLM; Gunnison RA

TRAILHEAD: Drive on CO 149 for either 20.2 miles south from US 50 or about 25 miles north from Lake City, and turn onto Indian Creek Road. This intersection is easily missed because there is no sign announcing the approaching junction. Drive the sometimes rough Indian Creek Road for 10.1 miles and park at the road-end trailhead. Two-wheel-drive vehicles should have no problems unless it has been unusually wet.

can; otherwise, walk on rocks, not plants, whenever possible. If you are crossing trailless tundra in a group, spread out to minimize the chance of the same plants being trampled over and over again.

The circuit climbs the cirque's northwest wall on an obvious path that cuts up the steep, grassy slope. A half mile of serious climbing will bring you to the plateau's 12,500-foot crest. From here, walk south, then walk east around the edge of the cirque and enjoy the many flowers at your feet, the shimmering waters of the Powderhorn lakes, and one of the most all-encompassing vistas of central Colorado. There is no better La Garita Range panorama than this, and there is also a spectacular view of Uncompahgre Peak. Across the vast gulf of the Gunnison Valley stand Grand Mesa, the Elk Range, and the Sawatch Range. Even the northernmost line of the Sangre de Cristo peaks can be admired from this lofty platform. Keep a sharp eye out for deer and elk, which often wander across the tundra, as do domesticated sheep. To the north and south, a long line of cairns leads away from the cirque rim, which invite limitless wandering. Otherwise, continue to follow the cirque rim until you reach a prominent depression in its southeast wall. A faint trail winds steeply down the talus below and into the cirque adjacent to the lower Powderhorn Lake. From here you can either return to your camp or head back to the trail and the trailhead.

San Luis Peak

Located far from any town or highway, the La Garita Wilderness remains one of Colorado's least-known places. One of the first units designated after the passage of the 1964 Wilderness Act, the La Garita forever preserves the heart of its namesake range, one of the San Juans' most distinctive and beautiful regions. Bold peaks cloaked with tundra wildflowers and peaceful valleys dotted by dozens of beaver ponds rule the landscape, while roaming herds of deer and elk far outnumber the few humans who explore these lonely heights. Crowning the wilderness is 14,014-foot San Luis Peak, whose inclusion in the state's "14'er" club makes it the La Garita's most popular hike. Popularity is relative though, and this least-attempted of Colorado's fifty-four highest hikes is rarely trod by more than a handful of people on any given day. Indeed, the extremely rare opportunity to stand alone atop one of the state's loftiest summits is in itself reason enough to attempt this journey. In the end, however, do not be surprised if the wonderful scenery and pervading sense of wildness are what make the La Garitas memorable.

The hike to San Luis's summit can be approached in one of two ways. The basic route takes an out-and-back course up the valley of Stewart Creek, while a longer alternative ascends Stewart Creek and returns via Cochetopa Creek, making a loop out of these parallel drainages. Neither trail is more crowded than the other, even though both the Colorado Trail (CT) and the Continental Divide Trail (CDT) include Cochetopa Creek in their routes. Both trails offer the same high-quality alpine scenery, and the two trailheads are within 0.3 mile of each other, thus eliminating the need for car-shuttle arrangements. Ultimately, determining which option you prefer is merely a matter of available time.

Departing the Stewart Creek Trailhead, the trail climbs easily up valley and enters the La Garita Wilderness almost immediately. Grassy meadows spread across the valley floor, and though set at a fairly high altitude, the sunny exposure can make for hot hiking. Beavers have been impressively busy in this vicinity, and quite a few dams block the stream's flow; the fortunate few who hike during the fringes of daylight may even spot one of these industrious critters making his way to work. Keep an eye out for

SAN LUIS PEAK

VIA STEWART CREEK

DISTANCE: 12.5 miles round-trip

ELEVATION RANGE: 10,450 to 14,014 feet

TOTAL ELEVATION GAIN: 3,600 feet

TRAIL CONDITIONS: Good trail with gentle to moderate grades until treeline; steep climber's path with loose scree to summit; snowfields possible until mid-July; exposed to poor weather

SEASON: Late June through September

USGS MAPS: Elk Park (1965); Stewart Peak (1979); San Luis Peak (1986)

ADMINISTRATION: Gunnison NF; Cebolla RD

STEWART CREEK–COCHETOPA CREEK LOOP

DISTANCE: 15.5 miles round-trip

ELEVATION RANGE: 10,350 to 14,014 feet

TOTAL ELEVATION GAIN: 3,700 feet

TRAIL CONDITIONS: Established trails with gentle to moderate grades below treeline; steep, often faint paths with sections of loose scree above treeline; snowfield and storm hazards

SEASON: Late June through September

USGS MAPS: Elk Park (1965); Stewart Peak (1979); San Luis Peak (1986); Halfmoon Pass (1986)

ADMINISTRATION: Gunnison NF; Cebolla RD

STEWART CREEK TRAILHEAD: From the intersection of US 50 and CO 114 (7.3 miles east of Gunnison), drive south on CO 114 for 19.7 miles. Turn right onto CR NN14 (signed Old Agency Work Center) and continue on this good gravel road, passing a junction at mile 3.4 to arrive at the junction of CR 15GG at mile 6.8. Turn right here (signed Stewart Creek Trailhead) and drive this rough but passable dirt road. Stay to the right where the road splits at mile 4.1, bear right again at mile 13.7, and then bear left at mile 15.8 and mile 17.7. Park at the signed trailhead at mile 20.1.

EDDIESVILLE TRAILHEAD: Continue past the Stewart Creek Trailhead and park at the road's end, which is 0.3 mile farther. Be sure to turn right and cross Stewart Creek, avoiding a private ranch entrance.

freshly felled aspen in the small stands dotting the lower valley walls.

The trail finally reaches the cover of the subalpine forest about 2 miles into the trip, and it begins a steadier ascent shortly after passing a stock fence. The hike's next mile can be arduous, as the forest is somewhat monotonous, and the 0.5-mile string of beaver ponds that would seem to offer scenic variety instead provide a prolific breeding ground for swarms of mosquitoes. The steepening valley walls, which have transformed from forested ridges into the cliff-lined flanks of two massive peaks—Baldy Alto and Organ Mountain—entice you onward, nonetheless.

Though not represented on the Stewart Peak map, the trail crosses to the south bank of Stewart Creek near the 3-mile mark, not long after passing a rotting log cabin. Planks and logs aid this ford, as they do a second one a short distance upstream. The forest thins above this second crossing, and subalpine meadow appears in the vicinity of several tiny brooks. The easy walking finally ends at the 4-mile mark, and the last very steep 0.5 mile brings you to treeline. Notice the appearance of bristlecone pine—the hardy species that has proven to have a life expectancy of several thousand years—within the last few dozen yards of forest.

The next 0.5 mile of pleasant hiking allows you to admire the alpine environment of the La Garitas while pressing onward. Dense willow thickets blanket the stream banks and lower mountain flanks, while emerald tundra spreads across the higher slopes. Carefully study the surrounding ridges and summits for a possible glimpse of the deer and elk herds that often graze here. Bighorn sheep also inhabit the wilderness, though they are rarely seen. San Luis's summit makes a brief appearance from behind the intervening ridge, but it quickly disappears from view as the trail nears the beginning of a steep ascent out of the Stewart Creek drainage. The trail fades into a faint climber's path as it makes its way up slope, and cairns mark the mile-long route onto San Luis's east ridge. The tundra provides a colorful wild-flower display, and, huffing and puffing up the ridge, you'll have ample opportunity to admire alpine bistort, purple fringe, and the beautiful blue alpine forget-me-not, which is especially striking when set against a back-drop of orange lichen.

San Luis's massive, rounded summit finally comes into view as you climb onto the 13,100-foot saddle between Stewart and Cochetopa Creeks. From here it is a straightforward 0.75-mile hike to the summit, as the climber's path traverses steep scree below a false summit before finally gain-ing the crest of the peak. From this vantage, it is easy to see why the La Garitas were given a Spanish name that means "the lookout"—much of northern San Juan country and the Gunnison Valley, Sangre de Cristo Range, Sawatch Range, and Elk Range fall within the splendid panorama.

Return to the 13,100-foot saddle and either retrace your route down Stewart Creek or turn southward and descend into Cochetopa Creek. There is no official trail down these fairly steep but easy slopes, though a faint path should be discernible all the way to the drainage floor, a 1.5-mile hike away. Timberline is reached here, and the Colorado and Continental Divide Trails (CT/CDT) intersect at this point. Now it is a long, leisurely, 7-mile downstream hike to the trailhead. Much like Stewart Creek, this drainage is the essence of wilderness, with pretty meadows, dense forest, and abundant wildlife. If you have an extra day, set up camp near timberline and hike a few miles farther into the heart of the La Garitas, where even lonelier splendor awaits.

Conejos Headwaters

The rumor had been floating around the mountains for decades: Offi-cially, the San Juans—and the whole of Colorado—had been without grizzly bears since September 1952, when the last known silver-tip had been shot up near the headwaters of the Los Pinos, deep in the heart of the Weminuche. But those who wandered the mountains often thought differ-ently. Could that have been a griz spotted in the Four Mile Creek area in the

CONEJOS HEADWATERS

THREE FORKS PARK

DISTANCE: 4.6 miles round-trip

ELEVATION RANGE: 10,250 to 10,350 feet

TOTAL ELEVATION GAIN: 150 feet

TRAIL CONDITIONS: Flat, easy trail

SEASON: Late May through mid-October

USGS MAPS: Platoro (1967); Summit Peak (1966)

ADMINISTRATION: Rio Grande NF; Conejos Peak RD

HEADWATERS LOOP

DISTANCE: 14.5 miles round-trip

ELEVATION RANGE: 10,250 to 12,200 feet

TOTAL ELEVATION GAIN: 2,000 feet

TRAIL CONDITIONS: Generally good with gentle to moderate grades; trail is more faint and much steeper above timberline; several stream crossings; potential for snowfields through July

SEASON: July through September

USGS MAPS: Platoro (1967); Summit Peak (1966)

ADMINISTRATION: Rio Grande NF; Conejos Peak RD

TRAILHEAD: From the community of Platoro (22 miles from CO 17 via FR 250), travel north on FR 250 and turn left onto FR 247 after 1.4 miles. Follow FR 247, first avoiding a boat ramp after 1.2 miles and then bearing left at 3.9 miles before reaching the road-end trailhead at 6.2 miles. Both roads are graded gravel and are accessible to all vehicles.

late fifties? Or at the head of the Navajo River in the mid sixties? Or above Ute Creek in the late sixties? Conclusive evidence was never found, at least not until a cold September night in 1979, when a local outfitter was mauled by a grizzly sow near Blue Lake, on the Continental Divide headwaters of the Conejos River. Somehow, at least one of the great bears remained undetected for almost thirty years, wandering the lonely wilds of the South San Juans. That sow was killed in self-defense, and once again Colorado has been proclaimed grizzly-free. But now new rumors have started: Could that have been a grizzly in Starvation Gulch in 1990? Was it a griz above the Navajo River in 1993?

The South San Juan Wilderness preserves the deep, forested valleys; alpine lakes; and windswept peaks that line the Continental Divide from south of Wolf Creek Pass down nearly to New Mexico. Far removed from the state's gold fields, railroads, and centers of commerce, the South San Juans have remained as unscathed as any part of the southern Rockies, and while logging companies have been nibbling at its flanks throughout the twentieth century, the presence of the wilderness ensures that the heart of this region will remain pristine. The Conejos River is the primary watershed on the wilderness' east flank, and its twisty run out of the range begins in a series of beautiful glacial valleys. Trails climbing the north and middle

Lush old-growth forest along the Conejos River's north fork.

forks of the Conejos can be linked by a segment of the Continental Divide Trail (CDT) to create the South San Juans' premier weekend backpack. A quick and easy jaunt to Three Forks Park takes in lush subalpine forest, expansive meadows, and a segment of the beautiful river, providing an ideal morning stroll.

Either excursion begins by following the well-traveled path up the Conejos valley and into the wilderness. The trail alternates between cool forest and open meadow as it contours across the lower valley wall, some distance above the sinuous river. Other than a few muddy places and a couple of small brooks, there are no obstacles, and the hike is enjoyable for people of all skill levels. Three Forks Park is located where the north fork, middle fork, and El Rito Azul commingle to form the Conejos. The wide, flat valley is dotted by wildflowers, and the many ripples and eddies attract both anglers and picnickers. If the park is your destination, you may wish to go no farther than the junction of the Blue Lake Trail, 1.9 miles from the trailhead. Or you can continue another 0.4 mile and turn back where the north and middle fork trails diverge, 2.3 miles from the trailhead.

If your goal is to complete the loop, continue beyond this point on either of the divergent trails. The route is described in a clockwise direction (up the middle fork), but it can also be hiked counterclockwise if you prefer. If you continue up the middle fork, you must wade the north fork almost immediately, though this is usually no problem since the waters rarely roil more than calf deep. The flat meadow across the stream has a number of excellent, tree-sheltered campsites, making this an ideal place to base camp. The trail then briefly climbs through an exceptionally lush stand of subalpine forest before it contours onto the floor of a beautiful, meadowed valley. In the distance, the rugged peaks of the Divide line up in dramatic fashion, with the distinctive notch of Gunsight Pass being the most prominent feature. Columbine grow profusely on the rocky slopes adjacent to the trail, and deer and elk are often spotted grazing the lush grass.

The trail continues through the meadow, then climbs gradually through pockets of forest until reaching the spectacular Conejos Falls, some 2.5 miles above Three Forks Park. Though the waterfall—a 90-foot plunge into a deep-blue pool—has somehow been left off the Summit Peak map, it is among the most photogenic in the San Juans. The trail climbs around the falls, while the slopes that lead to its base are steep, slippery, and definitely dangerous—admire this cataract from afar. Above the falls, the trail stays on the forest fringe at first before it ascends more steadily through the forest above the middle fork. Several brooks and gullies are decorated by pretty flower displays, and a number of other cascades may be seen. Timberline is reached about a mile above the falls, and the last 0.5 mile to the Continental Divide Trail (CDT) provides some fantastic alpine scenery. The trail fades before it reaches the unsigned junction, however, and the CDT is hard to spot on the valley floor, as well. No problem—simply look for the trail that climbs up the north valley wall and make a direct beeline for it. Satisfactory camping is available in this vicinity, and the steep, 0.5-mile trek to Lake Ann is just one of the potential diversions for those who linger here.

The next 2.5 miles are simply an exemplary taste of the CDT, one of the world's classic alpine conveyances. The far-reaching panoramas, multitude of flowers, snow-melt ponds, and bracing air are magnificent, but sampling such a small segment is not unlike catching the aroma of a gourmet meal without the money in pocket to indulge yourself. This part of the hike ascends a high ridge that separates the middle fork from the north fork, with a grade steady but not steep, and the tread rocky in places. Once upon the ridge's apex, contour for a bit and enjoy the breathtaking panorama before you begin the steep, switchbacking descent into the north fork drainage. These sheltered slopes often hold snowfields well into July, and extreme caution must be exercised if any are present during your hike. The trail itself can be rough in places, and its representation on the Summit Peak map is not exactly accurate. Nonetheless, signs mark the junction of the North Fork Trail, and the hike becomes easier once more as you exit the CDT and begin the more gentle downhill leg of the hike.

At first, the North Fork Trail is hard to find on the grassy basin floor—contour around the east side of the basin, and the tread should become apparent within a few minutes. Passing timberline, the trail descends steadily through forested glades and small meadows and remains some distance above the north fork. When the trail levels into a shady subalpine grove, a number of stock paths diverge—stay on the lowest of these, and you'll soon be at the fringe of a fine meadow. The valley widens here, and the grassy valley floor and forested walls make for a very pastoral scene, especially when a herd of sheep dots the landscape. (Edward Abbey once unaffectionately referred to the woollies as "San Juan Range Maggots.") Midway down the meadow, cross the north fork (another easy wade) and enjoy a lengthy piece of level walking as you return to the shelter of the forest. After contouring above a small gorge, the trail finally resumes its steady descent, drops into Three Forks Park, and closes the loop 3.4 miles below the CDT. Retrace the first easy 2.3 miles to the trailhead.

Conejos Peak

Broad-shouldered Conejos Peak is a hiker's paradise of grassy slopes, gentle ridges, and sparkling lakes, which invite carefree wandering and peaceful contemplation. Tucked into the northeast corner of the South San Juan Wilderness, which is perhaps Colorado's most primitive corner, Conejos Peak features a more subtle grandeur than the dramatic spires and cirques found elsewhere in the San Juans. This, combined with its location far from any sizable town or paved road, means that Conejos Peak promises a degree of solitude that is increasingly more difficult to find.

Surprisingly, considering its lofty elevation, climbing the peak is not particularly challenging or exhausting. The trail is generally straightforward,

CONEJOS PEAK

DISTANCE: 6 miles round-trip

ELEVATION RANGE: 11,600 to 13,172 feet

TOTAL ELEVATION GAIN: 1,572 feet

TRAIL CONDITIONS: Moderate grade; trail indistinguishable in places, but otherwise good tread

SEASON: July through September

USGS MAP: Platoro (1967)

ADMINISTRATION: Rio Grande NF; Conejos Peak RD

TRAILHEAD: From the small community of Platoro, drive south on FR 250 for 6.1 miles (or about 17 miles north from CO 17) to the junction of FR 105 (Saddle Creek Road). Follow this road and bear sharply left at a junction 4.2 miles away. Continue another 2.7 miles and turn left onto FR 105.3A. This road, which leads into a large clear-cut, is rougher, but it is passable for most vehicles. Bear to the right after 0.4 mile and park at the trailhead, 100 yards away.

there are no raging streams to cross and few steep grades to climb, and there are no sections of tricky footing about which to worry. The greatest concerns are avoiding poor weather, which is a frequent and severe visitor to these high summits; and avoiding confusion, which can be caused by the USGS map's inaccurate portrayal of paths. In particular, do not attempt the "shortcut" trail—it looks logical on paper, but it never connects with the route to Conejos Peak and instead climbs steeply up another mountain on the opposite side of the basin.

It is ironic, perhaps, that this trail, which climbs into a spectacular wilderness area, starts in a vast clear-cut. Sadly, this is often the case with trails that lead into the South San Juans, as the lush forests that blanket the mountain slopes are irresistible to logging interests, which, at least in the past, have been readily supported by the Forest Service. Economic conditions have significantly curtailed logging operations in recent years, and hopefully any that occur in the future will be done in a less aesthetically destructive manner.

The trail climbs quickly out of the clear-cut, and after a brief section of forest, breaks into open meadow. Once into the meadow, the trail rapidly covers a lot of distance as it gently contours into the Saddle Creek drainage. Lush grasses and a sprinkling of wildflowers waving in soft breezes, the sweet balsam smell of scattered spruce, and the lyrical sound of distant rushing water typify the wilderness experience. The high, windswept ridge above the trail is home to a stand of bristlecone pine, which are not often found in the San Juans. Beautifully adapted to extremely harsh climatic conditions, the bristlecone survives where no other tree can, and does so for so long that, in some areas, it exceeds the life span of any other living entity.

Soon, the trail begins a more moderate ascent through a grassy basin before it arrives at the shore of Tobacco Lake, which is roughly 2 miles from the trailhead. Shaped like a tobacco pouch—at least according to those who bestowed the moniker—the lake is a sparkling gem tucked beneath the gentle ridges of the surrounding mountains. During the summer, herds of elk may often be observed grazing on the slopes both above and below the lake. Conejos Peak rises to the southwest of the lake, though it is no more distinctive than the other rounded summits visible from here.

To continue to the summit, follow a faint path around the north shore of the lake. The trail becomes more distinct as it climbs, in two short switchbacks, onto the fairly gentle slopes of the upper basin. One more long switchback brings you atop the ridge crest directly west of the lake, and after a traverse beneath a conical knob north of Conejos Peak, it is merely a few more steps to the summit. While this route is straightforward, the USGS map shows an inaccurate route beyond the lake, and several random cairns mark unofficial routes. So long as the weather cooperates, finding a route is easy since the summit is visible at all times; however, be careful to stay on the constructed trail as much as possible in order to minimize impacts to the fragile tundra.

The reward for attaining the summit is a spectacular full-circle view of the South San Juans, which encompasses the distinct U-shape of glacially carved valleys; the rugged peaks of the Continental Divide; countless acres of gently rolling, emerald-colored tundra; glistening lakes and tarns; and perhaps most pleasing of all, the absolute solitude of this vast wilderness, where for as far as the eye can see, nary another human soul is likely to be seen.

V-Rock Trail

The sweet musty smell of fall is inches thick under the hammock. It is a fragrance of aspen dust and honey and sunshine. The air is golden, as rich and sweet and heavy as an old Chateau d'Yquem. The trunks, reflecting the light and the fallen leaves, are gilded. The silence is soft and warm and full, between intermittent rustlings of gold

V-ROCK TRAIL

DISTANCE: 8.75 miles one-way

ELEVATION RANGE: 8,700 to 10,650 feet

TOTAL ELEVATION GAIN: 1,100 feet, with 2,000 feet of elevation loss

TRAIL CONDITIONS: Trail is infrequently maintained, with occasional poor or faint tread, mud, and downed trees; initial 1.5 miles are moderate to steep, remainder of grade is gentle; two easy unbridged stream crossings

SEASON: June through October

USGS MAP: Harris Lake (1984)

ADMINISTRATION: San Juan NF; Pagosa RD

BUCKLES LAKE TRAILHEAD: From the junction of US 84 and US 160 at Pagosa Springs, drive south on US 84 for 19.3 miles and turn left onto the gravel Buckles Lake Road (FR 663). Drive 7.3 miles to the trailhead at road's end.

OPAL LAKE TRAILHEAD: From the junction of US 84 and Buckles Lake Road, drive north on US 84 for 11.4 miles (7.9 miles south of the junction of US 160) and turn east onto the gravel Blanco Basin Road (FR 326). Continue for 9.5 miles and turn right onto Castle Creek Road (FR 660). Continue directly ahead at a junction that is 0.4 mile farther, then turn right onto Opal Lake Road (FR 23) after an additional 2.8 miles. The trailhead is 0.7 mile up this road.

tissue-paper wrapping up the glow of summer. . . . Nothing exists except motes of aspen dust glinting in a shaft of sunlight.

—Ann Zwinger
Beyond the Aspen Grove

The image painted by these words vividly describes one of the myriad pleasures offered by the V-Rock Trail, one of the unknown jewels of San Juan hiking. Traversing the southwest corner of the South San Juan Wilderness, the trail segment recommended here samples some of this beautiful area's most delightful features: old-growth spruce-fir forests; pastoral, Yellowstone-esque meadows; babbling streams; and aspen groves as lush and lovely as any in the southern Rockies. Best of all, the number of deer you encounter will probably exceed the number of other hikers on this quiet path.

Although it requires a car shuttle of more than 30 miles, this hike is best enjoyed as a one-way journey, which allows a single day to experience each of the hike's many beautiful scenes. If these arrangements can be made, it is best to start at the Buckles Lake Trailhead, as the amount of elevation gained is only half the amount lost. If a shuttle cannot be arranged, an out-and-back overnighter is highly recommended. In this case, a start at the Opal Lake Trailhead might be preferred; while the ascent is more substantial in this direction, the overall grade is gentle, and the summit of V-Mountain is a satisfying destination.

Aspen leaves swirl down a secluded San Juan brook.

Excellent campsites are available throughout the hike, and water is plentiful. Hikers desiring a simple out-and-back day hike will find either end of the trail to be equally rewarding.

Though there may be several cars parked at the Buckles Lake Trailhead, solitude lovers should not be discouraged—most of these people are only walking to the lake, which is 0.5 mile distant via an adjacent four-wheel-drive road. The V-Rock Trail passes through a wire gate and follows a now-closed road around a small meadow. After 100 yards or so the trail branches to the right—the junction should be obvious but may be unmarked, so pay close attention. The rough path immediately begins a sustained, sometimes steep ascent and continues in this manner until it crests the summit of V-Mountain, 1.25 miles distant. This leg of the hike gains 1,000 feet of elevation, and the rocky and sometimes muddy tread can make this a real blood-warmer. This section is nonetheless pleasant, with groves of aspen, scattered meadows, and ever-increasing vistas to spur you upward.

The summit of V-Mountain—actually a long, flat-topped ridge that is faced by a prominent cliff known as V-Rock—marks not only the wilderness boundary, but also the conclusion of the hike's only substantial ascent; with minor exceptions, the miles ahead are level or gently descending. The dramatic peaks that encircle the upper Blanco Basin frame the view across the grassy meadows of the ridge, while the slopes below are lapped by an ocean of aspen. Considering these extensive stands, it would seem logical to save this hike for the golden days of autumn. This time of year is indeed spectacular, but do not discount the beauty of late spring, when the rich green of new leaves is mirrored by fresh carpets of ferns and shrubs, and the year's first wildflowers rise from the damp soil.

After tracing the crest of the ridge for 0.5 mile, the trail loops to the south, descends through a narrow stand of spruce, and enters an exceptional meadow—one whose beauty is instantly recognizable to hikers familiar with the backcountry of Yellowstone. Unlike the meadows of the western San Juans, which drape across precipitous peaks and whose deep green is splashed by a riot of wildflower color, this meadow features waving grasses soaked by meandering brooks; a ring of somber evergreens; and a backdrop of dark cliffs. Hikers who manage to find their way into this meadow at the fringe of daylight stand a good chance of observing deer, elk, coyote, and perhaps black bear grazing at the forest edge.

The trail stays in this meadow for about 0.75 mile before it climbs up a hill on its left flank. The trail is faint much of the way (and often very wet); however, if you keep to the north side, it should be easy to find a discernible path. This climb is brief, and after it turns more toward the north, the trail begins its descent into the Leche Creek drainage. The trail skirts bands of forest while it meanders through small meadows—this ambling is one reason why this is such a pleasant hike. Instead of ascending *this* peak, or following *that* gully, the trail seems to flow across the rolling terrain, seeking out a patch of flowers or an aromatic tree. This type of casual walking is somewhat rare in the rugged up-and-down world of the San Juans.

At the hike's 4-mile mark, the USGS map depicts a split in the trail, with either direction appearing to be a feasible route. There is no sign for this supposed junction, and this author could not locate a divergent trail in this vicinity—though it may have been hidden by a downed tree or patch of snow. In any case, the discernible path is represented by the map's western branch, and this route is easily followed. This path enters a more substantial spruce-fir forest, and several old signs that identify the CENTER STOCK DRIVEWAY may be seen. Within a mile of entering the forest, the trail breaks into another meadow and arrives at the signed Leche Creek Trail junction. Continue on the right fork, which is faint at first but quickly becomes distinguishable as it drops down to cross Leche Creek, a ford that will make for wet feet but few problems. If you were observant enough to locate the aforementioned trail option—and adventurous enough to follow it—you should rejoin the primary route at this point.

The character of the hike changes beyond Leche Creek, with wet meadows and spruce-fir forest replaced by drier grasses and young aspen. The terrain becomes rockier, and after the trail passes a small but pretty pond, there are several dry "sinkholes." The trail becomes more rolling for the next mile, and there are three short ascents before the trail returns to its steady descent. The craggy ridge on the eastern skyline looms closest to the trail at this point, as well. Though these battlements are composed of ancient volcanic mud and lava flows, they are known collectively as the Chalk Mountains. Interestingly, the streams that issue from this ridge are often opaque.

The third of the three short ascents is located at the 6-mile mark, and beyond this, there is only downhill travel for the remainder of the hike. The 1.5 miles between this point and Opal Lake are particularly enjoyable, as the terrain becomes lusher and the hike's best aspen groves are passed. The unbridged but easy crossing of Castle Creek at mile 7.0 is a fine place to linger, as the sweet aroma of aspen and the pleasant babbling of the stream have a narcotic effect. Beyond the creek, the trail bisects a long, sloping meadow and soon joins the Opal Lake Trail at an unsigned junction just below the lake. This pondlike body of water isn't the loveliest pool in the South San Juans, but it is worth the short diversion—especially when sunset paints the encircling cliffs a brilliant orange hue.

Opal Lake is 7.5 miles from the Buckles Lake Trailhead, and from here it is a little more than a mile to the hike's termination at the Opal Lake Trailhead. Below the lake, the trail hugs the south bank of White Creek, crosses on a sturdy fallen log, and enters a meadow where the final trail junction is located. Our route bears to the left, descends steadily (500 feet in 1 mile), exits the wilderness, and arrives at the trailhead. Hikers who have enjoyed the V-Rock Trail and wish to extend their journey through the South San Juan Wilderness may wish to explore the right fork. This very lightly used trail climbs steeply to the crest of the Chalk Mountains, loops behind the summit of Flattop Mountain, and descends into the Fish Creek drainage where it terminates at the end of FR 660, approximately 8 miles from Opal Lake.

Quartz Lake

In all, the South San Juans are more compact, less accessible, less well known, less peopled, and in every way less messed-over than the northern mountains. And [the] South San Juan Wilderness . . . is the vibrant heart of the place.

—David Petersen
Ghost Grizzlies

The South San Juan Wilderness, as is typical of the entire San Juan region, is rugged, resplendent country ripe with wildflowers, wildlife, and heavenly vistas—all of which make wandering alpine wilderness such a lighthearted pastime. What makes the South San Juans unique is that the opportunity for solitude is greater here than in just about any of Colorado's other flagship wilderness areas. Even the more popular wilderness trails are often people-free, and they can even be enjoyed with a comfortable level of seclusion on the most "crowded" weekends and holidays. The hike to Quartz Lake is one such example, and being one of the easiest, most direct approaches into the high country, it is a highly recommended introduction to what the South San Juans have to offer.

Though not a gut-buster, the trail climbs steadily, especially within the initial 1.5 miles. Gaining about 1,200 feet, this stretch of trail ascends through a small drainage before switchbacking onto the crest of a prominent ridge. The wildflowers that spread across these lower slopes are extravagant during the short summer season, with an informal trailside census totaling nearly thirty different varieties just within the hike's first few minutes. Once atop the ridge, the trail turns east and con-

QUARTZ LAKE

DISTANCE: 9 miles round-trip

ELEVATION RANGE: 9,950 to 12,100 feet

TOTAL ELEVATION GAIN: 2,700 feet

TRAIL CONDITIONS: Good tread; steady rate of ascent, though steep in a few places; potential for snowfields

SEASON: Mid-July through September

USGS MAP: Blackhead Peak (1984)

ADMINISTRATION: San Juan NF; Pagosa RD

TRAILHEAD: From the junction of US 160 and US 84 in Pagosa Springs, drive south on US 84 for 0.3 mile and turn left on CR 302 (Mill Creek Road). Drive this dirt road and bear right after 5.9 miles onto FR 665. Continue on FR 665 and continue straight at mile 2.5, left at mile 3.3, and left again at mile 6.8. The trailhead is located at mile 10.1, where a sign identifies the Little Blanco Trail. There is parking for a few cars on the right shoulder of the road.

tinues its ascent along the ridge crest while it bears directly toward the rugged Quartz Ridge. Snowdrifts, which often remain well into the month of July, can bedevil this traverse, and because the trail is narrow and skirts precipitous drop-offs, it may be advisable to wait until melt-out is complete before attempting this hike. Timberline is passed after a mile of ridge-top walking, and with the sheltering forest now behind you, the panorama spreads far into the distance, encompassing both the peaks of the Weminuche Wilderness and the mesa country of northern New Mexico.

Shortly past treeline, the trail veers off the ridge, traverses across a steep bowl at the headwaters of Sand Creek, and climbs through a narrow pass. This 0.5-mile ascent is the hike's steepest, but the flower-speckled tundra makes it enjoyable all the same. The real payoff is the panorama that unfolds at the top of the pass, which includes the spectacular heart of the South San Juan Wilderness, with craggy peaks and steep meadows spread high above the deep, heavily forested canyon of the Rio Blanco.

Beyond the pass, which carries the trail across Quartz Ridge, the ascent continues a short distance farther, then is followed by a quick descent across the ridge's steep eastern face and onto a broad saddle. This saddle separates the waters of Quartz Creek from the Rio Blanco and is the location of an unsigned but obvious trail junction. While our hike bears left and descends into Quartz Creek's headwaters basin, the trail ahead, which contours across a flower-filled alpine ridge, is worth wandering if time and energy permit. Otherwise, enjoy the final mile to Quartz Lake, which loses about 550 feet of elevation en route to the scenic pond. This mile is an alpine Shangri-la that is dotted with brooks and ponds and has glacially scoured bedrock broken by verdant tundra. Wildlife abounds, including elk, marmot, and pika, and possibly even mountain goat and black bear, while the vistas remain stunning every step of the way.

Rainbow Hot Spring

While the fires of the great San Juan volcanic fields are stoked no longer, a few embers still smolder deep within the earth, offering a subdued reminder of the region's once-violent past. Heating subterranean waters, it is this enduring geothermal energy that is responsible for the hot springs that dot the region. Nearly all of these springs—Ouray, Trimble, and Pagosa among them—have been developed to exploit their restorative powers. One of the few pristine exceptions is Rainbow Hot Spring. Considered by many to be Colorado's finest backcountry soak, the spring pours into a rock-lined pool to form a beautifully situated, natural hot tub on the bank of a wilderness river.

Because Rainbow Hot Spring is located within the boundaries of the Weminuche Wilderness, it is forever protected from development and commercialism. Located alongside the San Juan River's west fork, the spring is easily reached by hiking up a gently climbing trail. The hike is rewarding for its own sake, with many attractive river scenes, and towering forests, dense shrubbery, ferns, and wildflowers that will leave you wondering if you haven't mistakenly wandered into the heart of the Pacific Northwest. Because access is so straightforward, this hike is perhaps the most popular in the Weminuche. Do not come here seeking solitude; not unless you plan on traveling farther up valley and deeper into the wilderness. Be a conscientious visitor and minimize your impact, because whether you soak for an hour or camp overnight, you will have plenty of company.

The hike's first mile crosses the privately held Born's Lake Ranch on the gated roadbed. The owners make it clear that trespassing off the road's right-of-way will not be tolerated; please respect their wishes and do nothing that may jeopardize future public access. Once you return to public

RAINBOW HOT SPRING

DISTANCE: 9.5 miles round-trip

ELEVATION RANGE: 8,250 to 9,150 feet

TOTAL ELEVATION GAIN: 900 feet

TRAIL CONDITIONS: Generally gentle and smooth, though there are two short, steep ascents; mud can sometimes be a problem

SEASON: Late May through October

USGS MAPS: Saddle Mountain (1984); South River Peak (1984)

ADMINISTRATION: San Juan NF; Pagosa RD

TRAILHEAD: Drive east on US 160 for 13.9 miles from the junction of US 84 in Pagosa Springs. Turn left onto West Fork Road (8.8 miles west of the Wolf Creek Pass summit), then drive 3 more miles and park where the road is gated.

land, you'll quickly enter the Weminuche Wilderness, and after you traverse a pretty meadow, you'll cross Burro Creek on a footbridge. Beyond this point, the trail climbs gently while it maintains a position about 100 feet above the river. This portion of the hike is a botanist's delight of lush meadows and primeval forests. Fern and moss bask in the damp shade of the forest floor, with many varieties of bush and blossom spreading into the sunlight.

Descending suddenly, the trail briefly travels along the bank of the west fork before it crosses over via a long, sturdy bridge, which is 3 miles from the trailhead. A short distance farther, Beaver Creek is crossed, and the trail then makes a short, steep ascent onto a bench above the river's east bank. Once on this bench, the trail resumes its gentle ascent through the pleasant valley-floor forest. Above the towering trees, the canyon walls rise steeply overhead, and tiny cascades occasionally tinkle down their dark faces.

After the Beaver Creek Trail branches to the right (about 1.25 miles above the West Fork Bridge), the trail winds past three small gullies, each of which rarely holds more than a trickle of water. Just past the third gully, which is 0.5 mile beyond the trail junction, a series of smaller paths veer toward the river. These paths lead to the first of a group of campsites, and eventually to the spring itself, which is located right on the edge of the river at the bottom of a steep bank.

The hot spring issues from a crack in a rock wall just above the river, spouting forth a steady supply of 100°F to 110°F, slightly mineralized water. Two small pools have been constructed using river-rounded rocks to dam the spring's outlet; the warmest is a small, two-person pool situated just beneath the spring's source. A larger pool located on the riverbank can be tempered by mixing in a bit of the west fork's icy water; however, the brimming, runoff-laden river may render it inaccessible until July. Because soaking space is limited, you may need to wait for an open seat, especially on weekends and holidays. If so, enjoy a riverside rest spot or wander into a small meadow a short distance up valley.

Do not expect a commercial experience at this wilderness spring. There are no facilities, no on-site managers, and ultimately, no rules—skinny-dippers are to be expected. If you wish to stay overnight, the Forest Service requires that you use only designated campsites, which are comfortable but heavily impacted. Campfires are also prohibited in the area. Again, plan on having company, and because the sites are located within close proximity to one another, be sure to minimize noise and other disturbances.

Though this hike proceeds no farther than the hot spring, the trail continues and leads much farther into the wilderness, and it can be used to access several extended backpacking routes. The trail climbs through the west fork's rugged upper valley and passes brooding cliffs and several spectacular waterfalls en route to Piedra Pass and the Continental Divide, 7 miles above the spring. From Piedra Pass, it is possible to hike either north or south on the Continental Divide Trail (CDT), with paths in adjacent drainages easily utilized to create long, one-way excursions. A recommended loop uses an 8-mile, southbound portion of the CDT to connect with the Beaver Creek Trail, which can be followed back to the West Fork Trail at the aforementioned junction. This multiday loop features miles of beautiful, exposed alpine walking as well as lonesome meadows and expansive forests. You can expect little if any company on this wilderness journey.

Palisade Meadows

By a fortuitous combination of climate, topography, and geology, the canyons of the eastern Weminuche Wilderness are among the most verdant in the San Juans. Sculpted from dark, volcanic rock, these canyons are a paradise of crystalline cascades, mossy boulders, fern-covered stream banks, thick shrubbery, and lively wildflowers. Perhaps the most exceptional of these drainages is the canyon of Indian Creek, which spills out of Palisade Meadows before tumbling down a magnificent gorge. The garden path that winds along the creek is the perfect place to experience this veritable "pine-forest Polynesia."

The hike's first 2 miles penetrate the Weminuche Wilderness along the Williams Creek Trail, an important travel corridor up the Williams Creek drainage. At first, there is little indication of the lush glens ahead, as the trail climbs across a flood-ravaged area and onto the steep, rocky, canyon wall. The microclimate in this area is fairly hot and arid, with massive ponderosa pine, Douglas fir, and occasional aspen dominating the forest. The initial climb is fairly steep, but it moderates as the trail makes its way onto a narrow bench high above Williams Creek. Watch the opposite canyon wall for a glimpse of a magnificent, ribbonlike waterfall that usually remains until midsummer.

The trail switchbacks farther up the side of the canyon at the edge of a ragged gully far above the clear waters of the creek. The vegetation soon grows more verdant, and those with an eagle eye may spot ripe strawberry, raspberry, or thimbleberry during the latter part of August. A pair of small, moss-lined brooks are passed in quick succession, and a short, steep climb just after the second brook leads through a shallow gully and into a small meadow.

PALISADE MEADOWS

DISTANCE: 10 miles round-trip

ELEVATION RANGE: 8,400 to 10,800 feet

TOTAL ELEVATION GAIN: 2,600 feet

TRAIL CONDITIONS: Good trail throughout, but quite steep for much of the way; three unbridged stream crossings, with one being potentially difficult

SEASON: Mid-July through mid-October

USGS MAP: Cimarrona Peak (1973)

ADMINISTRATION: San Juan NF; Pagosa RD

TRAILHEAD: From Pagosa Springs, drive west on US 160 for about 2.5 miles and turn right on Piedra Road (FR 631). Drive this road for 21.3 miles, staying left at all intersections and following signs for Williams Creek Reservoir. Turn right onto FR 640, pass the reservoir, and park at the road-end trailhead at mile 4.5.

Turn onto the Indian Creek Trail where it diverges to the east in the middle of this meadow, and quickly descend 100 feet to the bank of Williams Creek. The easy hiking ends here, with the crossing of this icy stream being a potentially difficult obstacle. Once runoff has subsided in July, the ford should be no more than calf to knee deep, but the water is swift, and the streambed slippery—use caution. Once across, the trail immediately commences a steep, steady ascent up Indian Creek Canyon, gaining nearly 2,000 feet within the next 3 miles. The first half of this climb can be tedious as there are few pauses in the steep grade, and the tread is often muddy or rocky. While the initial 0.5 mile of this trail hints at the tropiclike greenery ahead, it soon climbs onto the sunny, south-facing slopes and returns to the realm of drier montane forest.

When the trail finally drops down to meet Indian Creek, the character of the landscape changes dramatically. Easily crossing the stream at mile 4.0, the trail enters a world of shady spruce, wildflower-carpeted hills, and mossy boulders. Especially enchanting is a small brook just opposite this ford, which the trail briefly follows—its gurgling waters pour over a steady succession of rocks and logs, all of which are softened by green mosses and lichens, while wildflowers abound on the banks above. The trail recrosses the stream 0.5 mile farther, after it passes a particularly dense collection of bittercress and bluebells. Just upstream from the second ford is a small but spectacular cascade, which can be admired from several vantages as the trail climbs through a steep avalanche-cleared swath on the slope above. After a small island of forest, the trail once again makes its way through the open meadows that sweep along both sides of the creek. This last 0.5 mile before the meadow is the hike's most scenic, with an endless succession of cataracts and cascades enlivening the stream while more mossy boulders and a rainbow of wildflowers drink from the spray on its banks. Even the black, hardened lava that forms pebbles, boulders, and small cliffs throughout the area seems to have been lifted straight from the forests of Hawaii.

Our hike concludes as the trail eases into the grassy, subalpine expanse of Palisade Meadows. This sloping field is a delightful place to picnic and relax, while several fine campsites can be found in the encircling subalpine forest. Backpackers will find this an ideal place to make a base camp in order to explore routes leading to the Continental Divide. As with the West Fork Trail, located above Rainbow Hot Spring, tying in the Continental Divide Trail (CDT) with other paths in nearby drainages can create various loops.

Piedra River

El Rio de la Piedra Parada is a relative rarity in Colorado: a montane ecosystem river valley that remains in its primitive state. For nearly a dozen miles the Piedra remains untrammeled, flowing through grassy meadows, past stately cottonwoods, beneath lush conifers, and through a dramatic box canyon—one of the rugged gorges that gives the Piedra its name, which means "river of the rock wall." The Piedra River Trail is the only conveyance through this beautiful country, and the hiker who explores it will enjoy the river's clear pools and murmuring rapids, excellent opportunities to observe wildlife, long stretches of solitude, and pastoral scenery.

The Piedra River Trail provides opportunities for both great hiking and backpacking. If you wish to spend only a day on the trail, you may start at either end and hike to a turnaround point determined by your level of interest and energy. If you are a hardier soul, you may choose to hike the entire length of the trail, assuming that a car shuttle has been arranged. Backpacking is the best choice for a through-hike, as there are dozens of outstanding campsites available. Backpacking will leave you ample time for angling, stone skipping, or simply relaxing by the river's edge.

PIEDRA RIVER

DISTANCE: 10.5 miles one-way

ELEVATION RANGE: 7,100 to 7,850 feet

TOTAL ELEVATION GAIN: 1,100 feet (downstream)

TRAIL CONDITIONS: Several short, though fairly steep climbs; good tread; no route-finding difficulties

SEASON: Mid-May through October

USGS MAPS: Oakbrush Ridge (1964); Bear Mountain (1964); Devil Mountain (1964)

ADMINISTRATION: San Juan NF; Pagosa RD

PIEDRA RIVER TRAILHEAD: From Pagosa Springs, drive west on US 160 for about 2.5 miles and turn right onto Piedra Road (FR 631). Drive on this road, which turns to gravel after 6 miles. Stay to the left at a junction that is 6.5 miles beyond the end of the pavement, and you'll arrive at the trailhead just beyond the Piedra River bridge, a total of 15.7 miles from US 160. Park in the lot on the left side of the road, just past the road junction adjacent to the bridge, not in the parking area on the right side of the road, next to the river.

FIRST FORK TRAILHEAD: From Pagosa Springs, drive west on US 160 for about 23 miles and turn right onto First Fork Road (FR 622). Drive this gravel road for about 12 miles, until it crosses the Piedra River. The trailhead is adjacent to the bridge.

The trail is well constructed, though hardly level, and it rolls above the north bank, frequently gaining small bits of elevation in order to avoid obstacles near the river. The most significant climb—a gain of 500 feet—is located where the trail traverses high above the narrow confines of the Second Box Canyon, near the trail's lower end. The uppermost 3 miles of trail offer the gentlest grades, and thus the easiest hiking. Keep in mind that the lower elevations of the Piedra allow for hiking both earlier and later in the season than elsewhere in the San Juans. In particular, this is an outstanding trail for an autumn journey. One word of caution: Ticks are very common in the grassy meadows along the Piedra. Until the end of July, take appropriate preventive measures and check yourself often while hiking here.

Hiking downstream ultimately offers the least amount of climbing; thus, the hike described here begins from the upper trailhead. From here, the trail initially traverses a grassy meadow before it turns toward the river as it enters a short but very impressive gorge—a dramatic introduction to the canyons ahead. For the next 0.5 mile, rugged limestone cliffs rise high above the trail and the river, combining with verdant shrubs and conifers to make a very beautiful scene. Almost as abruptly as it constricted, the canyon widens again into a fairly broad valley, and the lush undergrowth gives way to broad, grassy meadows.

The trail crosses Williams Creek on a new footbridge about 1.5 miles from the trailhead. The next 1.5 miles of hiking continue across the gentle floor of the valley and past the greatest number of potential campsites. During spring and early summer, the meadows are sprinkled with a variety of wildflowers, ranging from dandelions to irises. The river meanders through the valley in a series of ripples and pools, and ancient cottonwoods line its banks. The lower valley walls are covered in rich stands of ponderosa, which give way to spruce and aspen as the slopes rise higher. Wildlife is often spotted along the way: deer and coyote are most frequently seen, while elk, black bear, and mountain lion are rarer sights. Additionally, the truly observant may catch a glimpse of a river otter, a species that has been reintroduced to this section of the Piedra.

Three miles from the upper trailhead, the Piedra Stock Trail branches to the left; descends to the river, which it crosses on a sturdy steel bridge; then climbs out of the Piedra Valley. A 0.5-mile stretch of gentle meadows on the south side of the river, which has the potential for several more nice campsites, may be accessed via this bridge. The Piedra River Trail continues on the north bank, beginning a short climb before dropping in a pair of switchbacks to a bridged crossing of Weminuche Creek. The character of the valley changes downstream from this point: The flat, grassy meadows give way to forested slopes, which drop somewhat steeply to the river. The trail climbs to about 50 feet above the Piedra and stays roughly at that elevation over the next 1.5 miles. The effect of "slope aspect" is particularly pronounced in this section of the canyon. On the south-facing slopes that the trail traverses, direct exposure to the sun creates a warm and dry environment that is perfect for stands of ponderosa pine and Gambel oak. The shady north-facing slopes on the opposite side of the river are cooler and moister, thus they are more suited for Douglas fir and Colorado blue spruce, as well as denser shrubbery and a fair amount of moss.

The trail breaks back into meadows about 5 miles from the upper trailhead and climbs gradually for the next mile until it drops to a crossing of Sand Creek. The Sand Creek Trail branches right just before the descent to the creek, while another trail branches to the right just beyond the bridge. The vicinity of Sand Creek offers the last good camping opportunities for the remainder of the hike. Sand Creek also marks the temporary end of easy hiking, as the trail begins a rather steep climb about 0.5 mile below the confluence. Over the course of the 0.5-mile ascent, almost 500 feet of elevation is gained in order to avoid the rugged inner gorge of the Second Box Canyon. The trail stays at this contour for the next mile and offers only the occasional peek at the upper walls of the gorge before it begins a moderate descent. After passing Davis Creek at mile 8.5, the grade eases, and the trail returns to near river level. The final 2 miles of the hike are fairly level, remaining about 100 feet above the river. The ponderosa forest is pretty, and the river can easily be accessed in numerous places. A short final descent brings you to the confluence of the First Fork and the lower trailhead.

Emerald Lake

This journey is an excellent introduction to the beautiful variety of the Weminuche Wilderness. The popular trail follows the Los Pinos River through a strikingly beautiful valley dotted with meadows and stands of ponderosa and cottonwood; continues up rushing Lake Creek, whose banks

EMERALD LAKE

Los Pinos River

Distance: 12 miles round-trip

Elevation Range: 7,850 to 8,200 feet

Total Elevation Gain: 350 feet

Trail Conditions: Flat, easy trail throughout; initial 3 miles are on private property; popular with horse-packers

Season: Mid-May through October

USGS Maps: Vallecito (1964); Granite Peak (1964)

Administration: San Juan NF; Columbine RD

Emerald Lake

Distance: 20 miles round-trip

Elevation Range: 7,850 to 10,050 feet

Total Elevation Gain: 2,200 feet

Trail Conditions: Above the Los Pinos River, the trail includes extended moderate grades; popular with horse-packers

Season: Mid-June until early October

USGS Maps: Vallecito (1964); Granite Peak (1964); Emerald Lake (1973)

Administration: San Juan NF; Columbine RD

Trailhead: From the intersection of US 160 and CR 501 (Vallecito Road) in Bayfield, drive north on CR 501. After 8 miles, turn right to remain on the paved road, then bear to the right toward Vallecito Reservoir at mile 8.8. At a junction 4.5 miles farther, stay straight—although some maps may depict the right fork as a shortcut, it ends on private property and does not connect with the correct road.

are alternately lined by aspen, spruce, and colorful wildflowers; and finally emerges at Emerald Lake, which sparkles beneath a backdrop of rugged peaks. Backpackers will find ample opportunity to locate the perfect campsite, while anglers will be drawn to the countless ripples and eddies of the Los Pinos and the sweeping shore of the lake, which is one of the state's largest natural bodies of water.

The first 6 miles of trail follow the valley of the Los Pinos River (commonly called by its English translation, "the Pine"), whose flat floor allows for easy walking. With an altitude in the 8,000-foot range and an elevation gain of only 300 feet, this section of trail is ideal for an introductory backpack as well as late spring and autumn hikes. Due to high visitor impact, camping is quite limited in the vicinity of Emerald Lake and is restricted to designated sites only. Instead, plan on camping along either lower Lake Creek or the Los Pinos River. The first 3 miles of trail cross the private property of Granite Peak Ranch. Please respect the owner's rights by staying on the trail. Use of this trail is heavy, particularly on weekends and holidays, so it is especially important to practice low-impact techniques. Keep in mind that the trail is popular with horse-packers, so be prepared to yield to them.

Leaving Pine River Campground, the trail stays to the left side of the valley, away from the river, while it passes through the ranch. Two gates are passed en route—please leave them as you find them. While access to the river is prohibited during these first miles, the scenery is nonetheless quite pleasing. The trail passes through a nice mixture of meadow and forest, while the flat valley floor contrasts markedly with the steep walls that guard its sides. As the trail first nears the bank of the river, 3 miles from the trailhead, public land begins. An additional 0.5 mile brings you to the wilderness boundary.

Continue on the main paved road, which circles around the far shore of Vallecito Reservoir until it turns to gravel 6.5 miles from the previous junction. Pine River Campground is 5.8 miles farther—the large trailhead is just beyond, at the road's end.

The Los Pinos is one of the few places in Colorado where wilderness protection extends to such a low elevation, and the experience of walking through a primitive piece of montane ecosystem is one of the highlights of the trail. Tall cottonwoods line the banks of the river, grassy meadows and ponderosa pine spread across the valley bottom, and the canyon walls are cloaked in dark conifers and a scattering of aspen. Beaver ponds and associated wetlands draw a variety of bird and animal life and provide a mirror for the surrounding scenery. The best campsites are in the meadows along the river, which provide level sites and room for several parties. Try to minimize impact by using existing sites, refraining from fires, and packing out all garbage.

About 5.8 miles up the river, the trail crosses Lake Creek, and a short distance beyond the bridge is the Emerald Lake Trail junction. While the upper Los Pinos River is enticing, our route turns left and begins climbing along the creek. Though not steep, the trail ascends steadily through shady forest. There is a respite from the grade about 2 miles from the junction, where the trail enters a series of lush meadows. The last decent camping sites before the lake are here, though the marshy and often buggy conditions make for less-pleasant sites than those adjacent to the Los Pinos. Above the meadows, the moderate grade resumes, and the trail passes through several avalanche paths. These slopes, which are cleared of encroaching trees each winter, provide a sunny home to a variety of subalpine wildflowers. The climb steepens a bit more as the trail enters shady forest, then slackens once it reaches Little Emerald Lake at mile 9.75. The much larger Emerald Lake is just 0.25 mile farther.

Autumn reflections in a beaver pond along the Los Pinos River.

The result of an ancient landslide that blocked the valley and dammed Lake Creek, Emerald Lake is about 1.5 miles long, 0.5 mile wide, and nearly 250 feet deep. The lake's setting is quite dramatic, with sheer walls of gray granite rising more than 2,000 feet above its dark green waters. On its western shore, a long cascade spills down a cliff and into the lake with a roar. A fringe of forest wraps around the lake like a shawl, while the literal apex of the scene is the high peaks that stand at the head of the valley.

The fishing is among the primary reasons that Emerald Lake is such a popular destination, and despite the pressure, anglers are not often disappointed. The Division of Wildlife asks that only artificial flies and lures be used and that catch-and-release be practiced. Possession is limited to two fish, 14 inches or less. Upstream from the lake, Lake Creek is closed to angling from January 1 to July 15 each year, to protect spawning fish.

While most hikers will be content with a spot along the lake to enjoy its beautiful scenery, the trail does continue along the east shore of the lake and into the upper valley. The 3-mile walk from Emerald Lake to Moon Lake is recommended. The additional 1,500 feet of climbing is rewarded by austere alpine scenery, spectacular wildflowers, and thundering waterfalls.

Beauty doesn't always come in the grand vista; sometimes it's found right on the forest floor.

MOUNTAIN BIKING

The road, if it can be called a road, lay along the river, once or twice crossing it. The river was nothing but a chain of wild cascades. The road was but a track over and among piles of huge rocks. The teams were sometimes taken off and the wagons pried up and raised by levers, to get them over impassable places.

—Margaret A. Frink, August 27, 1850
From the diary published in *Covered Wagon Women 1850*

There can be little doubt that, of the many hardships faced by the first west-ward pioneers, the very act of traveling across the land caused some of their greatest daily difficulties. The deplorable condition of roads and trails—where they existed—often resulted in the death of their livestock, damage to their wagons and other belongings, and simply made their lives miser-able. Yet despite the difficulties, a tide of humanity rushed into the moun-tains and valleys of the West, with every person seeking their literal and figurative pots of gold. It's quite ironic that, beneath this historical backdrop, today's westward rush is built at least in part upon the continued existence of rotten roads and treacherous trails. Recreation is today's gold, with mountain bikers prospecting for the nastiest, gnarliest paths on which to pedal being a large part of the latest tide. The technological advancements of today's bicycles, complete with intricate gearing, alloy frames, and knobby tires, make traveling even the roughest corners of the West not a hardship, but an exciting adventure. And with hundreds of miles of decrepit mining, logging, and ranching roads—not to mention scores of twisting trails—it is only natural that the San Juans have become one of the mountain-biking community's new meccas.

Hermosa Creek

With trails like these, it's easy to understand why Durango has become ground zero for the mountain-biking explosion of the last decade. The Her-mosa Creek Trail is especially popular in a town where the large number of nearby rides—all scenic and exciting—has been enough to make some of the country's best mountain bikers become residents. Widely considered one of Colorado's most enjoyable single-tracks, the trail careens down a roadless canyon; winds past rushing streams, grassy meadows, and cool forests; and has long stretches of effortless coasting punctuated by enough "grunt climbing" to keep you honest. Technically, this is one of the easier single-tracks you will find, and though it can get crowded, it is a fine place to experience off-road mountain biking for the first time.

Unless you are driven by loop rides and would like to add another 30 miles to your bike's odometer, plan on arranging a car shuttle and enjoying Hermosa Creek as a one-way, downstream adventure. Do not, however, as-sume *downstream* means the ride is all downhill. There are a number of short

A summer shower freshens a Sneffels Range columbine bouquet.

Shimmering aspen trees on a late summer afternoon.

A foggy dawn on Molas Pass after a long, stormy night.

The San Juans's rich volcanic soils and frequent showers give life to a dazzling display of wildflower color.

Gilpin Peak and the crags of 13,000-foot Blue Lakes Pass.

Only lichens thrive among the rocks of Hurricane Pass.

The subtle play of light turns a common forest scene into a work of art.

The Sound Democrat Mill and the expansive tundra of Placer Gulch.

Lush gardens at the base of Bridal Veil Falls.

November's first light highlights the awesome beauty of Wilson Peak.

July still finds Sloan Lake to be fringed with snow and dotted by ice.

Crystalline streams and carpets of flowers spill down the slopes below Black Bear Pass.

A small piece of San Juan sky reflects in a pond near the virtual headwaters of the Rio Grande.

uphill pulls and one sustained ascent; in all, count on about 1,200 feet of elevation gain to go with your 2,200-foot descent. Though the track becomes narrow in places, there are few technical difficulties. The tread is smooth, and other than a few jutting roots and tight side-hill traverses, there is little that will make even a novice want to dismount. The intermediate skill rating is more a factor of the ride's overall length and the number of minor obstacles than any individual challenge.

The ride commences by following an old double-track out of the open valley of Hermosa Park and down into the narrow valley of Hermosa Creek. Though gently descending, the track can be rocky in places, forcing you to check your speed. The valley begins to narrow as you pass your third cattle guard and East Cross Creek, about 1.8 miles into the ride. Continuing downstream, the trail soon enters a very pretty little gorge with limestone cliffs, which shelter a lush montane forest of spruce and fir. Named after the Spanish word for "beautiful," Hermosa Creek is certainly an appropriate moniker.

The trail swings across Hermosa Creek on a good bridge that is 4.8 miles from the trailhead. Be careful not to blow by this turn, as the Elbert

HERMOSA CREEK

DISTANCE: 18.7 miles one-way
ELEVATION RANGE: 7,600 to 8,850 feet
TOTAL ELEVATION GAIN: 1,200 feet (with a 2,250-foot descent)
TRAIL CONDITIONS: Single- and double-track trail; several sustained climbs; trail is narrow in places
SKILL LEVEL: Intermediate
SEASON: June through October
USGS MAP: La Plata County, Sheet 1 (1975)
ADMINISTRATION: San Juan NF; Columbine RD

HERMOSA PARK TRAILHEAD (UPPER ACCESS): From the intersection of US 160 and US 550 in Durango, drive north on US 550 for 27.5 miles and turn left onto FR 578 (Hermosa Park Road) just past Purgatory Ski Resort. A half mile up FR 578, bear right to avoid the ski area parking lot, then bear right 2.8 miles farther and bear left 0.5 mile after that. Turn left and park at the large trailhead, which is a total of 8.9 miles from US 550.
HERMOSA CREEK ACCESS (LOWER ACCESS): From the US 550/US 160 junction, drive north on US 550 for 10.5 miles, turn left at the community of Hermosa, and then immediately turn right onto FR 576. Drive on FR 576 for 4.2 miles and park at the end of the road.

Creek Trail continues directly ahead for a spell before it turns east and climbs out of the canyon. Climb a small hill beyond the bridge, then enjoy a

mile of smooth coasting before the trail crosses Hermosa Creek once more. After this second bridge, the trail narrows and contours across a steep hillside above the rapidly descending creek. Use caution here, as occasional obstacles or a general lack of concentration could result in an unpleasant "soil-sampling" experience.

The trickiest riding ends as the trail veers away from the creek to cross a dry gulch, 8.5 miles from the trailhead. Though narrow in places, the trail remains mostly level as it winds in and out of small gulches, bumps over occasional rocks and roots, and generally provides a great ride. After passing a fourth gate, the trail crosses Elk Creek at mile 10.3, then climbs over and descends a small hill to intersect the right-branching South Fork Trail at mile 11.1. Little Elk Creek is crossed 0.5 mile farther, and the trail continues a gentle up-and-down routine for another 2 miles after that, before it drops more steeply to intersect the Clear Creek Trail, 10.4 miles from the trailhead. Stay to the left, and you'll soon arrive at Dutch Creek.

Within the last few miles, you should have noticed the type of ecosystems present along the trail change from the spruce, fir, and aspen communities to Gambel oak and ponderosa. Elevation plays an important role in determining plant distribution, and the 8,000-foot contour is the rough boundary that divides moister, cooler forests from the warmer, drier ones in the southern Rockies. The Hermosa Creek drainage, one of the larger, non-wilderness, roadless areas in Colorado, is actually one of the most ecologically diverse places in the San Juans, with a complex combination of elevation, aspect, and soil type resulting in highly varied plant cover within relatively small areas. In particular, the primitive, low-elevation forests along Hermosa Creek are favored haunts of most San Juan wildlife species, including deer, elk, mountain lion, and black bear. Such a wealth of wildlife draws a large number of hunters, so be careful to make your presence known should you be riding during hunting season.

The least enjoyable part of the ride is upon you as you begin a steep, mile-long ascent beyond Dutch Creek. The first third of this climb can be tortuous; the remainder is just a grind. Relief comes when the Dutch Creek Trail is intersected at mile 15.1. Though the trail has climbed enough to reenter a cooler aspen forest, the trail soon returns to the scrub oak as it makes a long, smooth descent across hillsides that blaze spectacularly crimson during late September. The winding descent continues past Stony Gulch and Jones Creek, and, at about 18.5 miles, the trail passes a large information board for anglers. Just after this sign, look for a left-branching trail, which climbs a short distance to arrive at the Hermosa Creek Trailhead and journey's end.

Lime Creek Road

Before it was rerouted, US 550 once followed the route of Lime Creek Road, which today is a quiet, backcountry route that twists and turns through thick aspen groves, past large beaver ponds, and into the shadowy depths of Lime Creek Gorge. Though still used by the occasional automobile sightseer, this sometimes-rough dirt road is now a highly enjoyable bike ride that takes in many pretty scenes, including a neck-cramping panorama of the West Needle Mountains. Though the road climbs steadily for much of its length, the lack of traffic and its wide, generally reliable alignment make it an excellent family ride. Be sure to allot enough time to rest, picnic, and perhaps fish along the bank of beautiful Lime Creek.

It is possible to create a 20-mile loop by combining Lime Creek Road with US 550's ascent of Coal Bank Pass, though heavy traffic makes this of questionable enjoyment if you are the type of casual biker uncomfortable with cars, trucks, and motor homes whizzing by at high speeds. Less harrowing is to make this an out-and-back ride of about 23 miles, with a start possible at either end of the road thanks to dual access of US 550. You'll probably wish to finish the hardest

---

LIME CREEK ROAD

DISTANCE: 11.4 miles one-way
ELEVATION RANGE: 8,750 to 9,800 feet
TOTAL ELEVATION GAIN: 1,550 feet
TRAIL CONDITIONS: Dirt road with light traffic; moderate grades; rocky in places
SKILL LEVEL: Novice
SEASON: Mid-May through October
USGS MAPS: Snowdon Peak (1972); Engineer Mountain (1975)
ADMINISTRATION: San Juan NF; Columbine RD

CASCADE CREEK ACCESS: From Durango, drive north on US 550 for 29 miles (or from Silverton, drive south on US 550 for 19 miles) and turn onto FR 591, Lime Creek Road. Park in the large pullout on the right.
WEST LIME CREEK ACCESS: Drive north from Durango for 37.5 miles (or south from Silverton for 10.5 miles) until Lime Creek Road reintersects US 550. Park here.

---

riding on the outbound trip, so the ride described here starts from the Cascade Creek access. If you are crafty and arrange a car shuttle, a one-way ride from the West Lime Creek access means you'll be coasting for the majority of the ride—though a sustained, 400-foot ascent midway through will ensure at least a nominal workout.

The ride begins as the road crosses a cattle guard and begins to roll through open meadows and past scattered stands of aspen. There has been some development in the area within the past few years, and several new vacation homes have been built here, though the last of these are left behind where the road crosses tiny Mill Creek and makes a short switchback a mile into the ride. The next 3 miles are very pleasant: The road climbs gently through aspen forest and past several large ponds. Pause at a pond for a few minutes, and you may be lucky enough to glimpse one of the resident beavers; if not, you'll at least enjoy fine reflections of the surrounding mountains.

At mile 4.1, the road makes a sharp left turn and enters the deep canyon of Lime Creek. US 550 was rerouted over Coal Bank Pass in the late 1950s because of dangerous avalanches and persistent ice that plagued this portion of the road. Though masonry retaining walls still exist, there is little else to suggest this was once the main auto route across the San Juans. You'll enjoy a 1.5-mile downhill coast as the road drops 400 feet to the floor of the canyon. Other than a few rocky places, there will be little to distract you from admiring the impressively imposing West Needle Mountains, which culminates more than 4,000 feet overhead at the summit of North Twilight Peak. A swath of demolished aspen on the opposite canyon wall is the result of a particularly destructive 1993 avalanche.

After reaching the bank of Lime Creek, the road climbs easily for the next 2 miles, offering many fine places to stop, rest, and enjoy the clear, rushing waters. A break here will renew your strength for the last 4 miles of the ride, which climb high above the creek through stands of aspen and eventually into the higher realm of the subalpine evergreen forest. A jog past Coal Creek signifies that US 550 is near, which is where Lime Creek Road ends after 11.4 miles. Unless you plan to attack Coal Bank Pass, retrace your tire tracks from this point.

Placer and Picayune Gulches

Classic San Juans. That is the best way to describe the high country at the head of the Animas River, which includes a pair of beautiful alpine valleys, Placer and Picayune Gulches. Above timberline for all but a few minutes, the looping four-wheel-drive road that connects these two drainages showcases the dramatic mountain scenery and rich mining history of the region. The road is rocky and can be very steep in places, but this is an otherwise straightforward ride that can be completed within a few hours by most intermediate-skilled bikers. However, you'll want to schedule the better part of an entire day for this loop, as there are so many old mines to explore, meadows to wander, rocks to ponder, and vistas at which to marvel that the ride itself becomes secondary. Just be sure to keep an eye to the sky, because there is no shelter from the afternoon storms that regularly brew amongst these peaks.

PLACER AND PICAYUNE GULCHES

DISTANCE: 9.9 miles round-trip

ELEVATION RANGE: 10,750 to 12,750 feet

TOTAL ELEVATION GAIN: 2,000 feet

TRAIL CONDITIONS: Rough, rocky four-wheel-drive road; steep grades in places

SKILL LEVEL: Intermediate

SEASON: Mid-July through mid-September

USGS MAP: Handies Peak (1975)

ADMINISTRATION: BLM; San Juan RA

TRAILHEAD: The trailhead is located at the ghost town of Animas Forks, which is 12.2 miles upstream from Silverton at the headwaters of the Animas River. Take CO 110, which soon becomes CR 10, east from town, and follow the signs to Animas Forks. The last few miles are rough in places, but most cars should be able to make it without difficulty.

Even before you mount your bike, you'll want to take some time to wander around the abandoned town site of Animas Forks, an archetypal western ghost town. Founded in approximately 1880, the town was a thriving mining community until 1917. Among the ruins is a large concrete foundation near the river—this is all that remains of the Gold Prince Mill, which, in the short decade it existed, was the state's largest ore-crushing facility. The small, windowless wood structure near the foundation was the jail; it is said that the bars of one of the interior jail cells still existed up until just a few years ago. The most impressive building is the famed Walsh House, a two-story structure complete with a bay window. San Juan lore has long held that the building was once home to Thomas Walsh, owner of the Camp Bird Mine (and father of one-time socialite Evelyn Walsh McLean); however, there is no evidence that he lived here or anywhere else in town. Several other old houses can be examined, and towers of the aerial tram that carried ore from the Gold Prince Mine may also be seen.

Once you have satisfied your curiosity at Animas Forks, ride west out of town on the four-wheel-drive road, which climbs along the west fork of the Animas River. The road is somewhat rocky but climbs only moderately to start. The picturesque Bagley Mill, located 0.7 mile above Animas Forks, is a worthy stop. The mill is said to be one of the earliest and largest prefabricated structures in the state, and if you peek into its shadows, you'll still see the numbered beams that facilitated the building's reconstruction. Above the Bagley Mill, the road traverses the mouth of Placer Gulch. This 0.5 mile is slightly gentler and not as rocky, and the surrounding slopes are colorfully decorated with wildflowers.

The road branches at mile 1.2; bear left and begin the climb into Placer Gulch. A half mile up the gulch, the road continues on a new alignment created in 1998. The old road is now closed to vehicles; however, it can still be ridden by bike if so desired. Because it is no longer maintained, expect washouts, rockfall, and generally rougher going. The newer road climbs a brief, steeper pitch before it eases into a gentler traverse of the gulch's lower slope. After passing through a recent mined-lands reclamation project, you'll reach the remnants of the Gold Prince complex and return to the original road, 2.9 miles from Animas Forks. Pedaling back down the old road for 0.5 mile in order to visit the Sound Democrat Mill is a mandatory diversion. The mill, which was built in 1905, probably contains more of its original equipment than any Colorado mining relic. Carefully take a look inside the building, which is being restored by the Bureau of Land Management, and you'll see the old pulley wheels that held the heavy ore-crushing stamps as well as a set of copper-plated shaker tables. (A visit to the Mayflower Mill outside of Silverton will give you an idea of how this equipment was used.) Outside the mill, enjoy a good look around the gulch, where numerous other mines and related structures sit in the shadows of Treasure and California Mountains.

Back at the Gold Prince, which consisted of several structures, including the upper terminal of an aerial tram and a boardinghouse that once housed 150 men, continue up two sets of steep, rocky switchbacks to arrive at a small but very beautiful basin, which is directly beneath Hanson Peak. Another 0.5 mile of steep pedaling brings you to a saddle high above Parson Gulch. This saddle, which is 4.9 miles above Animas Forks, offers absolutely stunning views to the south, including the rolling peaks of the Continental Divide and the snow-streaked crags of the Grenadier Range.

The ride's apex comes just beyond the saddle, with a welcome piece of smooth, rolling road traversing the top of Treasure Mountain's southeast ridge. (Before beginning the descent into Picayune Gulch, you may want to scramble the last 250 feet to its summit.) Heading down into Picayune Gulch, you'll pass many small mines and prospect pits, and at a sweeping curve, you'll enjoy a fine look at the sculpted summit of Niagara Peak as well as the ride's best flower fields. A half mile after a tight switchback turns you toward the mouth of the gulch, you'll pass the remains of the Treasure Mountain Mine. This mine, located 7.5 miles from Animas Forks, saw its greatest development in the 1930s, and the attendant structures date from this era.

The ride becomes almost harrowing beyond the Treasure Mountain Mine, as the road plummets out of Picayune Gulch and into the upper Animas drainage. The section just below treeline is the worst, and only a good set of brakes and a steady grip on the handlebars will keep you upright as the road dives 300 feet in a very rocky 0.5 mile. Relief comes at mile 8.5, where the four-wheel-drive road intersects CR 10 below Animas Forks. Turn left and begin climbing once again, staying along the valley floor as you cross the river and pass a pair of divergent tracks. Traffic is heaviest in this final part of the loop, but because vehicles travel slowly, you'll have no problems. Bear left when the road forks at mile 9.2, and pedal another 0.7 mile to arrive back at Animas Forks and the completion of the loop.

Black Bear Pass

So, do you want to test your mountain-biking mettle? Do you think you can conquer a relentless climb at an oxygen-starved altitude? Are you willing to ride the meanest, most feared pass in all of the Colorado Rockies? If so, saddle up and take the Black Bear Pass test. Don't let the short distance of the ride fool you. Straining ceaselessly, you'll pedal up the massive mountain wall west of Red Mountain Pass and gasp your way through cascading

BLACK BEAR PASS

RETURN TO RED MOUNTAIN PASS

DISTANCE: 6.4 miles round-trip

ELEVATION RANGE: 11,050 to 12,840 feet

TOTAL ELEVATION GAIN: 1,790 feet

TRAIL CONDITIONS: Four-wheel-drive road; steep except for brief portions; rough and rocky at times

SKILL LEVEL: Advanced

SEASON: Mid-July through September

USGS MAP: Ironton (1955)

ADMINISTRATION: San Juan NF; Columbine RD

THROUGH TO PANDORA MILL

DISTANCE: 9.3 miles one-way

ELEVATION RANGE: 9,000 to 12,840 feet

TOTAL ELEVATION GAIN: 1,790 feet (with a 3,840-foot descent)

TRAIL CONDITIONS: Four-wheel-drive road; very steep both in ascent and descent; rough and rocky at times; very tight switchbacks

SKILL LEVEL: Advanced

SEASON: Mid-July through September

USGS MAPS: Ironton (1955); Telluride (1955)

ADMINISTRATION: San Juan NF; Columbine RD; Uncompahgre NF; Norwood RD

RED MOUNTAIN PASS ACCESS: Drive US 550 to the summit of Red Mountain Pass, which is between Ouray and Silverton. Park just south of the pass in a large gravel pullout.

PANDORA MILL ACCESS: Drive east from Telluride on CO 145 Spur (Colorado Avenue) and park at the old Pandora Mill, which is located at pavement's end, about 2 miles from town.

స్ఠస్ఠస్ఠ

meadows and past sparkling waterfalls. The satisfaction you feel once you reach the crest of Black Bear—if you make it—will only be surpassed by the breathtaking panorama that spreads before you. Such satisfaction is but an hors d'oeuvre for the maniacal daredevils who find their greatest glory in surviving the hair-raising descent back to the trailheads below.

There are two options by which to ride Black Bear Pass. The most straightforward is to pedal up from Red Mountain Pass, then return via the same route. A longer option entails riding over the pass and descending through Ingram Basin, past Bridal Veil Falls, and arriving at the Pandora Mill, just east of Telluride. The requisite car shuttle for this longer option is a time-consuming task. If you drive a standard passenger car, you're faced with a 64-mile drive to Telluride via paved roads through Ridgway and Placerville. If you have a four-wheel drive, you can shorten the distance—but not the time—by using nearby Ophir Pass. A third option is to drive Black Bear Pass itself, though this is the least favorable choice because the steep, rough, narrow, and often scary road is considered to be the most challenging pass to drive in the entire state. You will need to be experienced with mountain off-highway driving techniques, have a four-wheel-drive vehicle with a short wheelbase, and possess steel nerves. Furthermore, the road is one-way westbound from the top of the pass to Bridal Veil Falls, meaning that the shuttle vehicle must be driven in the same direction as the recommended ride, thus creating more of a support-vehicle situation. If you do shuttle via Black Bear, keep in mind that the biker will probably be able to complete the descent off the pass much more quickly than the driver will.

The ride starts steeply with only a few respites, and it remains that way until it crests Black Bear Pass, 3.2 miles away. Begin by following the dirt road that veers away from US 550 on the west side of Red Mountain Pass, quickly passing underneath a set of power lines before winding upward across flower-carpeted slopes. The road is rocky and rutted in places and will continue in the same condition for the duration of the ride. The only hope for smoother tread comes in the first mile, where a mining operation sometimes grades the road for trucks that serve it. The first brief breather comes 0.9 mile into the ride, where the road flattens just prior to splitting into two branches. Take the right fork and enjoy a great view of a lovely waterfall as you climb steeply into almost continuous wildflower meadows. Vistas become ever more impressive, and several small creeks can be seen cascading off of rock outcroppings as you slowly progress up the steeply switchbacking road.

The grade eases once again as the road climbs into Mineral Basin, 2 miles above US 550. There are several small tarns, a couple of abandoned mines, and many wildflowers among the rock-strewn and snow-streaked mountains that encircle the basin. Be sure to look back over your shoulder every once in a while—such great views of the Grenadier Range, among other high peaks, are often hard to come by. The road braids into a number of rough tracks, though the most heavily traveled route is not difficult to identify. Compared with the grade over the first 2 miles, the last mile or so to the pass is almost a relief—though the very high altitude saps much of your remaining energy.

When you finally get to the pass, you'll probably want to dump your bike and collapse among the rocks and tundra that surround you. Even the icy breezes will feel good after the tireless work of the last 3 miles. The view that opens before you is of unsurpassed beauty. Peaks north and south of the pass limit the panorama in those directions, but the westward scene overlooking Ingram Basin is dominated by Mount Sneffels, while the sea of mountains to the east unfolds like a series of waves, with the Red Mountains being the nearest in a line of peaks that stretch as far as the Needles.

A fog-shrouded cascade pours out of Mineral Basin.

Whichever way you plan on continuing—either back down to Red Mountain Pass or on to Pandora—you'll be faced with a very rough and unyielding descent. Flex your hands before you start out, because they are about to get a serious, brake-clenching workout. If you are continuing westward, the road descends across the headwall of Ingram Basin then contours more gently across the cirque's northern flank. Ingram Lake and more flowery meadows make the basin a place to linger. Below the turnoff to the Black Bear Mine, the road steepens considerably, and it becomes especially treacherous after several switchbacks carry it to the lip of the basin. After crossing Ingram Creek and passing a series of old mining ruins, the road begins its most famous stretch: Steep, extremely tight switchbacks carry the road down the face of a very steep mountain wall—one so steep that Ingram Creek becomes a long and exceptionally spectacular cascade.

The most frightening part of the ride ends where the road intersects Bridal Veil Basin Road, about 3.5 miles below Black Bear Pass. In the final 2.5 miles below this junction, the road continues its switchbacking ways, though the grade is wider and not nearly so treacherous. You may actually be able to look up from your handlebars to admire Bridal Veil Falls just to the south. At 365 feet, it is Colorado's tallest and perhaps most beautiful waterfall. The building perched at the brink of the falls is an old powerhouse now restored as a private residence. After pausing at the falls, you'll negotiate a few more switchbacks, contour below the rugged cliffs of Ajax Peak, and then face one last rough, downhill pitch to arrive at Pandora. You've survived—now go reward yourself with some refreshment in Telluride.

La Plata Canyon

The La Plata Mountains are a distinct group of peaks at the southwestern edge of the San Juans. Rising sharply above the oak- and juniper-dotted mesa country of the surrounding foothills, their colorful summits and verdant alpine meadows are true to the expected scenery of the region, while their somewhat isolated position makes their high ridges an ideal place to seek dramatic vistas. The progressively rougher dirt road that climbs La Plata Canyon, which cuts right through the heart of the range, is a popular bike ride with locals and visitors alike. In as few as twenty minutes, you can get out of Durango, be on your bike, and on your way.

LA PLATA CANYON

DISTANCE: 18.8 miles round-trip

ELEVATION RANGE: 8,750 to 11,600 feet

TOTAL ELEVATION GAIN: 2,850 feet

TRAIL CONDITIONS: Gravel road turns steadily rougher until becoming a rocky four-wheel-drive road; unrelenting grade is sometimes steep

SKILL LEVEL: Intermediate

SEASON: Mid-June through mid-October

USGS MAPS: La Plata (1963); Hesperus (1963)

ADMINISTRATION: San Juan NF; Columbine RD

TRAILHEAD: Drive 11.4 miles west from Durango on US 160 and turn right onto CR 124 (La Plata Canyon Road). Drive another 4.7 miles, pass the burg of Mayday, and park at a large pullout at the end of the paved portion of the road.

La Plata Canyon Road is rough at times—particularly in its upper reaches—but is otherwise without many technical obstacles. The ascent is unrelenting, and while it is truly steep only for limited durations, the overall elevation gain makes this ride a serious workout. Your greatest difficulty will be to avoid choking on the dust from cars that stream up and down the road, especially on weekends. While the upper few miles are limited to slow-moving four-wheel-drive vehicles, most cars can travel the first 6 miles at a fairly high speed. For this reason, be especially observant of the "rules of the road." If you want to avoid the heaviest traffic, try a midweek ride (especially during the early morning), or wait until after Labor Day, when most tourists have returned home.

As the road starts into the narrow, steep-walled portal of La Plata Canyon, it maintains an easy, smooth course that is adjacent to the modest La Plata River. The canyon floor is lush: Tall cottonwoods line the river and the road, and thick stands of aspen stretch up the mountain walls. Long avalanche gullies, usually graced by trickling brooks, pass by at regular intervals, and there are several nicely developed camping areas. About 3 miles up canyon, the road enters the site of La Plata City, where several summer cabins are interspersed among more historic structures. First described by Spanish explorers who skirted the area in the mid-eighteenth century, the La Platas were named for the silver riches they hoped to find. While such treasure eluded them, the name proved prophetic when both silver and gold were discovered and extensively mined during the late nineteenth century. Many ruins and prospect pits dot the canyon, and several can be examined at different points on the ride. The most impressive is the large, rotting wood structure of the Gold Prince Mill, which can be observed across the canyon at mile 4.4, just after you pass the remnants of an old chimney.

While the ascent has been generally gentle until this point, that will soon change. In the miles ahead, the road is more than twice as steep as before. As progress is made up canyon, the surrounding peaks become more imposing, and wildflowers become more profuse. Avalanche gullies become more numerous as well, and some may hold snow in their run-out zones until the middle of summer. The road becomes much rougher about 6 miles above Mayday, and the next mile or so will weed out less determined bikers.

After passing Columbus Basin Road at mile 7.5, you will come upon the most challenging portion of the ride, which has steep grades and very rough tread. Fortunately, this part of the road is restricted to four-wheel-drive vehicles, so at least you don't have to worry about traffic. Fortunately, too, this part of the ride is the most scenic: Tall mountains, beautiful meadows, and several small waterfalls spread around you. A short distance after splashing through the creek-size waters of the La Plata River, the road breaks above timberline and enters Cumberland Basin, 9 miles up the canyon. The road actually becomes easier to ride—at least temporarily—as it passes several mines and makes its way to the rear of the basin. The last 0.25 mile onto the ridge above the basin is more challenging, but the climactic payoff at the top makes it all worthwhile: Spread northward before you is a 100-mile line of peaks that stretch from the San Miguel Range to the South San Juans. Southward, across the head of the canyon, the sculpted peaks at the crest of the La Platas stand in bold relief above flower-filled meadows and beneath deep-blue skies. This is truly one of the most impressive panoramas in the San Juans.

The recommended ride ends here, but there are options for bikers who want more. One is to ride another mile to Kennebec Pass to enjoy its even more expansive eastward vistas. A second option is to ride a very rough mining track across the east face of Snowstorm Peak and down into Columbus Basin, which creates a short, experts-only loop. A third possibility is to pedal either the Colorado Trail (CT) or Junction Creek Road (accessible via a short trail from Kennebec Pass) down the steep eastern flanks of the La Platas and into Durango.

Echo Basin

The numerous old mining and logging roads that crisscross the western slopes of the La Platas offer a number of mountain-biking possibilities. One of the best is the loop through Echo Basin, an easy leg-stretcher that is ideal for bikers of any skill level. There is only a modest volume of vehicle traffic and no challenging obstacles. Aspen cloak much of the route, while a handful of pretty meadows permit fine views of Mount Hesperus and the La Plata Range.

From the T-Down Park Trailhead, begin pedaling up FR 566, which climbs moderately through scrub oak and scattered pockets of aspen. One mile and some 500 feet higher, the road splits into the loop that encircles Burnt Ridge and traverses Echo Basin. Bear to the right, and after a brief bit of steeper climbing, enjoy far-reaching vistas to the west, which encompass the Montezuma Valley, Mesa Verde, and the distinctive Sleeping Ute Mountain. The grade moderates as it curves closer to the middle fork of the Mancos River, though it does become more rocky and rutted in places. Unfortunately, a small quarry and several recent clear-cuts detract from the otherwise enjoyable montane scenery.

The ride's steady but reasonable ascent ends about 3 miles after the beginning of the loop. Cresting a small saddle at this point, the road begins an easy, winding descent into Echo Basin. Small meadows throughout the area are usually filled with flowers, particularly in early summer when marsh marigold and buttercup spread across the damp ground beneath melting snowbanks. The La Plata Range's highest peaks fill the eastern skyline, with the tallest, most distinctive being 13,232-foot Mount Hesperus.

This beautifully banded summit is prominent on the eastern horizon from as far away as northeastern Arizona, especially during the ten months of the year when it is covered by a glistening blanket of snow. So striking is Hesperus—even from afar—that it is considered one of the four sacred peaks of the Navajo people.

The road continues through and then out of the basin on an easy grade, and while it is occasionally rough, the ride remains easy and enjoyable. Pockets of spruce are interspersed among the meadows, and Hesperus commands the skyline until the road begins to turn in a westward direction. After doing so, the forest becomes one predominately of aspen, and the tall canopy of quaking leaves—either green or gold—add another scenic dimension to the ride.

Continue past the turnoff for the Owen Basin Trail 7 miles after the beginning of the loop, and then begin a gentle, 0.75-mile climb into the open meadows of Lucy Halls Park. The Owen Basin Trail is a new route that climbs into the basin just south of Hesperus, which even from this vantage point is obviously a very scenic destination. Thick with wildflowers, Lucy Halls Park is a nice place to relax and picnic, provided that the mosquitoes can be tolerated. The next 1.5 miles beyond the meadow roll gently and smoothly through tall aspen before closing the loop. Bear right and speed back down the first mile of the ride to return to T-Down Park and your waiting vehicle.

Galloping Goose Trail

The nostalgia of railroading remains one of the romantic attractions of the San Juans. Many decades ago, rails penetrated all corners of the range, connecting the mines and towns that dotted their flanks with the rest of the civilized world. While the days of boomtown riches are long past and most of the railroads are but a distant memory, this era comes to life once again in a few precious places. The Galloping Goose Trail is one such place. Built on the long-abandoned grade of the Rio Grande Southern Railroad (RGS), the trail traces the line's serpentine course from Telluride to Ophir and on to Lizard Head Pass. Looking beyond your handlebars, it is easy to pretend for just a moment that you are riding the rails of yesterday. Feel the rhythmic swaying of the cars, the clackity-clack of the rails, the billowing clouds of smoke, and the soulful wail of the whistle. Imagine, as you pass the remains of trestles, water tanks, and other structures, the herculean task of transporting people and goods through such difficult and spectacular terrain.

As mining riches began to wane in the early twentieth century, the Rio Grande Southern began looking for more economical ways to transport the rapidly shrinking cargo of goods and people that sought the railroad's service. The solution was an odd-looking contraption that was soon nicknamed the Galloping Goose—a 1936 Pierce-Arrow automobile welded to a boxcar and set onto the rails. In all, seven Geese were constructed, plying the line for more than twenty years. Today, there are Geese on display in Telluride and Dolores, and the Colorado Railroad Museum in Golden has two, both of which are still operable. It is in fond remembrance of these unique machines that this trail has been named.

The Galloping Goose Trail is a recent addition to the San Juans' trail system, and thanks to the hard work of the Forest Service and other interested groups and individuals, it can be rated among the best. Several roads intersect the route; thus, the trail can be ridden in segments, and a ride can be tailored to your individual time and energy allotment. Because of this, the following description is outlined on a segment-by-segment basis. To complete the entire journey, it is necessary to ride a winding, 1.1-mile section of the moderately busy CO 145. While the remainder of the ride can be enjoyed by people of all ages, families with small children may wish to avoid this section. The long-range goal is to complete a trail bypass of the highway, but definitive plans for this have yet to be completed. Small posts that bear a distinctive Galloping Goose logo mark most of the route.

TELLURIDE TO SOCIETY TURN

Society Turn is located at the western edge of the flat-floored hanging valley in which Telluride is located. The site, which is marked by the junction of CO 145 and CO 145 Spur, was given its name because it was a turnaround used by Telluride's elite when they took carriage rides. Between town and Society Turn, the valley floor is largely private property, and the exact grade of the Rio Grande Southern Railroad (RGS) cannot be traced. However, there are two other bike routes through this section. The River Trail is an interesting single-track that winds along the extreme south edge of the valley. There are only a few challenges on this trail, but it does cross private property, and careful attention must be

TELLURIDE TO SOCIETY TURN

VIA THE RIVER TRAIL
DISTANCE: 3 miles one-way
ELEVATION GAIN: Less than 100 feet (150 feet on return)
TRAIL CONDITIONS: Single-track; muddy at times
VIA THE TOWN TRAIL
DISTANCE: 2.8 miles one-way
ELEVATION GAIN: 100 feet (on return)
TRAIL CONDITIONS: Paved bike path

TRAILHEAD: There is a large parking area on Mahoney Street, about 0.2 mile south of CO 145 Spur on the west edge of Telluride. The River Trail intersects Mahoney Street on the opposite side of the river from the parking area, while the Town Trail intersects Mahoney Street adjacent to CO 145 Spur.

paid in order to stay on the correct path. The alternate is the Town Trail, a recently constructed, paved bike path that parallels the highway into Telluride (CO 145 Spur). This trail is nearly flat and is very popular with bikers, walkers, and in-line skaters. Its route is straightforward.

The River Trail starts as a continuation of the path that follows the San Miguel River through Telluride. Continue westward on the crushed-gravel path as it leaves town and becomes a regular dirt trail. The grade is easy, though the occasional rock and root demand concentration. After about a mile, the trail forks, and the appropriate route bears left and climbs slightly. This junction is on private property and may be marked with a small sign. Just after this junction, the trail crosses a somewhat tricky side-hill—novices may wish to walk this short stretch. The trail now remains slightly above the valley floor and passes through a nice forest of aspen and spruce. After about 2.5 miles, the path crosses tiny Prospect Creek, which marks a split in the route. The main path continues directly ahead on the grassy valley floor and soon arrives at a step gate at CO 145 at the end of the Town Trail, which is directly across from Society Drive. The other option is more obscure, but it's especially pretty: Ride a few yards to the left, parallel to the creek and a small ditch, until you intersect a path that climbs somewhat steeply up a hill. This climb, which lasts only a few minutes, brings the trail onto a narrow bench. The remaining distance to Society Turn traverses this bench, which is beneath a beautiful aspen grove, before it ends at a step gate over a fence adjacent to CO 145. To continue on the Galloping Goose, ride 100 yards north on the shoulder of the highway until you arrive at Society Drive and the end of the Town Trail.

SOCIETY TURN TO ILIUM

Because the RGS mainline was routed up the valley of the San Miguel's south fork en route to Lizard Head Pass, a spur had to be built in order to provide rail service to Telluride. This section of the Galloping Goose traces this spur as it descends out of Telluride's hanging valley and winds to the floor of the south fork, 500 feet below. The steady, 4 percent grade promises an exhilarating downhill coast, or an honest—but not grueling—climb. Watch for rocks and other obstacles along the route, and be cautious as you turn into small ravines near the top of the grade, as washouts have made the trail rough in places. As you gather speed on this descent, think of the day back in 1907 when Engine 19 flew out of control while descending this grade, eventually reaching nearly 60 mph before flying off the tracks. Fortunately, the engineer and fireman were able to jump from the speeding locomotive before it crashed. The mangled tender remained at the wreck site for decades afterward. A post opposite the entrance to the

SOCIETY TURN TO ILIUM

DISTANCE: 3.25 miles one-way

ELEVATION GAIN: 500 feet (on return)

TRAIL CONDITIONS: Single-track; several small washouts and rock obstacles; gravel road

TRAILHEAD: From the junction of CO 145 and CO 145 Spur west of Telluride, drive south on CO 145 toward Lizard Head Pass. After only 0.25 mile or so, turn right onto the road adjacent to the Conoco gas station. Follow this road past the gas station and pass the small signpost that signifies the start of the Galloping Goose Trail. There is parking just beyond the gas station, at a large gravel pullout.

aforementioned Conoco (a short distance west of CO 145) marks the upper end of the trail. The lower end of the trail intersects South Fork Road; turn right at this point and ride down this lightly traveled road for 0.5 mile to reach the old community of Ilium, a present-day church camp.

ILIUM TO OPHIR

Though the initial third of this section follows a gravel road, this is arguably the most interesting portion of the Galloping Goose, both in terms of history and scenery. Leaving the floor of the South Fork Valley, this section of the Rio Grande Southern Railroad (RGS) grade climbs steadily up the west wall of this glacially carved valley, passes through beautiful stands of aspen, traverses beneath impressive cliffs, and allows wonderful vistas of the surrounding peaks. Many traces of the RGS remain, including the remnants of two spectacular trestles and stretches where the railroad ties are still in place. As a ride, this section is particularly enjoyable since the grade is easy and the trail surface is generally smooth. In the short distances where the trail must bypass the remains of the collapsed trestles, the tread can become tricky— and quite narrow. The last 0.5 mile of trail in this section has begun to be rerouted in order to avoid the access and engineering obstacles between Old Ophir and the Matterhorn Campground. However, a 1.1-mile gap has yet to be completed, thus forcing riders to use the shoulder of the highway.

ILIUM TO OPHIR

DISTANCE: 7 miles one-way

ELEVATION GAIN: 1,150 feet

TRAIL CONDITIONS: Gravel road and single-track; occasional rocks and other obstacles; generally gentle grades; two washouts bypassed by short sections of steeper grades and narrow tread; steeper single-track in the last 0.5 mile

ILIUM ACCESS: From the CO 145 and CO 145 Spur junction west of Telluride, drive west on CO 145 toward Placerville. After 2.6 miles, turn left onto South Fork Road (FR 623), which is signed Ilium. Drive 2.1 miles and park at the intersection of Sunshine Mesa Road, which is right at the community of Ilium.

OPHIR ACCESS: From the CO 145 and CO 145 Spur junction, drive south on CO 145 toward Cortez. After 7.4 miles, pass the junction of South Fork Road (signed Ames) at Old Ophir. Drive 0.6 mile farther and park at a large pullout on the north side of the highway. The presently unmarked terminus of the constructed trail is on the other side of the highway.

❀❀❀

Starting from Ilium, the road makes a short, moderately steep climb before it turns south and gains the route of the RGS mainline. From here, the smooth, lightly traveled road climbs at an unwavering 3 percent grade, slowly gaining elevation above the valley floor. The aspen stands that cloak this valley wall are among the most dense in the San Juans, and when autumn turns their leaves to gold and orange, this ride becomes especially magical. After 2.2 miles, the road makes a sharp switchback to the right, while the Galloping Goose continues directly ahead, passing a vehicle barrier to remain on the unaltered alignment of the railroad.

About 0.5 mile from the vehicle barrier, the trail crosses the Ames Slide, an area of frequent mudslides and avalanches that caused problems for the RGS for many years; a snowslide actually struck a train here in February 1925—fortunately, damage was minimal. The mudslide problem was greatly reduced in 1929, when the Forest Service removed beaver dams from atop the mesa, thus keeping the earth at the head of the gully from being constantly saturated. An old water tank stood just to the south of the slide—look for its concrete foundation on the west side of the trail. A half mile farther is the site of the now-collapsed Ames Gulch Trestle. This gorgeous, 254-foot-long, 80-foot-high wooden structure remained standing until 1979, when a vicious windstorm blew it to pieces. Use caution on the narrow section of trail that winds through the gully to rejoin the railroad grade on the far side.

The following 2 miles cross beneath the sheer face of the Ames Wall, a high cliff that has become popular with rock climbers. This portion of the RGS was particularly susceptible to snowslides, and the track was often blocked for weeks at a time. On two separate occasions—1908 and 1925—freight trains were hit by avalanches here, and cars were swept to the bottom of the slope, more than 300 feet below. This section of the trail retains many railroad ties—please do your part to preserve them by staying on the dirt track and not riding on them. Keep an eye out for rocks, which occasionally fall onto the trail from the cliffs above. After rounding the curve at Windy Point, the trail bends into a ravine and comes to the collapsed Butterfly Trestle, which spanned the rushing waters of the San Miguel's Lake Fork. This structure was one of the largest on the RGS, with a total length of 338 feet and a height of about 60 feet. It was also one of the most troublesome places on the line, since floods damaged the trestle on numerous

 136

occasions. The entire structure had to be rebuilt after a disastrous 1909 flood caused by the failure of the Trout Lake Dam. Within a year of its reconstruction, a locomotive derailed and crashed off the trestle, causing extensive damage to both the structure and the engine. The Forest Service hopes to build a small bridge here at some point in the future, but for now, backtrack from the edge of the trestle abutment until you find a track that drops down to the stream, which is crossed on a narrow plank. Follow the Galloping Goose posts back up to the grade on the other side and continue toward Ophir.

A mile above the old Butterfly Trestle is the site of the RGS's most impressive piece of engineering: the Ophir Loop. Because the upper Lake Fork valley hangs steeply above the floor of the Howards Fork (where these two forks meet, the South Fork is born), the railroad was forced to extend some distance up the Howards Fork canyon before curving back at a higher contour to gain the lip of the upper valley. The only way to accomplish this feat was to build a great trestle across the Howards Fork, construct as tight a 180 degree turn as possible, rebridge the Howards Fork, and continue up the mountainside above—in the opposite direction as the track directly below. Once completed, this portion of the line had hundreds of feet of wooden trestle, and elsewhere the track bed was carved directly from the steep bedrock of the canyon wall. Sadly, the great trestles of the loop are long gone, and because of the landscape's alteration by CO 145, second-growth forest, and the pile of tailing from Silver Bell Mine, you'll have a difficult time picturing the track's layout as you pedal up the grade. Because the trestles are gone, you'll need to bear right onto a road that climbs somewhat steeply off of the railroad grade, then almost immediately swing to the right at a four-way intersection. At this point, you'll return to the old track alignment above the upper abutment of the Ophir Loop. Watch carefully for Galloping Goose signs, as crisscrossing roads can make this a confusing area to navigate. The Galloping Goose Trail follows the old railroad grade for only another 100 yards or so above this intersection before it bears off to the left on a steeply switchbacking section of single-track. After passing a large water tank, the trail follows an underpass to the other side of the highway. The trail winds a short distance farther, skirts an old flume, then ends on the shoulder of the highway, opposite from the pullout where you parked.

OPHIR TO LIZARD HEAD PASS

DISTANCE: 7 miles one-way (5.9 miles one-way if the CO 145 section is eliminated)

ELEVATION GAIN: 1,000 feet (or 700 feet)

TRAIL CONDITIONS: Moderately busy paved highway (which can be eliminated); gently climbing dirt roads

MATTERHORN CAMPGROUND ACCESS (ELIMINATING CO 145 SECTION): Drive south on CO 145 for 1.7 miles past the Ophir Pass turnoff and park in a gravel pullout on the right, opposite a minor dirt road that branches to the left. If you reach the Matterhorn Campground, you've gone 0.1 mile too far.

LIZARD HEAD PASS TRAILHEAD: Located atop the pass, about 12 miles south of Telluride via CO 145.

OPHIR TO LIZARD HEAD PASS

Bikers who attempt to complete the entire course of the Galloping Goose Trail will need to ride a 1.1-mile section of CO 145 from the site of the Ophir Loop to the point where the RGS grade is reintersected near Matterhorn Campground. Because the highway has moderate traffic, and because there is little in the way of a shoulder on which to ride, caution should be exercised. Families may wish to skip this portion of the ride, instead beginning at the Matterhorn Campground access, where the remaining 5.9 miles to the pass are well suited to riders of even modest abilities.

Pedal away from CO 145 on the quiet dirt road, taking care to avoid a private driveway as you start. The road, though rocky at times, climbs easily along the east side of the valley, skirts the edge of Matterhorn Campground, and stays within the cool shade of a pleasant aspen grove. After passing Priest Lake about 1.2 miles above CO 145, the road continues through a small gully and arrives at Trout Lake 0.5 mile farther. At this point, turn left at a T intersection and ride along the north shore of this large and lovely lake. Trout Lake was enlarged by a dam so that water could be piped to the community of Ames, which rests on the floor of Howards Fork Canyon, just below the Butterfly Trestle. Here, the water was funneled into a power plant where the world's first supply of commercial AC electricity was produced. Trout Lake Dam failed catastrophically in 1909, but today the lake is placid once again, providing water for the still-operating power plant and mirroring the spectacular peaks visible in all directions.

Though a number of vacation homes now surround it, an old water tower remains standing near the lakeshore, thanks to a restoration project initiated by concerned citizens. After admiring this structure, continue around the upper end of the lake, where the road continues its gentle ascent. A final treasure comes 3.5 miles above CO 145, where the grade crosses the Lake Fork. Here, in defiance of a century's worth of snow, stands the last intact RGS trestle. The road now circles behind it, and traffic of any kind is prohibited on the teetering structure. Above the trestle, subalpine forest lines the grade for 1.5 miles, and then the final mile of the Galloping Goose traverses the open meadows atop Lizard Head Pass. Before completing your ride, stop and wander the grassy fields, admire the surrounding mountains, and wonder what it must have been like to arrive here by train, so many years ago.

Wilson Mesa

Traversing the northern flank of the San Miguel Range, the Wilson Mesa Trail has become a favorite with the local mountain-biking community, which is drawn to its outstanding scenery and twisty roller-coaster course through aspen-covered hillsides, steep gullies, and open meadows. This is a challenging ride, including numerous rocks, roots, logs, mud holes, and streams obstructing the trail as well as hair-raising descents and heart-pounding climbs. However, amid the adrenaline-inducing obstacles, there are long stretches of smooth, easy single-track—the type of biking that is the essence of the sport.

While the word *mesa* would seem to indicate that the ride is fairly level, it is not. Smack dab in the middle of the ride is Bilk Creek, and it is the rough descent into—and grueling ascent out of—this valley that makes this ride the exclusive realm of skilled bikers. Because roads intersect the trail at either end, it is possible to arrange a car shuttle and eliminate the need to face the Bilk Creek drainage twice. Route-finding on this ride is not difficult—simply stay on the best trail at

> **WILSON MESA**
>
> **DISTANCE:** Approximately 6.5 miles one-way
>
> **ELEVATION RANGE:** 9,200 to 10,000 feet Total Elevation Gain: 1,300 feet (2,400 feet round-trip)
>
> **TRAIL CONDITIONS:** Single-track; steep in places; numerous obstacles, including roots, rocks, and logs
>
> **SKILL LEVEL:** Advanced
>
> **SEASON:** Mid-June through mid-October
>
> **USGS MAPS:** Gray Head (1953); Little Cone (1953)
>
> **ADMINISTRATION:** Uncompahgre NF; Norwood RD

SUNSHINE MESA TRAILHEAD: From the intersection of CO 145 and CO 145 Spur near Telluride, drive west on CO 145 toward Placerville. After 2.6 miles, turn left onto the mostly gravel South Fork Road (FR 623) and drive 2.1 miles. Turn right onto the dirt Sunshine Mesa Road (still FR 623), then drive 3.7 miles, bear left, continue another 1.8 miles, and park at the signed trailhead. The last 1.8 miles can be rough, but the road is passable by all vehicles.

WEST WILSON MESA TRAILHEAD: From the CO 145/CO 145 Spur intersection, drive west on CO 145 toward Placerville. Turn left on Silver Pick Road after 5.9 miles, drive 3.2 miles, bear left, and continue another 0.7 mile to reach a somewhat tricky four-way intersection. Make a soft right, avoiding the left-bearing main road and a hard right–bearing private road, to continue toward Silver Pick Basin. The West Wilson Mesa Trailhead is 2.2 miles farther.

any junction—but the nearly fifty-year-old Gray Head map does not completely depict the present trail alignment. It is important to remain on the correct track during this ride, because several divergent trails head into the Lizard Head Wilderness, where bicycles are prohibited.

From the Sunshine Mesa Trailhead, the ride starts up a gated road that climbs easily across a heavily wooded slope. In less than a mile, a small sign identifies the start of the true Wilson Mesa Trail and the beginning of single-track riding. Drop onto the right-bearing trail and begin a protracted descent to the floor of the Bilk Creek drainage. The trail descends quickly and winds around sharp corners and various wipeout-inducing obstacles. If you manage to stay upright, you'll find yourself at a creek about 2 miles from the trailhead. Cross a sturdy bridge, then bear right at a trail junction. A sign here indicates mileage for the Wilson Mesa Trail, but its totals are not accurate.

The trail then parallels Bilk Creek downstream for 0.5 mile before it intersects a track that is marked as Wilson Mesa Trail on the Gray Head map. Long unused, the other trails have faded enough so that our "left turn" appears as a seamless continuation of a single trail. The floor of this little valley is open and grassy and provides an excellent opportunity to peer up toward Bilk Basin and the rough peaks that encircle it, including the distinctive spire of Lizard Head. The steep climb out of the Bilk Creek drainage is the most tiresome part of the ride, which gains about 800 feet in 1 mile. Only the most physically fit do not have to dismount and walk at least some portion of the climb. Fortunately, the ascent is made through a mature stand of aspen, whose shade-producing canopy provides some respite from the baking sun. If you plan to ride back to the Sunshine Mesa Trailhead, you'll find this section of trail to be fairly obstacle-free, and any obstructions that do appear (particularly downed aspen boles) can be cleared as you climb upward. A small pond about halfway up the grade is a good place to rest. Its calm waters perfectly mirror the summit of Wilson Peak, one of the San Juans' most attractive mountains.

The apex of the ascent comes at a pretty meadow some 3.5 miles from the Sunshine Mesa Trailhead. From this point, the trail maintains roughly the same contour for the remaining 3 miles of the ride, with the only hills being short dips and rolls through minor drainages. This last portion of the ride is some of the best mountain biking in the San Juans. The trail twists and turns through a mixed aspen-conifer forest, splashes through a few creeks, and has just enough technical challenge to maintain the interest of experienced bikers. Herds of deer and elk can sometimes be spotted in the area, as well.

At mile 5.5, bear left to avoid an abandoned trail, then quickly bear right to avoid an unmaintained track that leads into the wilderness. Silver Pick Road and the West Wilson Trailhead are less than a mile farther. Unless you have a vehicle waiting, return via the same route once you reach the road. If you wish to extend the ride, the Wilson Mesa Trail continues west for another 7 miles to Fall Creek Road, and it has much the same scenery and challenge as the section you just completed.

Last Dollar

Bikers who seek a more peaceful alternative to serpentine single-tracks and bone-jarring, cliff-hanging mining routes will find Last Dollar Road to be ideal. Skirting the western flank of the Sneffels Range, this picture-perfect back road winds through bucolic ranch country and pretty aspen groves, with unhindered mountain vistas at every turn. Though easy in terms of technical challenge, its sustained ascent can tax bikers of average fitness. If a round-trip ride from one end of Last Dollar Road to the other seems overly ambitious, either arrange a car shuttle or simply turn around at the ride's ridge-top apex. To avoid traffic, plan an early-morning or weekday ride.

LAST DOLLAR

DISTANCE: 16.3 miles one-way

ELEVATION RANGE: 8,800 to 10,650 feet

TOTAL ELEVATION GAIN: 1,850 feet

TRAIL CONDITIONS: Dirt roads; rocky for a few short stretches; sustained, moderate grades

SKILL LEVEL: Novice

SEASON: June through October

USGS MAPS: Sams (1967); Gray Head (1953)

ADMINISTRATION: Uncompahgre NF; Norwood RD

DALLAS DIVIDE ACCESS: From Placerville, drive for 12 miles on CO 62 (or 11 miles coming west from Ridgway) to Last Dollar Road. Park on the shoulder of this road just after making the turn.

SHEEP CREEK TRAILHEAD: From CO 145, drive CO 145 Spur east toward Telluride. In less than 0.25 mile, turn left onto Last Dollar Road. Drive about 2 miles and veer right onto the gravel road just outside the airport entrance. Continue another 1.75 miles until you reach the signed trailhead.

While this is an enjoyable ride from either end of Last Dollar Road, this route begins at Dallas Divide. Pedaling up the smooth gravel road away from CO 62, you'll ascend gently through an aspen-lined ravine and pass several private homes before you break onto the open ranch land atop Hastings Mesa. These pastures, which begin about 1.3 miles into the ride, are dotted with livestock, and during early summer, a bright display of wildflowers. A seasonal explosion of arrowleaf balsamroot makes late June an especially beautiful time to ride here. Rolling hills forested by dense stands of aspen rise above these meadows, and the spectacularly rugged heights of the Sneffels Range tower in the distance. A mile of level pedaling atop this portion of the "mesa" allows you to fully appreciate this postcard scene.

Bear right to avoid a private driveway at mile 2.5 and pass the long-abandoned remains of a picturesque barn and homestead. After crossing Willow Creek, continue to ride across another 2.5 miles of gently rolling terrain, which feature scattered stands of aspen and flower-filled pastureland. The steep western face of the Sneffels Range looms just to the east, and as you ascend beyond the Hay Creek drainage, aptly named Lone Cone comes into view. Five miles into the ride, turn left at an intersection and continue along Last Dollar Road as it first descends into a shallow draw and then climbs moderately past lovely aspen groves and peaceful grasslands. The road now becomes rougher, and after splashing across Alder Creek at mile 6.3, the climb becomes more difficult. This prolonged ascent takes the road from pasture to aspen forest, and finally into stands of conif-

A Fourth of July electrical storm clears from Hastings Mesa and the Sneffels Range.

erous forest. Though the grade is tiring, the ever-increasing elevation provides expansive vistas to the west, which on clear days stretch as far as
Utah's La Sal Mountains and the eastern edge of the Colorado Plateau. A
nice place to rest and admire the panorama is at mile 9.0, where the view
from a small meadow includes the San Miguel River canyon and the western horizon. This is a logical turnaround for bikers who are unable to
arrange a shuttle or are unwilling to tackle the return ascent out of the San
Miguel drainage.

The unrelenting climb continues another mile until the road reaches
its apex atop a ridge on the east side of Last Dollar Mountain. The view
southward from here stretches across the entire length of the magnificent
San Miguel Range, including Wilson Peak and Lizard Head. As you begin
to descend at a fairly rapid rate across the meadowy slopes of a steep ravine,
be sure to take your eyes off the horizon long enough to spot the occasional
rocks and ruts that lie ready to invert your bike—and your view. After crossing tiny Summit Creek and passing a pair of old log cabins at mile 11.7, the
road begins a 0.5-mile traverse across the lower margins of a broad talus

slope. This is the most technical part of the ride; slow down so that these sharp rocks don't puncture a tire.

The 2 miles below the talus are among the most pleasant of the ride, as the road winds through lush aspen groves and small meadows beneath Whipple Mountain (which draw autumn leaf-peekers from around the region). Gaining steam once again, the road drops into the Gambel oak ecosystem at mile 14.0, and after it passes (another) Willow Creek, it begins to contour across grassy slopes en route to the floor of the Deep Creek drainage, 16 miles from Dallas Divide. Pastoral meadows front the imposing peaks that ring the horizon. Continue directly ahead at a road intersection adjacent to the creek and pedal a final 0.3 mile up a moderate grade to arrive at the large Sheep Creek Trailhead. This is the recommended southern terminus of the ride, but Last Dollar Road does continue another 3.7 miles past numerous houses and the Telluride Airport before it intersects CO 145 Spur.

Red Mountain District

Five weeks ago the site where Red Mt. now stands was woodland mesa, covered with heavy spruce timber. Today hotels, printing offices, groceries, meat markets, a telephone office, saloons, dance houses are up and booming; the blast is heard on every side and prospectors can be seen snowshoeing in every direction.

—The Ouray *Solid Muldoon*, 1883
As quoted in *Mountain Mysteries, the Ouray Odyssey*
by Marvin Gregory and P. David Smith

Romantic images of the Wild West come to life as you pedal through the boomtowns gone bust in the Red Mountain District, one of the San Juans' richest silver-mining centers of the nineteenth century. Ghost towns, forgotten railroads, and dozens of abandoned mines are scattered about the pretty valley, which lies beneath the colorful summits of the Red Mountains. If your mountain-biking interest leans more toward admiring the interesting and the beautiful and less the seeking of hair-raising thrills, then this easy ride will likely become an oft-remembered favorite.

A few words of warning are appropriate for this ride: First, resist the urge to explore off the beaten path, as many of the old mining claims in the area remain private property. Entering any of the mines and buildings along this route could not only constitute trespassing, it would also risk damage to the rickety structures and injury to yourself. Be sure to carefully adhere to the following route, as it is easy to become sidetracked by the web of mining roads that lace the area. Second, be on the lookout for old nails, pieces of wire, and other scraps of metal along the road that could potentially flatten your tires or cause injury.

Ride up the minor dirt road that vectors away from US 550 at the aforementioned switchback and passes underneath a power line. Very soon, you'll cross Red Mountain Creek on an old bridge; pause here and study the orange water that flows down this highly mineralized watercourse. Red Mountain Creek is naturally tainted by the iron oxides found on the slopes of the Red Mountains; however, effluent from the tailing piles of the Idarado Mine—which loom just upstream—contributes significant mineral concentrations. Such water-quality issues are among the lasting legacies of the mining boom, and even today a concerted effort is being undertaken by mining companies and public agencies to mitigate environmental damage. Pay attention throughout the ride, and you'll identify several examples of their efforts.

After winding around a small, forested knob, bear left where the road forks, 0.8 mile from US 550. Pedal uphill another 0.1 mile to arrive at Guston, the site of a small community that is centered around a wealthy mine of the same name. Guston is marked by several well-preserved structures, including a sturdy ore-loading bin. The Guston claim operated from 1882 until 1897, and at the peak of production in 1890, the community's population was three hundred.

RED MOUNTAIN DISTRICT

DISTANCE: 5.8 miles round-trip

ELEVATION RANGE: 10,275 to 11,000 feet

TOTAL ELEVATION GAIN: 725 feet

TRAIL CONDITIONS: Dirt roads; moderate grades in places; sharp objects and other hazards near the mines

SKILL LEVEL: Novice

SEASON: June through mid-October

USGS MAP: Ironton (1955)

ADMINISTRATION: Uncompahgre NF; Ouray RD

TRAILHEAD: From Ouray, drive south on US 550 for 10.2 miles and park where a small dirt road diverges from the highway at the second set of switchbacks above the flat expanse of Ironton Park.

Leaving Guston, take a right fork and climb easily for another 0.25 mile to arrive at the Yankee Girl head frame. This highly scenic structure—the most prominent in the district—is all that remains of a much larger complex that included a power plant with twin smokestacks. The most productive claim in the vicinity of Red Mountain Pass, the Yankee Girl Mine is said to have produced anywhere from $3 million to $12 million in silver, gold, lead, and copper over the course of its existence. The head frame housed the pulley and power plant for the "skip" (or hoist), which was lifted up and down a shaft that serviced workings located more than 1,000 feet beneath the earth's surface.

Continuing beyond the Yankee Girl, the road roughly traces the grade of the Silverton Railroad. Not to be confused with the present-day Durango & Silverton Railroad (which actually uses the tracks of the old Denver & Rio Grande Western line), the Silverton was one of the three "pocket lines" built by Otto Mears to serve mines in the Red Mountain District, Animas Forks area, and along Cement Creek. The engineering skill required to create a feasible railroad among these tremendous mountains was considerable. The line, which became operational in 1888, included a pair of switchbacks and a mountainside turntable, and it was even to be extended to Ouray until it became evident that the extreme topography and ravaging snowslides of the Uncompahgre Gorge were unconquerable.

A quarter mile beyond the Yankee Girl, our ride forks left, briefly leaves the old railroad grade, and switchbacks up to the site of the Genessee-Vanderbilt Mine. Despite having ore that wasn't as rich as surrounding claims, the mine still managed to produce about $1 million. This mine was operational as late as the 1940s, and much of the remaining equipment dates from this era.

Drop off the tailings mound of the Genessee-Vanderbilt and bear left to return to the gentle railroad grade 1.7 miles above US 550. Though rocky here and there, the road ahead climbs easily toward the site of Red Mountain and the National Belle Mine, both 2.4 miles from the trailhead. This stretch of the ride offers the best overview of the surrounding valley as well as a great look at the three Red Mountains. These bulky peaks are gigantic piles of volcanic rubble that, due to subsequent hydrothermal activity, are composed of iron oxides that "paint" the mountains in varying shades of ochre. Right after a rain shower, especially in late afternoon, the Red

Mountains almost glow, and they are particularly photogenic when the valley's aspen turn autumn gold.

When you reach the town of Red Mountain, veer left and climb past a squat wooden structure, which was the old town jail. The road traverses the heart of town, though very few buildings remain visible. As the *Solid Muldoon* dutifully reported in 1883, Red Mountain was a classic Rocky Mountain boomtown that sprang up overnight and quickly became one of the region's most important communities. More than six hundred people resided there in 1890, but economic troubles and fires in 1892 and 1895 whittled down the town's population so much that by 1900, only thirty souls remained. Much of what remained burned in 1937, and the once-peaceful meadow became silent once more.

The large mine that rises above the town site was the National Belle Mine. Marked by a striking head frame of its own, the National Belle has a special place in Colorado's mining lore. Ernest Ingersoll, a writer for *Harper's Weekly,* reported the events at the mine in July 1883:

> . . . *a workman broke through the walls [of the mine] into a cavity. Hollow echoes came back with the blows of his pick, and stones thrown were heard to roll a long distance. Taking a candle, one of the men descended and found himself in an immense natural chamber, the flickering rays of the light showing him the vaulted roof far above, seamed with bright streaks of galena and interspersed with masses of soft carbonates, chlorides and pure white talc . . . They crept through [an] opening into an immense natural tunnel . . . in which they clambered over great bowlders [sic] of pure galena, and mounds of soft gray carbonates, while the walls and roof showed themselves a solid mass of chloride carbonate ores of silver . . . It would seem as though Nature had gathered her choice treasures from her inexhaustible storehouse, and wrought these tunnels, natural stopping places and chambers, studded with glittering crystals and bright minerals to dazzle the eyes of man in after ages, and lure him on to other treasures hidden deeper in the bowels of the earth.*

In all, the National Belle produced more than $9 million and was for a time one of the most famous mines in the country.

The ride's last 0.5 mile climbs steadily past the National Belle and a smaller claim called the Hero. Cresting at exactly 11,000 feet, the road then drops slightly and arrives at US 550 0.25 mile north of Red Mountain Pass. While you can complete a loop by riding US 550 back to the trailhead (2.6 miles away), heavy traffic, an extremely sinuous highway alignment, narrow (or nonexistent) shoulders, and a dearth of guardrails combine to make this a potentially troublesome idea. It's much better to retrace the dirt-road route to your vehicle.

Cimarron Valley

Much like the Last Dollar country, the Cimarron Valley is classic "West," a paragon of the regional image so often represented in books, magazines, and pickup-truck commercials. Idyllic pastures unfold across the valley's lowest reaches, while its walls and higher slopes are densely forested and shadowed by impressive ridges and craggy peaks. The long country road that climbs through the valley (and eventually crosses Owl Creek Pass and descends into the Uncompahgre River drainage) is in general a wonderful place to pedal away a day. But it is the incredible stands of aspen that make this road—and the ride—so special. Touring an area that is highly regarded by fall-foliage aficionados from around the state, this San Juan bike ride is at its prettiest during the latter half of September and the first week of October.

CIMARRON VALLEY

SILVER JACK
DISTANCE: 38.6 miles round-trip
ELEVATION RANGE: 7,050 to 9,000 feet
TOTAL ELEVATION GAIN: 2,000 feet
TRAIL CONDITIONS: Dirt roads; moderate grades; moderate traffic
SKILL LEVEL: Novice
SEASON: June through October
USGS MAPS: Gunnison County, Sheet 6 (1975); Montrose County, Sheet 2 (1979)
ADMINISTRATION: BLM; Gunnison RA; Uncompahgre NF; Ouray RD

OWL CREEK PASS
DISTANCE: 41.2 miles one-way
ELEVATION RANGE: 7,000 to 10,100 feet
TOTAL ELEVATION GAIN: 3,200 feet
TRAIL CONDITIONS: Dirt roads; moderate grades; moderate traffic
SKILL LEVEL: Novice
SEASON: Mid-June through mid-October

Though lengthy, the ride follows a regularly maintained dirt road that is suitable for novice bikers. The overall elevation gain is considerable, but the rate of ascent is rarely steep and is often broken by stretches of level riding.

Potential problems are limited to washboards, dust, and traffic. Because this scenic valley has several campgrounds and is home to Silver Jack Reservoir—a well-known fishery—the road is occasionally busy. Most people limit their visits to weekends and holidays, so plan your ride for the quieter days of midweek. Two options for biking the Cimarron are presented here: A round-trip ride up the Cimarron Valley as far as the east fork bridge lets you take in some of the prettiest scenery without the need to organize a lengthy car shuttle. If a car shuttle can be arranged, the second option is to continue over Owl Creek Pass and drop into the Uncompahgre Valley. This route offers even more variety as well as some spectacular Sneffels Range vistas. That you can readily tailor this ride to fit your available time and energy is one of its nicest features: You can create shorter rides by driving farther up valley before beginning to pedal.

USGS MAPS: Gunnison County, Sheet 6 (1975); Montrose County, Sheet 2 (1979); Ouray County, Sheet 2 (1975)

ADMINISTRATION: BLM; Gunnison RA; Uncompahgre NF; Ouray RD

CIMARRON RIVER ACCESS: From Montrose, drive east on US 50 for approximately 20 miles and turn right (south) onto Cimarron River Road (FR 858), which is signed SILVER JACK RESERVOIR AND OWL CREEK PASS. Park where convenient near this intersection. Be sure to turn on Cimarron River Road, not Little Cimarron River Road, which intersects US 50 about 0.25 mile farther east.

UNCOMPAHGRE RIVER ACCESS: From Ridgway, drive north on US 550 for 1.8 miles and turn right (east) onto CR 10, which is also signed SILVER JACK RESERVOIR AND OWL CREEK PASS. Park where convenient near this intersection.

Beginning from US 50, Cimarron River Road ascends gently along the cottonwood-lined river and passes hay fields and contented livestock. After 2 miles, the road swings across the river and begins climbing more steadily away from the river and up the valley's western slopes. The grade eases somewhat during mile 5.0, and soon the rugged pinnacles at the Cimarron headwaters come into view. After bearing left at mile 5.8, you'll ride through a short piece of rough road where recent slumping has caused significant damage. Beyond this minor obstacle, the road continues through scenic ranch landscapes, dips through shallow draws, and rises over gentle hills for the next 7 miles.

You'll enjoy some nice views of the rugged cliffs that line the valley's rims as the road contours back toward the river. At mile 14.5, the road recrosses the Cimarron and enters the national forest. A steadier climb commences once more, and the pastures of the lower valley are replaced by thick forests of aspen, fir, and spruce. After skirting tiny Beaver Lake at mile 15.1, the road enters a magical stretch of almost 4 miles, where unbroken groves of towering aspen rise above damp wildflower gardens and small brooks. Though autumn is the most spectacular time to visit an aspen grove, there is much beauty to be found here throughout the summer: Shafts of light fall through the thick, green foliage and illuminate clumps of columbine and thickets of bluebell. This is just one of many inspiring scenes possible here.

After you pass the various roads that lead to Silver Jack Reservoir and its associated campgrounds, you'll cross a cattle guard and emerge from the forest into a grassy meadow. A half mile of level pedaling brings you to the junction of East Fork Road, and after you bear right and ride 0.1 mile farther, you'll come to the east fork bridge, 19.3 miles above US 50. Whether this is your destination or not, you'll want to pause here and gaze over the forested slopes and the intricately carved pinnacles and cliffs that line the surrounding valleys. A respite along the bank of the river is a relaxing way to prepare for your return or continuing journey.

Less than 0.25 mile above the east fork, you'll pass Middle Fork Road and cross the middle fork of the Cimarron River. From this point onward, the ascent will proceed more steadily, and the road will become rougher due to washboards, potholes, and the like. Notice that as you gain elevation spruce and fir become more prominent, as deep winter snows and cooler temperatures mark this area as the upper limit of the aspen forest ecosystem. After turning into the west fork drainage, the road crosses the stream (mile 23.0) and climbs through somber pine forests beneath the hulking spire of Chimney Rock. Bear right to avoid West Fork Road at mile 25.6, and ride 0.25 mile farther to arrive at the top of 10,114-foot Owl Creek Pass. Dense forest prevents any far-reaching vistas at this point.

It's almost all downhill from here as the road winds down into the Owl Creek drainage. There is an impressive view of Chimney Rock and Courthouse Mountain at mile 26.5, and shortly thereafter, you'll find yourself immersed in an aspen forest once more. After passing a left-branching road at mile 28.4, you'll have to endure a moderate 0.5-mile ascent before descending at a rapid pace again. Avoid another divergent road, then abruptly exit the aspen forest, make a sweeping left bend, and turn into a small overlook just off the road. Spread before you is rolling pastureland, hillsides of Gambel oak (which turn a remarkable crimson in early October), and the distant crest of the Sneffels Range.

After soaking up the view, turn back onto the main road and proceed through the home stretch. After leaving the national forest at mile 33.5, the road crosses Nate Creek and descends through its shallow gully before it drops into the Cow Creek Valley, where there is a fine view of the high peaks of the Uncompahgre Wilderness. Bear right at mile 35.8, continue downhill, cross Cow Creek, and arrive at another junction at mile 37.3. Bear to the left and ride directly toward the Sneffels massif, then climb gently for a few moments and pass yet another left-branching road. At mile 40.3, bear right one last time and enjoy a final mile of easy riding through open pastures to arrive at US 550.

Alpine Loop Backcountry Byway

Bring your thesaurus, because you'll not get halfway around the Alpine Loop Backcountry Byway before exhausting your bag of superlatives. Recently named one of the top ten mountain-bike rides in the country by a well-known travel magazine, the Alpine Loop is everything spectacular about the San Juans wrapped up into one tidy package. Circling through the very heart of the range, the loop offers views of high peaks, acres upon acres of flower-studded tundra, scores of old mines, several ghost towns, and countless waterfalls, alpine lakes, and aspen forests. However, you'd better be acclimated to the altitude, because not only will you cross two of the state's highest passes in the course of this nearly 50-mile ride, you'll also climb as high as the Grand Canyon is deep.

The ride follows established roads for the duration, though road conditions run the gamut. You'll spend time on paved highways; smooth gravel; and rocky, muddy, four-wheel-drive tracks. You'll need only intermediate biking skills to negotiate the loop's technical obstacles, but this is not a "moderate" ride in terms of overall difficulty. Have you ever biked 50 miles through steep, rough, mountainous country? Ever considered riding up a hill more than a mile high? Unless you are quite strong, it may be better to plan this as a two-day ride, with a camp located somewhere near the ride's midpoint. If the thought of fully loaded panniers leaves a bitter taste in your mouth, you might want to arrange for someone else to drive a "support vehicle."

ALPINE LOOP BACKCOUNTRY BYWAY

DISTANCE: 48.2 miles round-trip

ELEVATION RANGE: 8,650 to 12,950 feet

TOTAL ELEVATION GAIN: 5,700 feet

TRAIL CONDITIONS: Roads of varying condition, ranging from pavement to rocky; wet four-wheel-drive tracks; immense elevation gain, with steep grades for extended distances; includes a 10-mile section above timberline with no shelter from storms; moderate traffic

SKILL LEVEL: Intermediate

SEASON: June through September (depending upon how quickly the passes are plowed)

USGS MAPS: Hinsdale County, Sheet 1 (1978); San Juan County (1975)

ADMINISTRATION: BLM-Gunnison RA; BLM-San Juan RA; Gunnison NF; Cebolla RD

TRAILHEAD: In Lake City, turn west off CO 149 onto Second Street (signs indicate the Alpine Loop), proceed 2 blocks, and turn left onto Henson Creek Road. Drive 0.7 mile and park at the Alpine Loop Byway information pullout/ATV staging area.

You'll need to be watchful of traffic, as its inclusion in the National Scenic Byway System has made the Alpine Loop a premier tour for four-wheel-drive enthusiasts. You can expect a steady stream of jeeps, sport utilities, and trucks throughout the ride. Fortunately, where the road is smooth it is also wide, so faster traffic can easily pass. The roads are most narrow where they are rough, and here, vehicles usually travel no more than 5–10 mph. However, expect to eat a little dust in the lower portions of the loop.

Though ultimately a matter of personal preference, riding the loop in a counterclockwise direction is recommended because the mountain scenery unfolds a tad more spectacularly if you head up the Lake Fork Valley. Furthermore, riding the circuit in this direction allows you to tackle the loop's roughest sections with downhill momentum rather than during an already-challenging uphill grunt. Despite this recommendation, begin your ride at the ATV staging area about a mile up Henson Creek from Lake City—yes, you'll have to immediately retrace your route back to town, but this is the most logical parking facility on the loop.

Once you have pedaled back to Lake City, turn south on CO 149 (beware of the nonexistent shoulder) and ride toward Lake San Cristobal. In 2.2 miles, turn right to remain on the Alpine Loop and continue to ride along the paved road that skirts the shore of the lake. One of the larger natural bodies of water in Colorado, Lake San Cristobal is less than a thousand years old. When a great mass of saturated earth sheared off Mesa Seco about seven hundred years ago and again about three hundred fifty years ago, the resulting debris dammed the waters of the Lake Fork River and filled the nearby valley. The yellowish earth near the lake's outlet readily identifies the face of the landslide.

After winding along the lakeshore for almost 2 miles, the road continues to climb easily up the broad Lake Fork Valley. Four miles above CO 149, the pavement ends, and the Alpine Loop forks to the right and enters a short, shallow gorge of gray volcanic rock. The gravel road ahead remains a nice riding surface, and the surrounding scenery—which features aspen groves across the entire south valley wall—becomes steadily more dramatic. After you pass Williams Creek Campground at mile 9.8 and cross the Lake Fork River 0.25 mile farther, the road reveals a particularly beautiful portion of the valley. A series of incredibly rugged peaks rise above rich pastures, and the Continental Divide traces the ridge along the Lake Fork Valley's south rim.

Two miles farther, the road recrosses the Lake Fork and quickly passes Mill Creek Campground. Another mile of easy riding takes you to an important junction not far from the site of Sherman, an old mining camp that is now being replaced by summer homes. Sherman marks the confluence of the Lake Fork, Cottonwood Creek, and Cataract Creek, three precipitous gorges that cut through extremely steep mountains. The Alpine Loop branches to the right and begins a 3-mile section known as the Shelf Road. Though it clings to the face of sheer cliffs, the tread of this part of the road is fairly smooth, and after the initial mile, not steep at all. Because vehicles can suddenly appear around the tight, blind corners of Shelf Road, you'll want to pull off the main road often. Use these opportunities to admire the awesome scenery surrounding you.

The road contours back onto the valley floor at the lower end of Burrows Park, a long, flat meadow tucked directly between the 14,000-plus-foot summits of Sunshine, Redcloud, and Handies Peaks. Trailheads for hikes to these peaks are located at mile 18.9. The road ahead maintains a steady but reasonable grade as it continues another 2.5 miles through Burrows Park. Keep an eye out for abandoned mines and numerous waterfalls on either side of the valley. As you near the upper end of the park, be sure to peek over your shoulder for a nice view of Sunshine and Redcloud.

It's rockier going as you pedal through a mile of subalpine forest above Burrows Park and arrive at the American Basin junction at mile 22.5. If you have the energy, the road into the basin (which ends about 0.75 mile above the junction) rewards you with one of the San Juans' prettiest prospects. Back on the main route (bear right at the junction), the road commences a much

It is still winter in July at the crest of Engineer Pass.

steeper ascent across a slope of colorful wildflowers. After crossing a small stream, you'll pass the remains of the Tabasco Mill and climb through four tight, steep switchbacks. Once above these turns, you'll have climbed past the final fringe of subalpine forest and into the alpine tundra ecosystem. You now begin a 10-mile segment of alpine biking, which is not only fantastically beautiful but is also quite exposed to blustery winds and stormy weather. Keep an eye out for developing thunderstorms—you wouldn't want to be sitting atop your metal-framed bike when the lightning starts dancing, would you?

You now have a mile to go until you crest the 12,620-foot summit of Cinnamon Pass, which is 26.8 miles above the trailhead. The ride regresses into a grueling, oxygen-starved climb, and while the tread isn't too rough, it is often wet with snowmelt. Indeed, the road over the pass is open before mid-July only because Hinsdale and San Juan County road crews attack it with plows as soon as the last winter snows have fallen, sometime in mid-May. Relief comes once you reach the pass, and a well-deserved break is appropriate in order to catch your breath and admire the glorious scenery. The austere summits that have loomed far overhead for most of the ride are now within arm's reach, and you feel on top of the world.

You'll quickly gain speed as you drop off the west side of the pass and into a small, tundra-carpeted basin. The road remains fairly smooth at first; however, once you exit the basin and begin to descend into the Animas River drainage, you'll have to contend with large rocks and loose talus. Take it slow through here, as punctured tires—or worse—are quite possible in this rough terrain. An important intersection comes 2.1 miles below Cinnamon Pass; bear right and begin your ascent of Engineer Pass. Unfortunately, the 1,400 feet of elevation you've just descended must now be regained en route to Engineer. As you begin the long, rocky, uphill grind, you'll at least have all the magnificent scenery you can handle. The slopes around you are the best of the Alpine Loop's wildflower gardens, there are several nearby cascades, and you'll enjoy a bird's-eye view of the Animas Forks ghost town and surrounding mine structures.

After a pair of short switchbacks, you'll pass a small, icy tarn known as Denver Lake, which is the recognized headwaters of the Animas River. Exactly 2 miles past the previous intersection, another important junction presents itself. Again, bear to the right (the left fork is also part of the Alpine Loop; it descends into the Uncompahgre Gorge and meets US 550) and begin the most challenging ascent of the ride. Climbing through a series of rocky switchbacks, you'll gain almost 800 feet in the initial mile before the grade moderates in the second mile to arrive at the scenic and altitudinal climax of the Alpine Loop, a 12,950-foot knob on the west ridge of Engineer Mountain. From this amazing vantage, you can gaze upon the vast collection of peaks that make up this corner of the San Juans, including the Sneffels Range, the Grenadier Range, and all of the beautiful, mine-studded mountains in between.

From the short spur that leads out to the knob, continue around the northwest flank of Engineer Mountain. You'll actually descend about 100 feet to arrive at Engineer Pass, which is 33.2 miles from the trailhead. Engineer is one of the highest vehicle-accessible passes in North America, and the view from here befits such a lofty perch. Though they are somewhat obscured from the knob-top vantage, the expansive tundra fields of American Flats—crowned by the great horns of the Uncompahgre and Wetterhorn Peaks—now dominate the eastward panorama.

With the ride's long ascents now behind you, point your bike down the east flank of Engineer Pass and into the Henson Creek drainage. The road takes a sinuous course through the basin at the headwaters of this creek, and the occasional snowmelt-fed mud holes can be interesting obstacles. In the 2.5 miles below the pass, you'll descend about 1,400 feet, so keep a close grip on your bike and a tight rein on the brakes. Like the country surrounding Cinnamon Pass, the mountains and tundra that encircle you in this valley are spectacular at every turn.

In the following mile, you'll pass a series of right-branching four-wheel-drive tracks, including one that leads to the site of Rose's Cabin, a historic stage stop and lodge for travelers making their way between Lake City and Ouray. Continuing down Henson Creek, the road is rather rocky, and you'll have to really slow down to maintain control. The road gradually improves as you descend steadily along the north side of the valley. The 3-mile stretch below the Rose's Cabin area is filled with plunging cascades, stands of aspen, and views of towering mountains. Be sure to stop at Whitmore Falls (7 miles below Engineer Pass) and walk a short distance to the scenic overlook of this raging plunge.

The descent mellows considerably below the falls, and you soon find yourself in an open meadow at the confluence of Henson Creek and its north fork. This small park was the site of Capitol City, which founder George T. Lee envisioned as the administrative center of the state. Lee even went as far as constructing an ornate brick mansion to be used as the governor's residence (being cast in the governor's role was part of his vision). Unfortunately, the town's 120 residents couldn't wrest the designation from Denver, and like most other San Juan silver camps, Capitol City eventually faded from existence. It's probably a good thing, too—could you imagine how far the ball would fly if the Colorado Rockies had a stadium in this 9,700-foot-high meadow?

The Capitol City site is 9.1 miles below Engineer Pass and 42.3 miles from the start of the ride. From here, it is only another 8.1 miles of gentle downhill coasting and easy pedaling to reach the trailhead. The smooth gravel road closely hugs the bank of boisterous Henson Creek for most of this distance, only climbing above the water at the site of the Ute-Ulay Mine, the Lake City area's most prominent claim. Shortly thereafter, you'll arrive at your car, tired but satisfied.

Saguache Stagecoach Road

Virtually unknown to the outside world, the ravines and ridges north of the La Garita Range are perfect for thrilling mountain-bike adventures. Laced with abandoned logging roads, ranching tracks, and, in this case, a historic stagecoach route, this remote corner will thrill bikers with exciting, roller-coaster topography; rocky creeks; mud holes; roots; and downed logs—a veritable mountain-bike obstacle course. Though not as spectacularly beautiful as other San Juan locales, the biking here is every bit as good, and solitary to boot.

Despite all of the obstructions, only intermediate technical skills are needed to enjoy this ride. Because its most difficult portions are on old four-wheel-drive roads, and because the few steep hills are short and spread apart, the obstacles can be reasonably negotiated. Simply slowing down will go a long way toward easing this ride's challenges. Though the first half of the ride follows a well-maintained forest road, traffic is very light, and once you reach the rougher half of the loop, the depreciated condition of the "roads" makes them impassable by most full-size vehicles. At most, you may come across someone riding an all-terrain vehicle (ATV) or perhaps another biker, though most likely you'll not see another soul.

Begin the ride by pedaling up FR 788, which climbs very easily through the valley of Los Pinos Creek. The surrounding country is very pretty, with grassy pastures and sagebrush flats spread across the gentle drainage floor, and a mixed montane forest of aspen, spruce, and fir growing in thick stands on the surround-

SAGUACHE STAGECOACH ROAD

DISTANCE: 18.5 miles round-trip

ELEVATION RANGE: 9,200 to 10,300 feet

TOTAL ELEVATION GAIN: 1,500 feet

TRAIL CONDITIONS: Gravel road and extremely rough double-track; short, steep grades; many obstacles, including mud holes and downed logs

SKILL LEVEL: Intermediate

SEASON: June until mid-October

USGS MAP: Saguache County, Sheet 1 (1979)

ADMINISTRATION: Gunnison NF; Cebolla RD

TRAILHEAD: From the intersection of US 50 and CO 114 (7 miles east of Gunnison), drive south on CO 114 for 19.7 miles, then turn right onto CR NN14. Drive this good gravel road for 3.4 miles, then turn right onto CR KK14. Drive this road, which eventually becomes FR 788, for 7.4 miles, and park on the shoulder of the road adjacent to a Forest Service interpretive sign for the Saguache Stagecoach Road and a divergent four-wheel-drive track.

ing ridges and hills. A surprising variety of wildflowers grow among the sage, especially after a wet spring, when large tracts of land are tinted blue by an exploding iris population. The first intersection you'll reach is at 1.4 miles; continue straight ahead and maintain an easy grade, keeping a lookout for a large waterfall that is visible across the valley at mile 1.9. Beyond this, the road maintains the same easy, smooth character for the next 6 miles. Winding past several small creeks, you'll continue across both open sagebrush country and through large aspen groves. This area is a perfect example of a rainshadow ecosystem. Though winters are bitterly cold and brutally windy, snowfall is minimal and the ground may remain bare for much of the winter, making this an important winter habitat for large mammals such as elk and deer. Conversely, summer afternoons in the sage flats can be bone dry and scorching hot, so bring extra water.

The gravel road crosses Los Pinos Creek at mile 8.2 and intersects a minor vehicle track (FR 599) 0.1 mile later. Turn right and proceed back down valley on its western edge. Climbing gently through a small gap, the road then enters an extended expanse of sagebrush known as Pinto Basin. The road is little more than a double-track, though it is generally smooth and enjoyable to ride. The real adventure begins at mile 10.6, where the road enters an aspen forest and becomes much rougher. You'll have to fight your way across many deep ruts, over large rocks, and past quite a few large roots. The once-gentle road rolls more steeply, with lengthy ascents broken by short, steep descents down rough slopes. After passing through a wire gate at mile 12.1 (as with all gates, leave this one open or closed as you found it), you'll plummet wildly toward School Section Creek. Keep your speed under control, because this ford sneaks up on you and is extremely rough, with very large rocks and very deep mud.

The road climbs away from the creek and ascends steadily through a small gully. The track is faint where it crosses a damp meadow, but it soon becomes obvious as you return to the forest. Both aspen and conifer populate this area, and many downed trees obstruct the road. The 1.5 miles it takes to get from the creek to the top of a rocky hill are perhaps the most tedious of the ride, during which you'll slowly crawl past stumps, rotting timber, and large rocks. When you finally reach the crest of the climb (the ride's high point), it's back down another steep rock garden and on to a junction. Turn to the right and begin a short climb on another rough track (FR 808). This road follows the old Saguache Stagecoach route, which traversed the isolated country between Saguache and the Lake City area. Not much is known about this particular conveyance, but it is likely that service started sometime in the 1870s and ended within a decade or so.

The short climb ends 0.1 mile beyond the junction, and the track turns down another forested ravine, where some of the ride's most daunting obstacles are located. Extensive blow-downs and some treacherous ruts must be negotiated on a fairly steep descent, and you must pass through a pair of wire gates. About 1.5 miles below the top of the last hill, you'll enter an especially pretty aspen-lined gully with a small brook. Pay attention to the road though, as this is some of the rockiest terrain yet. You'll dip down and cross Miller Creek at mile 16.7, and after enduring another short but steep ascent, continue a steady downhill spin. The Saguache County map recommended for this ride does not accurately depict the remaining 1.8 miles of road, but regular posts and an obvious right-of-way will keep you on the right track. Any diverging tracks have been officially closed to motor vehicles, and all are marked as such. The ride's difficulty eases significantly in this last section, and regular earthen "water-bars" make for very fun riding and an opportunity to "catch air." After traversing another small sage flat, you'll descend into a narrow gully, make a couple of quick turns, and arrive at your vehicle. Watch out for the ill-placed wire gate just before the road!

Jarosa Mesa

Rare is the opportunity to bike atop the Continental Divide, but that is exactly the treat in store for you as you traverse the rough road on top of Jarosa Mesa. Unlike the serrated peaks that compose the Divide throughout most of the San Juans, Jarosa (pronounced ha-RO-sa) Mesa is a broad, upland plateau that reaches heights well above 12,000 feet. A ride here provides plentiful opportunities to appreciate the expansive willow thickets, profuse wildflowers, tundra ponds, and large elk herds that define the local environment. Best of all, this high, alpine platform permits an unobstructed look across a large part of the San Juans, with peaks in the Weminuche, La Garita, and Uncompahgre Wildernesses visible throughout the ride.

JAROSA MESA

Distance: 15 miles round-trip

Elevation Range: 10,900 to 12,300 feet

Total Elevation Gain: 1,400 feet

Trail Conditions: Rocky four-wheel-drive road; one steep, rough hill at ride's end; trail exposed to storms

Skill Level: Intermediate

Season: July through September

USGS Maps: Slumgullion Pass (1986); Lake San Cristobal (1964)

Administration: Rio Grande NF; Divide RD

Trailhead: Summit of Spring Creek Pass, on CO 149 (16.9 miles south of Lake City or 31.1 miles north of Creede).

Overlooked by most local bikers, Jarosa Mesa is a quiet and highly scenic tour.

With the exception of the ride's last mile, which gains more than 500 feet on a steep hill of mud and loose gravel, the route is surprisingly mellow for a journey along the Continental Divide. However, it is one of the most rock-strewn roads you will find, and you'll be dodging around and jolting over boulders throughout the trip—you'll really appreciate your bike's shocks, if you have them. Be forewarned that nearly the entire ride is above treeline and is exposed to blustery winds and developing thunderstorms. Your best bet is to make this an early-morning adventure and finish by noon.

Starting at Spring Creek Pass, pedal up the dirt road that continues west from the trailhead parking area. The initial climb is somewhat steep, but it quickly moderates as the road winds through scattered meadows and the upper fringes of subalpine forest. Vehicular traffic is very light; however, because the road is a segment of both the Continental Divide Trail (CDT) and the Colorado Trail (CT), you may pass an occasional backpacker. There are many colorful wildflower displays in both open meadows and under the forest canopy, and looking back over your shoulder, you'll have a nice view of 13,383-foot Baldy Cinco and the western flank of the La Garita Range.

Breaking into open tundra at mile 2.5, the road remains rough, especially where it skirts several talus fields. Fortunately, the grade is nearly flat at this point, and it is easy to admire the bouquets of columbine growing among the rocks. With the enveloping forest now behind you, the view broadens to include the arc of the Continental Divide, which swings south around the headwaters of the Rio Grande and across the crest of the Weminuche Wilderness. A final group of trees—and the last shelter from storms—is passed at mile 4.1.

The road maintains its easy grade across the open tundra for another 2 miles. By mile 5.0, our ultimate destination—a 12,300-foot knob marked by a small radio facility—becomes visible on the low northwest horizon. The road becomes smoother at this point, and the panorama even more expansive. Bear to the right, avoid a faint track at mile 5.7, and arrive at a more distinct junction at mile 6.5. The ride's grand finale is now before you: pedal the middle of three branching roads, aiming for the summit of the aforementioned knob, which is now directly ahead. With an ascent of about 500 feet over the last mile, this is the most challenging part of the ride. The tread is sometimes muddy and includes pockets of loose gravel. Take your time and persist—the payoff is worth the effort.

The grade eases as you near the crest of the hill, and the road ends upon arrival at the radio facility. The vista before you is an unsurpassed panorama of the central San Juans, which includes not only the Weminuche and La Garita peaks, but most of the gorgeous peaks surrounding the Lake City area, including Wetterhorn, Uncompahgre, Sunshine, and Redcloud. Directly below you is the upper valley of the Lake Fork River and the shimmering body of Lake San Cristobal. Blanketed by a colorful variety of tundra wildflowers, this sunny summit is a wonderful place to enjoy a picnic and a lengthy rest before jumping on your bike and bouncing back down to the trailhead.

Bachelor Historic Loop

The cliffs are solid silver—
With wondrous wealth untold,
And the beds of running rivers
Are lined with the purest gold.
While the world is filled with sorrow,
And hearts must break and bleed,
It's day all day, in the day-time
And there is no night in Creede.
                              —Cy Warman

Among the greatest rip-roaring mining camps of the old West, Creede is the legacy of Nick Creede's 1890 discovery of a fabulously rich lode of silver ore. In the months that followed, hundreds of men came to the canyons of Willow Creek, crawling through every nook and cranny in hopes of making their own strikes. Family members and merchants—as well as the gamblers, con artists, and prostitutes common to any self-respecting boom-town—came soon thereafter, and a community was born. For more than a century, despite fires, floods, depressions, and bad fortune, Creede has managed to survive. The surrounding hills, however, are now silent, the raucous "get-rich-quick" atmosphere but a distant memory. The mines of the rush now rot silently among the deep canyons and windswept ridges above town.

BACHELOR
HISTORIC LOOP

DISTANCE: 16.9 miles round-trip

ELEVATION RANGE: 8,800 to 10,700 feet

TOTAL ELEVATION GAIN: 1,900 feet

TRAIL CONDITIONS: Gravel road throughout; one short, steep climb, but otherwise moderate grades; light to moderate traffic

SKILL LEVEL: Novice

SEASON: June until mid-October

USGS MAPS: Creede (1986); San Luis Peak (1986)

ADMINISTRATION: Rio Grande NF; Divide RD

TRAILHEAD: Park anywhere in the town of Creede—the large gravel pullout off CO 149 at the south edge of town is a good choice. CO 149 enters and exits the south side of Creede at two different points; this pullout is on the side of town nearest Lake City, and it's marked by an interpretive sign on the east side of the highway. Mileage begins from this point.

Mount your bike, and prepare to ride among these ghosts of yesterday.

The Bachelor Historic Loop weaves together a series of gravel roads that wind through the heart of the Creede Mining District, which creates a circuit of compelling historical interest and beautiful mountain landscapes. Maintained for passenger cars, this loop is also an outstanding bike route with no technical challenges and only a few steep climbs, all of which are of short duration. Though one of Creede's best attractions, this remote town receives less tourist traffic than almost any other San Juan community, and thus vehicular conflicts are rare. Just in case, a midweek or post–Labor Day ride may be desirable. Before beginning this ride, be sure to pick up the informative *Bachelor Historic Tour* brochure produced by the Rio Grande National Forest and Creede/Mineral County Chamber of Commerce.

From your Creede parking spot, ride to the north end of town and into the canyon of Willow Creek. (If you start at the aforementioned suggested parking area, be sure to avoid a right turn on CO 149 and instead continue northbound toward the mouth of the canyon.) A vertical gateway that is as dramatic a backdrop to be found in any western mining town, the sheer, brooding cliffs of the canyon rise nearly 1,000 feet overhead as you make your way into the narrow drainage, which is 1 mile above the recommended parking area. A half mile farther, Willow Creek splits into its east and west forks. The road splits here as well, and our tour continues up the west (left) fork. This now-vacant confluence was the one-time site of North Creede, which once bustled with wagon and railroad traffic.

The last light of a fading season shines through a golden aspen grove.

The road becomes much steeper upon entering the West Willow Creek drainage. The spectacularly situated site of the Commodore Mine is gained almost immediately, and a break to admire the remaining structures is a nice way to regain your breath. The Commodore was one of the district's greatest producers, and it had more than 200 miles of tunnels that honeycombed the canyon walls. The "ore house" that overhangs the road was used until the 1970s. As with all mines and structures on this ride, resist the urge to explore too closely, as most are extremely dangerous and nearly all are private property.

Beyond the Commodore, the road climbs the "Black Pitch"—the ride's steepest section. Fortunately, the grade eases rather quickly, otherwise you might find yourself plummeting back into the Bone Yard, which is what miners named the curve just below this grade, the site of many a wrecked wagon and destroyed pack animal unable to negotiate this grueling hill. The abandoned site of Weaver—a small community that served the surrounding mines—is passed at mile 2.8, and a short distance farther is the Amethyst Mine, one of the richest silver mines ever established in the Silver State. Legend has it that a stubborn burro was the cause for this mine's 1891 discovery by prospector Theodore Renniger. When his animal failed to budge, Renniger took a seat, examined a piece of rock, and ultimately became a part of history.

The road climbs steadily up the Nelson Creek drainage for nearly a mile above the Amethyst Mine and passes the upper end of East Willow Creek Road before it turns sharply to the left and contours back toward West Willow Creek. Though mines become less frequent as you proceed up valley, aspen groves, small meadows, and numerous beaver ponds highlight a beautiful slice of subalpine scenery. After another 2 miles of gently rolling terrain, you'll come to an intersection just before the road swings sharply left and crosses the creek. The right branch represents a 4.4-mile (round-trip) spur that is included within the ride's mileage total. This easy diversion takes you to the site of the Equity Mine; though no structures remain to be seen, a pretty vista up the willow-lined valley of West Willow Creek allows you to gaze as far as the gentle slopes of the Continental Divide. From road's end at the Equity Mine, coast back down to the main road and turn right to continue the loop.

Climbing gently, the road contours across the upper flanks of Bachelor Mountain for 2 miles to gain its broad summit, which is 12.2 miles into the ride. Though aspen and spruce forest line the road for most of this climb, there are nice views of the La Garita Range near the top. Dropping slightly into a small meadow, you'll arrive at the site of Bachelor, another of the many communities that sprang up around the Creede area. More than a thousand people resided here, and in 1892, many refugees from fire-ravaged Creede came here until their town could be rebuilt. A century later, there is little more than a few faint foundations to indicate a town of any size once prospered here.

The ride is now a long, enjoyable coast as the road begins to descend the south flanks of Bachelor and Bulldog Mountains. Just after passing the Rat Creek four-wheel-drive road at mile 13.4, you'll traverse the upper reaches of Windy Gulch and simultaneously enjoy a bird's-eye view of Creede. Winding down the mountainsides, the road stays within open meadows that permit unimpeded vistas up and down the beautiful Rio Grande valley. After keeping to the main road at all previous junctions, you'll want to make a quick side trip to Creede's cemetery at mile 15.7. This 0.8-mile (round-trip) diversion (also included in the ride's mileage total) leads you to an archetypal boomtown graveyard. You could spend a good hour or more wandering this cemetery, examining the many old headstones, and pondering life and death on the frontier. Remember that this cemetery remains the burial place for Creede's residents, so please be respectful of all the graves and any mourners that you may encounter.

Don't miss the Bob Ford grave, which is just north of Creede Cemetery. One of the West's legendary figures, Ford is alleged to have been the man who shot Jesse James in the back a decade before the founding of Creede. Having escaped the revenge of the remaining James gang, Ford eventually wound up the "boss" of Creede, which he "governed" from his drinking and gambling establishment. Though the exact circumstances are disputed, Ford himself was shot in the back (a nice example of poetic justice) by Ed O'Kelly, a man of questionable reputation who happened to be the town marshal of Bachelor. Ford's burial was the biggest event in Creede's short history and was reportedly attended by all of the town's gamblers, scam artists, and prostitutes. It is said that in lieu of flowers, shots of whiskey were poured into Ford's open grave. When Ford's body was later relocated to his home in Missouri, legend has it that the body of another murderer was dumped in its place to save the undertaker from having to dig another grave.

When you are done looking around the cemetery, pedal back to the main road and continue coasting another 0.5 mile until you arrive at CO 149 and, shortly thereafter, the parking area.

Treasure Mountain

Unlike Durango and Telluride, the Pagosa Springs area remains relatively undiscovered by mountain bikers. One reason for this is that much of the surrounding mountain country falls within the Weminuche and South San Juan Wilderness areas, where bicycles are prohibited. Another is that a great deal of the remaining land has been extensively logged, and most bikeable roads tend to wind through and between unsightly clear-cuts. However, *never* think in absolutes, as there are always exceptions to the rule. There are some real gems hidden in the nearby hills, and none sparkle more than the Treasure Mountain Trail. An exciting single-track through beautiful scenery, this ride is one of the best-kept secrets in the region.

By tying in an old logging route called Wolf Creek Road, this ride allows you to pedal from the west side of Wolf Creek Pass, across the upper flanks of Treasure Mountain, and down to the floor of the majestic East Fork valley. Wolf Creek Road is a fairly rough four-wheel-drive track that climbs steadily through expansive clear-cuts. Gaining about 1,000 feet in a little more than 3 miles, this route offers enough elevation gain and technical challenge to satisfy even the advanced rider. However, it is the long, twisting, 3,000-foot descent into the East Fork valley that makes this ride so remarkable. Sure, there are a few rocks and roots, a respectable amount of mud, and even a clothes-liner or two, but this surprisingly smooth single-track is ideal for intermediate bikers looking for a few hours of fun. The trickiest part of the ride is a short section of side-hill traverse across some fairly steep slopes—a challenge that will overwhelm a novice biker. Otherwise, the biggest obstacle is arranging a car shuttle between the two trail access points—it's a long, hard ride back up Wolf Creek Pass.

Unless you're a maniac who would rather gasp your way up mountains than coast down them, you'll want to start at US 160 and Wolf Creek Road. Descending about 100 feet, you'll coast for 0.25 mile on a gravel road. Just after you cross Wolf Creek itself, turn left and begin climbing into a large clear-cut. Though few people would sing the scenic praises of such logged areas, this one actually has a few positive attributes, including a healthy wildflower population and some nice vistas of the waterfalls that tumble down the opposite valley wall. Old roads lace the area, though the proper route is easily identified by the mountain-bike markers recently installed by the Forest Service. The two most significant intersections come at mile 1.1, where you bear left; and mile 1.8, where you turn right. Above this second intersection, the road becomes much rougher, and it will remain so until it climbs onto a distinct saddle at mile 3.5. Separating Treasure Mountain from the Continental Divide, the saddle is the ride's high point and is a good place to view peaks in both the Weminuche and South San Juan Wilderness.

Before you now is 7.5 miles of nearly continuous descent, which is a veritable carnival ride of forests, brooks, meadows, and mountains. Continue on the road at first, then branch to the left at mile 4.0. Descending slightly, the road skirts the edge of a large meadow (a great place to spot elk, especially in the morning), then climbs gently once more. The road finally peters out 0.5 mile farther, when it arrives at the brink of a steep gully just below the summit of Treasure Mountain. The mountain takes its name from a classic—if not clichéd—tale of lost treasure. Local lore has it that a party of French trappers, in possession of a quantity of gold, was attacked by a group of Utes. The survivors buried their gold so that they could flee unencumbered, and when they later returned to reclaim their cache, it could not

TREASURE MOUNTAIN

DISTANCE: 11 miles one-way
ELEVATION RANGE: 8,200 to 11,150 feet
TOTAL ELEVATION GAIN: 1,050 feet
TRAIL CONDITIONS: Rocky four-wheel-drive road with moderate climb, then smooth single-track; some muddy sections with occasional rocks and roots; narrow sidehill traverse in places; rapid descent
SKILL LEVEL: Intermediate
SEASON: Late June through September
USGS MAP: Wolf Creek Pass (1984)
ADMINISTRATION: San Juan NF; Pagosa RD

WOLF CREEK PASS ACCESS: From the intersection of US 160 and US 84 in Pagosa Springs, drive east on US 160. After you pass East Fork Road at mile 9.4, continue up the west side of Wolf Creek Pass until you reach Wolf Creek Road at mile 19.7. Park at the gravel pullout at this intersection.
EAST FORK ACCESS: From the intersection of East Fork Road at US 160, drive the gravel East Fork Road for 6.5 miles until you spot a small sign that identifies the Treasure Mountain Trail. Park here, on the shoulder of the road.

❧ ❧ ❧

be located—and has not to this day. Not only has the rumor been so persistent as to yield the name of the mountain, it has led to a number of treasure-seeking ventures, including a recent plan to use remote sensing techniques.

The actual trail begins with a steep, sidehill traverse across a long avalanche gully before it enters dense timber and eases into a moderate descent. After a sharp left turn, the trail proceeds directly down the crest of a narrow ridge, then turns back across the mountain slope to splash across Treasure Creek at mile 6.5. The smooth trail continues along the bank of the creek for a short distance before it turns to the right, traverses back across a gentler slope, and intersects a smaller brook. After successfully negotiating this rough, muddy ford, the trail winds into an open, flower-filled meadow where thick bunches of trail-crowding false hellebore will slap and soak your legs. A faint junction comes at mile 7.25; the right fork contours across to Windy Pass, while we continue our descent to the left and into the east fork drainage.

Below the junction, the trail descends more gently and soon enters the ride's first stands of aspen. Though many bikers will miss its subtleties as they speed down the trail, the forest scenery throughout the length of the Treasure Mountain Trail is quite beautiful. Forest ecosystems are distinctly separated, and the differences between them are readily observable. The upper 3 miles of the ride descend through subalpine forest and across avalanche-gully meadows, and below this is a 2-mile stretch of exceptionally lush aspen groves. The trail then descends into the montane forest, where Douglas fir, ponderosa pine, and a few Gambel oak thickets line the path.

The trail winds quite a bit as it descends through the aspen zone, though the riding remains easy and very enjoyable. Coasting along, it's easy to become lost among the musty aspen smells and pleasant birdsong that surround you, but don't get too relaxed, as every so often there will be a twisted aspen bole stretched across the trail right at neck level—a spectacular wipeout waiting to happen. After slicing past another small meadow, the trail recrosses Treasure Creek at mile 9.75, then enters a 0.25-mile section of forest where both Douglas fir and ponderosa pine grow to great heights and tremendous girths. The final mile is slightly steeper than the previous few, and as you ease into the open meadows at ride's end, you'll enjoy a beautiful look at the pastoral East Fork valley and the rough peaks at its headwaters. As you coast to a stop at your vehicle, you'll probably think to yourself, "Too soon!"

As last night's storm clears to the east, another foot of snow settles on the peaks above Red Mountain Pass.

SKIING AND SNOWSHOEING

As winter descends, the San Juans capture an aura unlike that of any other season. The ragged edges of the topography become softer under a pillowy blanket of snow. The explosion of color found in the forests and meadows becomes a muted world of gray and white. The raucous crashing of rivers and streams is replaced by the whisper of wind and falling flakes. Whether you seek to silently glide through gentle meadows, venture into secluded basins and up snowbound peaks, or float down heavenly slopes, the winter environment is one of true beauty and peacefulness. Step into the bracing air and see for yourself.

Lime Creek

The gently sloping terrain traversed by the snowbound Lime Creek Road is an excellent venue to experience the winter landscape. With a combination of gentle grades and good snow conditions, even novices can enjoy the beautiful patterns and colors found among the forests and peaks of this highly scenic area. The rolling benches are home to a mixture of aspen glades, evergreen forest, and open meadow, while a backdrop of the craggy West Needle Mountains creates a setting of rugged grandeur. More skilled skiers may take interest in one of the several possible off-trail excursions that are nearby.

In general, the low elevation and sheltered forests of the area make this tour a good choice when avalanche or weather conditions prohibit safe travel in other areas. Winds are usually light, and on sunny days the temperature often warms above freezing. No avalanche hazard exists along the primary route, though skiing in the surrounding terrain could increase the danger. In those areas, be cautious of triggered slides in gullies and on steeper hillsides, especially when the avalanche hazard below treeline is rated high. Such topography, however, is easily avoided. Beyond the turnaround point, the road enters the Lime Creek Gorge, an area of steep slopes and several large avalanche paths. Advanced skiers interested in continuing into the gorge should do so only during periods of low avalanche hazard.

The tour begins near to where the road crosses Mill Creek, which is where winter maintenance typically ends. The tour continues on the unplowed roadbed, which climbs steadily—though not steeply—away from this drainage, and passes through an evenly mixed forest of aspen and spruce. Fanciful icicle displays appear where rivulets of snowmelt freeze on the rocks above the road. Indeed, given its southern exposure, freeze-thaw cycles occur on an almost daily basis, the result being an occasional mixed bag of snow conditions. On sunny days the snow can become mushy in places, while shadier areas retain a firm, dry snowpack. If you are using waxable skis, prepare for a variety of conditions.

You'll enter an open aspen grove about 1.5 miles from the trailhead, and soon you'll pass an active beaver pond. Beavers, once trapped nearly to extinction, are common in the San Juans once again. Second only to humans in the ability to alter the landscape, beavers have dammed several small brooks in order to flood this one-time meadow. They do not hibernate but instead live on a supply of aspen and willow branches collected during the summer. The family that inhabits this pond will breed in early winter, and a litter of "kits" will be born in the spring. Since they are nocturnal, beavers are rarely observed, though evidence of their presence is found in the remains of felled aspen in the groves that surround the pond.

The road now turns southward and climbs gradually up the side of the aspen-cloaked ridge to the east of the pond. Openings in the forest permit views of the distinctive summit of Engineer Mountain, Graysill Mountain's barren ridges, as well as the smallish Scout Lake and several associated ponds in the gently sloping terrain to the west. As the road crests the ridge slightly more than a mile beyond the beaver pond, it turns sharply to the left and enters the gorge of Lime Creek. The ski tour ends at this point, as the

LIME CREEK

DISTANCE: 6 miles round-trip
ELEVATION RANGE: 8,900 to 9,600 feet
TOTAL ELEVATION GAIN: 700 feet
TRAIL CONDITIONS: Gentle grades on a snowed-in roadbed
AVALANCHE HAZARD: None
SKILL LEVEL: Novice
SEASON: December through mid-April
USGS MAP: Engineer Mountain (1960)
ADMINISTRATION: San Juan NF; Columbine RD

TRAILHEAD: Drive on US 550, either for 29 miles north from Durango or for 19 miles south from Silverton, and turn south onto Lime Creek Road. Drive on this unpaved, often snow-packed road for 1.1 miles until winter maintenance ends, and park here. A four-wheel-drive vehicle may be necessary when Lime Creek Road is slushy or muddy. Additionally, no parking is allowed on the road after snow accumulations of 6 inches or greater until the road has been plowed. At such times, it is necessary to park at US 550 and walk or ski the 1.1 miles to the trailhead.

steep walls of the gorge present a significant avalanche hazard. However, the scenery from this prospect is unparalleled. On the opposite side of the narrow canyon, the massive ramparts of the West Needle Mountains tower nearly 4,000 feet overhead, while the shady canyon floor is more than 500 feet below. The long avalanche paths that trace its face and the plumes of snow that blow from its crest exemplify the winter inaccessibility of this rugged range.

While you can choose to make an easy return journey at this point, several off-trail options may interest skiers looking for a longer or more adventurous tour. One possibility is to explore the rolling glades directly south of Scout Lake. This area lends itself to casual skiing, but be careful about traveling too far down the increasingly steep slopes, which drop into the Lime and Cascade Creek drainages. A second option, which is suitable for intermediate or advanced skiers, is to follow the route of the summer trail to Potato (a.k.a. Spud) Lake. Though not marked for winter travel, a map, compass, and logic should make route-finding fairly easy. Diverge from the road adjacent to the large beaver pond, ski north, turn northeast, and climb along a small drainage. An ascent of 400 feet on this mile-long route is rewarded upon arrival at the snowbound lake, which is set beneath the rugged flanks of Potato Hill.

A third option is to create a 3-mile, off-trail loop through the glades south of lower Lime Creek Road. Though suitable for beginning skiers, the route is not usually tracked, and some route-finding will be required. Begin by skiing up the road about 0.5 mile from the trailhead, then turn into the gently rolling terrain to the south. Wind your way through the aspen and evergreen forest for a mile or so to a nice overlook high above Cascade Creek. Enjoy the view, then ski in a northwesterly direction and follow a fairly level contour until the route intersects Mill Creek. Use caution crossing the creek (snow bridges are often of dubious strength), then continue until you reach the plowed section of Lime Creek Road. Turn right, then ski (or walk) the 0.5 mile back to the trailhead.

Coal Creek

One of the most popular backcountry skiing routes in the San Juans, the upper Coal Creek drainage has earned its popularity by combining challenging terrain with superior snow conditions and attractive scenery. Telemarkers can choose from a variety of exciting routes, including open alpine bowls, acres of moderately sloped glades, and steep shots down heavily forested gully walls. Skiers simply interested in a tough but rewarding tour will not be disappointed with the scenery in the area, both near and far. Mature subalpine forest blankets much of upper Coal Creek, while the vista from the ridges above the drainage encompass the upper Cascade

Creek and Lime Creek valleys and the beautiful peaks beyond. The area deserves its reputation as one of the snowier places in the San Juans, and the fact that many of the best telemarking runs are on northerly aspects ensures high-quality powder for most of the winter.

Though the terrain around Coal Creek is suitable for both intermediate and advanced telemarkers, the route into the area from Coal Bank Pass is strictly the realm of the advanced skier. While the ascent itself is difficult, the more challenging problems are the steep sidehill traverses, navigation without benefit of marked trails, and a high avalanche hazard. The latter is a particular problem since the route from Coal Bank Pass immediately crosses a dangerous slope, which makes skiers susceptible to both natural and triggered slides. Avalanche hazard is also high along Coal Creek, especially along the steep gully walls near the floor of the drainage. In both places, avalanches have taken several lives. This is not the place to take risks—avoid this area when the avalanche hazard above and/or below treeline is rated as high.

COAL CREEK

DISTANCE: 5 miles round-trip to ridge (4 miles one-way for descent of Coal Creek)

ELEVATION RANGE: 10,300 to 11,750 feet

TOTAL ELEVATION GAIN: 1,100 feet, plus 350 additional feet in return to Coal Bank Pass if descending Coal Creek

TRAIL CONDITIONS: Steep, unmarked route through forested and gladed terrain

AVALANCHE HAZARD: High

SKILL LEVEL: Advanced

SEASON: December through April

USGS MAP: Engineer Mountain (1960)

ADMINISTRATION: San Juan NF; Columbine RD

TRAILHEAD: At the summit of Coal Bank Pass, which is about 30 miles north of Durango or 14 miles south of Silverton via US 550. Ample parking is available. Skiers who descend Coal Creek will intersect US 550 1.2 miles north of Coal Bank Pass. Either arrange shuttle transportation or walk this distance back to the trailhead.

From the large parking area atop Coal Bank Pass, ski north toward the steep avalanche path adjacent to the highway. Your immediate goal is to attain the ridge at the crest of this slope, and you have two options by which to accomplish this. The longer yet easier choice is to follow the summer hiking-trail route, which traverses the bottom of the slope before ascending the somewhat gentler slopes of a southeast-facing ridge. After a mile and approximately 500 feet of elevation gain, the trail breaks out of the timber and passes a small pond. This pond sits atop a small perch, located directly above the avalanche path that is visible from the parking area. Though the initial traverse is exposed to a high avalanche hazard, the remainder of this mile is mostly safe from slides. This traverse does require some steep sidehill skiing, which is especially tricky when extended periods of sunny weather create hard, suncrusted snow conditions on the south-facing slope. Because the area is so popular with local skiers, there is usually tracked trail, except immediately after a storm.

The second option is to climb directly up the steep slope north of the highway and crest atop the ridge just west of the aforementioned pond. Though this route is much shorter in distance, the skiing is much tougher. More importantly, this entire section is exposed to potential avalanches, and triggered slides are likely when the snowpack is unstable. The icy crust that can form after extended sunny periods is another potential problem, as keeping any sort of traction can be difficult in such conditions.

Once in the vicinity of the pond, the skiing becomes easier and more pleasant. The route climbs moderately along the north side of a small gully for about 0.5 mile and passes through a mixture of forest and glade. Upon exiting the gully, continue westward as you traverse across the first of the enticing slopes above Coal Creek. Be sure to stay well north of the cornice-shadowed slopes to the southwest, where extreme avalanche danger lurks. Telemarkers can diverge from the route at any time, either to begin a descent toward the bottom of the drainage or to try repeated runs on the open slopes northwest of Point 11,916. The vistas become increasingly eye-popping as the traverse nears treeline. The sheer northern face of Engineer Mountain is close at hand, while the massive peaks guarding the northern horizon—collectively known as the West Silverton Range—form a dramatic skyline. Depending on your location in the basin, you'll also enjoy glimpses of the West Needles, Needles, and Grenadiers.

Touring skiers will find the low ridge northeast of Engineer Mountain, culminating in Point 11,762, a worthy destination. These mostly open slopes offer the best western, northern, and eastern panoramas, and the looming summit of Engineer fills the southern view. At this point, you can choose to continue on the vast alpine slopes farther north or retrace your route to the pond. The easiest way to make the final descent to the trailhead is to follow the longer route down the ridge that is east of the pond, though even this will be challenging.

Skiers seeking to sample Coal Creek's telemark terrain can begin their descent almost anywhere in the upper basin—though ultimately you will want to stay on the south side of the creek once into the lower gully. The slopes in the upper basin are typically of moderate steepness and are a mixture of dense forest and open glades. As the gully begins to drop more steeply toward the east, simply traverse across the slopes above the creek until you find a tempting route, then point 'em downhill. As you near the drainage floor, traverse farther east again, then make another descent toward the creek. You can repeat this several times before you reach the highway, which is about 2 miles below the head of the basin. The gully becomes constricted by a small cliff within the final 0.25 mile before it intersects the highway, which requires you to ski very near the creek. Be wary of small but potentially deadly avalanches, which are easily triggered on the steep gully walls both here and in areas farther upstream. With planning, your ride will be waiting at the highway to whisk you back to the top of the pass for another go. Otherwise, enjoy the hike back uphill.

Molas Pass

At the very heart of the San Juans, the meadows of Molas Pass serve as a platform for some of the most awe-inspiring vistas in the Rockies. In all directions, a magnificent prospect draws the eye into a world of alpine wilderness. The stark, sculpted summits of Engineer Mountain, Grand Turk, Snowdon Peak, and the Grenadier Range each vie for individual admiration and combine to create a beautiful panorama. In terms of skiing terrain, Molas Pass deserves similar accolades. With the possible exception of Lizard Head Pass, few other places in Colorado can match the area's ideal combination of easy access, varied topography, dependable snow conditions, and fantastic scenery. With routes that traverse a variety of landscapes, from open meadows to frozen lakes and gladed mountainsides, myriad touring possibilities await the skier, regardless of ability.

The most logical way to describe the various routes is to lump them according to their trailhead. There are four different parking areas off of US 550, each within a mile of the Molas Pass summit. Each of these offer slightly different terrain and slightly different panoramas. Snowmobile usage on the pass has become more common in recent years, and as of the winter of 2000,

MOLAS PASS

DISTANCE: Variable; up to 5 miles round-trip

ELEVATION RANGE: Generally 10,500 to 11,200 feet

TOTAL ELEVATION GAIN: Variable; up to 700 feet

TRAIL CONDITIONS: Highly varied, from flat to fairly steep grades; excellent telemarking on some gladed slopes

AVALANCHE HAZARD: Variable; easily avoided in many areas, very high in others

SKILL LEVEL: Novice to advanced

SEASON: Late October through mid-May

USGS MAP: Snowdon Peak (1964)

ADMINISTRATION: San Juan NF; Columbine RD

TRAILHEAD: There are four possible trailheads; all are within a mile of the summit of Molas Pass. To reach the pass, drive on US 550 for either 7 miles south from Silverton or for 42 miles north from Durango.

the Forest Service was studying alternatives that would segregate motorized and nonmotorized recreationists. At any rate, there is usually plenty of untracked powder available, even days after the most recent storm. In fact, the snow conditions at the pass are among the most dependable in the region, with good skiing often possible from late October until May. Molas Pass is not well suited for stormy-day skiing, however, as its high elevation and open nature leave the area exposed to high winds and whiteout conditions. The avalanche danger throughout the area is variable—while much of the local topography is too gentle for the formation of avalanches, there are plenty of smaller slopes steep enough to present significant hazard. Additionally, the terrain above and below the pass steepens considerably. Always study the snowpack carefully if your planned route takes you into any area where slopes are steeper than 25 degrees.

The northernmost parking area is exactly 1 mile north of the pass summit, where a sign announces the beginning of the Molas Trail. Though this parking area may not be plowed during heavier snowfalls, it is usually cleared within a day. This is the best access to the gentle terrain east of the pass itself—the expansive meadows at the head of Molas Creek. A fine loop of 1 or 2 miles may be made in this area, though be careful not to drop too far down Molas Creek, which makes an increasingly steep descent into the Animas River Canyon. Also, avoid the tempting terrain adjacent to nearby Molas Lake, as it is private property. These meadows, which are interspersed with groves of spruce and fir, offer the finest views of the magnificent Grenadier Range. Carved from billion-year-old quartzite, the Grenadiers are among the most photogenic peaks in the San Juans. Avalanche

The last light of day paints the summits of the Grenadiers as another winter storm slowly clears away.

danger in the vicinity is minimal, and though some slopes could be susceptible to skier-triggered avalanches, these areas are easily avoided.

The next trailhead is located 0.6 mile farther south (or 0.4 mile north of the Molas Pass summit), where the snowbound Little Molas Lake Road branches to the west. This is one of the most popular routes in the vicinity; consequently, the parking area may be crowded. There is usually room to park on both sides of US 550, though be careful to not impede snowplow operations or other traffic. Little Molas Lake Road is an excellent 0.5-mile (one-way) route, and with minimal avalanche danger and only 100 feet of elevation gain, it is suitable for novices. Trees are scattered, which allows sweeping vistas of the surrounding peaks throughout the tour.

The terrain west of the frozen lake has good potential for several advanced routes. One option is to continue west of the lake for another 0.5 mile, then turn south to descend the steeper slopes above US 550. Though the vertical drop on these slopes is only 200 to 400 feet, they are well suited to telemarking, with both forested and open slopes to provide variety. When you reach the highway, it will be necessary to walk a mile or so back to the parking area or arrange shuttle transportation for repeated runs. The avalanche potential on these slopes is very high, and they should be avoided when the overall avalanche hazard is rated as high. Another possibility is to ascend the ridge northwest of the lake, then traverse across the slopes above the headwaters of Lime Creek. Mainly above treeline, the panorama in this area is particularly outstanding, but once again, the avalanche danger is quite high.

The third trailhead possibility is to park atop Molas Pass. The best choice on snowy days, it is usually plowed during storms. Novices may enjoy skiing toward the flat basin of Andrews Lake, which is about a mile southwest of the pass, or toward Little Molas Lake by following the gradually rolling ridge northwest from the parking area. Avalanche danger is minimal in both areas. The terrain east of the parking area is attractive for intermediate to advanced skiers. Fairly flat benches separate several short but steep pitches. The lowest flat is a small meadow bisected by Molas Creek just before it plunges into the Animas River Gorge. In all, there is about 700 vertical feet of prime telemarking available in this vicinity, though you will have to make the climb back up to the highway. Be sure not to descend too far down Molas Creek, and be cautious of the potentially high avalanche hazard.

The southernmost parking area is exactly 1 mile south of the pass, where the road leading to Andrews Lake splits to the south. The snowbound roadbed is another excellent route for novices, and the frozen surface of the lake, as well as the gentle meadows surrounding it, provide both beautiful and easy skiing. Another popular telemarking area is on the ridge just south of the lake, which offers more than 500 vertical feet of both open and gladed slopes. By skiing down the ridge farther west of Andrews Lake, you can add an additional 300 vertical feet before you traverse across the slope to return to US 550. Predictably, the avalanche danger on this ridge can be high.

South Mineral Creek

The South Mineral Creek valley is one of the more popular cross-country skiing routes in the San Juans, and justly so. This textbook example of glacial geology offers a gentle valley floor that extends nearly 5 miles into the midst of numerous spectacular peaks. Its valley walls rise steeply to culminate in wind-battered peaks thousands of feet overhead, while streams that issue from numerous hanging valleys freeze into striking displays of ice.

Despite a veritable gauntlet of avalanche paths, the valley tour is largely without difficulty and is often one of exceptional peacefulness.

Though novice skiing abilities will suffice, an awareness of avalanche hazard is necessary to ski in this valley. While the tour does not cross any terrain where a skier-triggered avalanche would be possible, it does cross the run-out zones of multiple large slide paths that streak both valley walls. These avalanche paths can produce slides large enough to sweep across the entire valley floor. Though avalanches of such magnitude usually occur only after intense snowstorms or prolonged periods of high winds, such slides can be expected several times during an average winter. For this reason, the valley should be avoided at times when the hazard for natural avalanche activity is high both above and below treeline. While nearby peaks help to shelter the valley from the strongest winds, it is often colder here than at other nearby locales. A natural "cold-air sink," the valley floor is typically several degrees colder than slopes just a few hundred feet higher. Furthermore, its towering southern flank keeps the valley floor in shade on most winter days. Though the colder temperatures ensure favorable snow conditions, it obviously makes warm clothing necessary.

The tour simply traces the route of South Mineral Creek Road, which is easily followed in its entirety. Little more than 75 feet of elevation is gained in the initial mile to the Mineral Creek bridge. Beyond the bridge, the road turns southwest into the true South Mineral Creek valley and continues to climb very gently, gaining only another 125 feet in the next 1.5 miles. The valley floor is a mixture of willow thickets, subalpine forest, and open meadow, and there are impressive vistas of the surrounding peaks from almost all points. Unless trail must be broken through new snow, this distance passes very quickly, especially for skiers well versed in "kick-and-glide" practices.

SOUTH MINERAL CREEK

DISTANCE: 9 miles round-trip

ELEVATION RANGE: 9,450 to 9,800 feet

TOTAL ELEVATION GAIN: 400 feet

TRAIL CONDITIONS: Gentle grades on a snowbound road

AVALANCHE HAZARD: High

SKILL LEVEL: Novice

SEASON: December through early April

USGS MAPS: Ophir (1955); Silverton (1955)

ADMINISTRATION: San Juan NF; Columbine RD

TRAILHEAD: From Silverton, drive 2.2 miles north on US 550. The trailhead is signed South Mineral Creek Road. Plowed parking is usually available on the west side of the highway.

The first avalanche path crosses the road a little more than 2 miles from US 550; the potential for natural snowslide activity should be carefully evaluated before proceeding beyond this point. Staying to the north side of the valley, the tour continues in much the same manner as before, with only a slight increase in gradient. The many avalanche gullies that streak the mountain walls serve as effective mileposts, and one stretches to the valley floor every 0.25 mile or so.

Four miles from the highway is the right-branching Clear Lake Road, which climbs steeply into areas of extreme avalanche hazard. Our route remains on the valley floor and proceeds an additional 0.5 mile until the turn-around point at the snowbound South Mineral Creek Campground. The scenery throughout this final distance is superb. Several nearby ravines feature spectacular icicle displays, some of which attract ice climbers throughout the winter. The valley is more constricted in this area, which serves to heighten the drama of the surrounding peaks, while the often free-flowing creek adds both visual and auditory beauty to the landscape. Perhaps most enjoyable is the sense of solitude, and the knowledge that the bustle of towns, highways, and other trappings of civilization is far away.

The amateur geologist has much to marvel at while admiring these scenes. Most obvious are the classic effects of Ice Age glaciation, which can be observed at every turn. The steep mountain walls and the flat valley floor combine to create a U-shape that is characteristic of glacial erosion, while the hanging valleys, high cirques, narrow arêtes, and horn-shaped peaks offer further evidence of the sculpting ability of great glaciers. The high peaks on the south side of the valley display striking bands of red rock; these are part of the Hermosa Formation, a group of sandstones that were formed at the base of the ancestral Rockies more than 300 million years ago. That this once-level rock formation occurs on summits exceeding 12,000 feet, while at the same time appearing at the 6,000-foot elevation of the Animas Valley floor just north of Durango, illustrates the power of mountain building. Even subtler is the fact that the "straight" character of the valley indicates that it traces a fracture created by the collapse of the Silverton Caldera, whose western edge was consistent with the present-day Mineral Creek Valley and the route of US 550.

The valley beyond the campground may be attractive to highly experienced skiers; however, it should only be attempted during good conditions and by those with expert knowledge of avalanche dynamics and safety. The grade is much steeper, and the route is exposed to avalanches continuously for almost 2 miles. Icy and densely packed avalanche debris only adds to the difficulty. The reward is a lovely meadow set beneath the looming bulks of Rolling Mountain, the Twin Sisters, and Beattie Peak, each more than 13,000 feet in height. The valley divides at this point, and both branches slope into vast alpine bowls. Expert telemarkers could spend days enjoying these slopes, though they are best left until spring, when snowpack consolidation often lessens the extreme avalanche hazard.

US Basin

Simply put, US Basin offers the finest backcountry skiing in the vicinity of Red Mountain Pass. The route into the basin is ideal for touring, with excellent snow conditions and spectacular vistas at every turn, while the basin and its surrounding peaks provide some of the best telemarking terrain to be found in this corner of the San Juans. Adding to the superlative quality of the area is the St. Paul Lodge, a rustic hostelry that features some of the most enjoyable (and accessible) winter backcountry accommodations in the state. Skiers with limited time to spend in the region would be well advised to mark US Basin a must-see on their itinerary.

With terrain that can be characterized as rugged, this tour is not suitable for inexperienced skiers. Much of the route climbs steeply, and there are many areas where avalanche danger lurks. The upper half of the tour is above treeline, which leaves skiers

US BASIN

DISTANCE: Up to 5 miles round-trip

ELEVATION RANGE: 11,050 to 12,350 feet

TOTAL ELEVATION GAIN: Up to 1,300 feet

TRAIL CONDITIONS: The trail is easily followed below treeline (often groomed to the St. Paul Lodge), but good route-finding skills may be required above treeline; moderate to steep grades; lower portion of trail traverses private property

AVALANCHE HAZARD: Moderate below treeline, high above treeline

SKILL LEVEL: Intermediate to advanced

SEASON: November through early May

USGS MAPS: Ironton (1955); Silverton (1955)

ADMINISTRATION: St. Paul Lodge and San Juan NF; Columbine RD

TRAILHEAD: Plowed parking is available at the summit of Red Mountain Pass, which is 10 miles north of Silverton or 13.5 miles south of Ouray via US 550.

The warmth of the morning light belies the bitterness of the air.

exposed to potentially high winds and blizzard conditions. The high altitude further conspires against the less fit.

For skiers unwilling or unable to accept these challenges on their own, staying at the St. Paul Lodge is a great option. Not only does the lodge offer comfortable accommodations and excellent food, Chris George, the proprietor, offers guided tours throughout the surrounding country. A renowned avalanche expert (Chris often teaches at the Silverton Avalanche School), he will ensure an enjoyable day of skiing with minimal hazard. Chris can even teach you to telemark in as little as a half hour. For information about accommodations, contact the lodge at P.O. Box 463, Silverton, CO 81433; (970) 387–5367.

To begin the tour, park at the summit of Red Mountain Pass, then walk about 100 yards south along the highway to a snowbound road that bears east. Begin skiing up this route, which is often groomed for guests of the lodge. The route almost immediately turns south and traverses beneath a short but steep cliff. If the avalanche hazard is high, avoid this area by skiing farther to the west, and you'll eventually return to the route as it turns into a small gully, about 0.5 mile from the highway. After 0.25 mile of fairly steep climbing on the floor of the gully, the groomed route bears sharply to the right and continues another 0.25 mile to the lodge. If you are not a guest, continue up the gully for another 0.25 mile, then turn sharply to the right as the road traverses the slope just above the lodge. Though either route will take you to nearly the same place, the proprietor requests that nonguests use only the upper route in order to minimize any disturbances to the lodge and his guests. Please remember to be considerate—the land surrounding the lodge is privately owned, and the skiing terrain is the commodity by which the proprietor makes his living. If you are not a guest, stay to the described route as you cross the property, and confine your turns to the public land located above treeline.

The tour continues to climb along the road, and it reaches treeline and the lower edge of the basin 0.5 mile above the lodge. There is another area of avalanche hazard in this stretch; however, it can be avoided if you climb up the shallow gully directly east of the lodge and traverse south to regain the road, which will now be above the hazardous slope. Though the vistas are impressive throughout the tour's length, they become truly inspiring as you approach treeline. The towering wall of peaks on the opposite side of the valley are as striking as any in the San Juans, where such sublime panoramas are not easily seen in the middle of winter.

By the time the basin is gained, telemarkers will be chomping at the bit, what with such vast quantities of untracked powder waiting on the slopes above. But not so fast—consider the potential for avalanches before proceeding any farther. The slopes above the basin floor are steep enough to slide at almost any point, particularly on the south wall, and once in the basin, there is no place to hide. Assuming the danger for natural and triggered slides is low, continue to climb up the drainage, using the path of least resistance to gain the ridge at the basin's far end. Though the skiing can be challenging, the alpine aura of the setting will have you grinning as you gasp for air.

The ridge, which stands at 12,300 feet, is the tour's destination, and with a superb panorama across the sea of snowy peaks that stretches toward the horizon, consider it the dessert of a gourmet backcountry repast. For expert telemarkers, the feast is just beginning, since hundreds of vertical feet of powder wait to be carved. The slopes of the basin are attractive, but the best terrain is farther north along the ridge. Ski along the crest, head north toward the summit of McMillan Peak, and then contour across its western slope to arrive near the top of a 1,000-foot slope of nearly unbroken white. Though the snow can be a bit wind-crusted in places, it is often ideal as you float back toward treeline. As always, be wary of avalanche terrain (which abounds on these slopes), and remember to respect private-property rights once you arrive at treeline.

The Meadows

THE MEADOWS

DISTANCE: 8.2 miles round-trip, with additional mileage possible

ELEVATION RANGE: 9,350 to 10,150 feet

TOTAL ELEVATION GAIN: 800 feet

TRAIL CONDITIONS: Gently climbing roadbed en route, then across level, open meadows; route-finding could be a problem in the meadows when visibility is low

AVALANCHE HAZARD: Moderate

SKILL LEVEL: Novice to intermediate

SEASON: December through March

USGS MAPS: Mount Wilson (1953); Dolores Peak (1953)

ADMINISTRATION: San Juan NF; Dolores RD

TRAILHEAD: From Rico, drive north on CO 145 for 6.6 miles (or south from Lizard Head Pass for 5.5 miles) until it intersects the unplowed FR 535, which is signed Dunton. Park on the shoulder of the highway at this junction. Space could be tight if there has been a recent heavy snowfall.

Though innocuously named, The Meadows are a fine ski touring destination. The meadows in question sit astride a narrow plateau, which separates the rounded summits of the Rico Mountains from the sharply angled San Miguel Range. This open country offers an extensive touring playground surrounded by many memorable vistas. The roadbed route leading to the meadows can seem long, but its easy grades and pleasant scenery make it an enjoyable experience in its own right.

The moderate avalanche danger comes from the steep open slopes above the route as it ascends the wall of the Dolores River Valley. Though there is little likelihood of a skier-triggered release, be sure to avoid this route when the potential for natural avalanche activity exists. The remainder of the route is easy to follow, and as aspen often shrouds it, makes a good stormy-weather tour. The meadows themselves are best enjoyed on sunny days: The surrounding panorama is one of the primary attractions, but the open terrain has few visible landmarks when fog or blizzard conditions exist.

From the trailhead, ski up the snowbound road as it begins a gentle but steady ascent of the valley's western wall. Except for scattered openings, the route burrows through lovely aspen groves and passes sandstone outcroppings and several small icicle displays. The reddish sandstone in particular adds a strong scenic dimension to the tour, its warm colors adding a rare contrast to the otherwise cold whites, blues, and greens of the winter landscape. This sedimentary strata tilts to the south, toward the heart of the upthrust of rock that created the Rico Mountains.

After 1.5 miles the road makes a sharp switchback and continues to climb. After another 0.25 mile the road turns sharply back to the left, and in short order it turns to the west and enters the narrow valley of Coal Creek, which is 2 miles from the trailhead. Having ascended about 700 feet above the valley floor, most of the tour's elevation has been gained by this point. The next 1.5 miles follow a nearly level contour, stay high on the valley wall, and pass through thick spruce timber—very enjoyable skiing.

After steepening somewhat within the last 0.5 mile, the road turns sharply and breaks into the eastern edge of The Meadows, 4 miles from the trailhead. The view from here is grand, with rolling mountains in all directions, including Dolores Peak and Mount Wilson, which abruptly rear out of a ring of evergreen forest. Roughly 1.5 miles long and 0.5 mile wide, The Meadows are a nearly flat expanse of open terrain that beckon to be explored. While some snowmobile traffic may be expected (the road above the community of Dunton is a popular route), there is plenty of space in which to seek peace and solitude, with good telemarking terrain located on the slopes to the north. Once you have had your fill, simply reski your tracks and enjoy a pleasant descent back into the Dolores River Valley.

Lizard Head Pass

With a unique combination of gentle meadows and precipitous mountain walls, Lizard Head Pass is unrivaled in terms of exquisite, though easily accessible, scenery. Unlike many alpine passes, which are often at the crest of steep ridges, Lizard Head Pass consists of a broad, slightly undulating expanse of meadows almost 3 miles in length. Contrasting with these

LIZARD HEAD PASS

LIZARD HEAD MEADOWS

DISTANCE: Up to 4 miles round-trip

ELEVATION RANGE: 10,000 to 10,200 feet

TOTAL ELEVATION GAIN: 200 feet

TRAIL CONDITIONS: Gently sloping meadows; no obstacles

AVALANCHE HAZARD: None

SKILL LEVEL: Novice

SEASON: Late November through mid-April

USGS MAP: Mount Wilson (1953)

ADMINISTRATION: San Juan NF; Dolores RD

GALLOPING GOOSE TRAIL

DISTANCE: 5 miles round-trip

ELEVATION RANGE: 9,900 to 10,200 feet

TOTAL ELEVATION GAIN: 300 feet

TRAIL CONDITIONS: Abandoned railroad grade with very gentle grades and no obstacles

AVALANCHE HAZARD: Low

SKILL LEVEL: Novice

SEASON: Late November through mid-April

USGS MAPS: Mount Wilson (1953); Ophir (1955)

ADMINISTRATION: Uncompahgre NF; Norwood RD

CROSS MOUNTAIN TRAIL

DISTANCE: 5 miles round-trip

ELEVATION RANGE: 10,000 to 11,800 feet

TOTAL ELEVATION GAIN: 1,800 feet

TRAIL CONDITIONS: Steeper climbing on a snowbound trail; route-finding skills are required

smooth fields are the rugged peaks, which are visible in all directions, particularly the imposing set of summits that soar on the eastern skyline. During winter, the pass is pounded by storm after storm, which funnel in from the southwest to drop tremendous quantities of light, dry powder. This combination of terrain and snow make the pass a superb choice for cross-country skiers of all abilities. Novices will enjoy circuiting through the meadows, while advanced skiers will find ample challenge in one of the routes that climb onto the alpine slopes surrounding the area.

Those making a first attempt at cross-country skiing will find that the meadow atop the pass offers the easiest routes. The terrain here is nearly level, and it's so open that there is no need to worry about obstacles. Plowed parking is available at the summit of the pass, even during snowstorms. There is no avalanche hazard in the immediate vicinity, though its open nature exposes the pass to blustery conditions on stormy days. As far as a particular route is concerned, the meadow is truly "choose your own adventure." Most people ski in a southerly direction from the parking area and stay near the forest on the eastern edge of the meadow. Easy skiing continues for about 2 miles in this direction. The first mile has almost no elevation change, while the second mile, where Snow Spur Creek begins its descent toward the Dolores River, is narrower and more sloping. In all, you'll lose 200 feet of elevation if you ski to the meadow's southern end. Snowmobilers sometimes use the area, which may be a distraction for some, though others will appreciate following their packed routes instead of having to break trail through deep snow.

The scenery throughout the area is beautiful, and when the skies are clear, the surrounding panorama is very impressive. The shining summits of the Rico Mountains rise to the south, high above the forested ridges that ring the Dolores River Canyon. The distinctive spire of Lizard Head, as well as other peaks to the west of the pass in the San Miguel Range, can be admired from the southern end of the meadow. Perhaps the most impressive vista is that to the north, where Yellow Mountain, Pilot Knob, the Golden Horn, and Vermillion Peak loom as if they were a jagged wall.

Another option for skiing in the vicinity of the pass is to follow the route of the Galloping Goose Trail from the summit down to the old wooden trestle across the Lake Fork of the San Miguel River. The route is easily followed, and with an elevation change of only 300 feet over 2.5 miles (each way), it is also suitable for novice skiers. Skiers who start from the pass will descend in elevation on the outbound portion of the tour and make the ascent on their return. If you find this to be less than ideal, you can drive to the trestle, ski uphill to the pass, and return with a downhill coast. To locate this trailhead, drive north from the summit of Lizard Head Pass and turn right onto North Trout Lake Road after about 2 miles. Drive down this normally snowpacked road for 1.9 miles and park adjacent to the trestle. Parking is extremely limited here; be sure not to block the nearby driveway.

The Galloping Goose Trail follows the route of the Rio Grande Southern Railroad, which was abandoned in 1952. Today, the route offers an

AVALANCHE HAZARD: Low below treeline, high above
SKILL LEVEL: Intermediate
SEASON: Late November through April
USGS MAP: Mount Wilson (1953)
ADMINISTRATION: San Juan NF; Dolores RD

TRAILHEADS: Lizard Head Pass parking area, which is 12 miles south of Telluride on CO 145, or the Cross Mountain Trailhead, which is 2.2 miles south of the summit of Lizard Head Pass. The Cross Mountain Trailhead is often unplowed until a day or two after a heavy snowfall, so be prepared to dig out a parking spot.

❧❧❧

exceptionally peaceful and scenic look at the country once traversed by steam locomotives on a daily basis. Starting from the summit of Lizard Head Pass, ski directly east for a few yards until you reach the obvious railroad grade that bears to the north. The first mile of the trail circles around the edge of a large meadow, where views of the distant Sneffels Range and the nearer slopes of Yellow Mountain are outstanding. Soon, the route turns to the east and descends across a slope covered by subalpine conifers and a smattering of aspen, all the while maintaining the steady 3 percent grade typical of a railroad. The nearly vertical north face of Sheep Mountain towers high above, presenting a form strongly reminiscent of peaks in the Canadian Rockies.

In a couple of places, the slope above the trail is bare and is possibly steep enough to slide when the avalanche hazard is extremely high. Though this is rare, use caution. Otherwise, the trail is typically more sheltered from windy conditions than the meadow atop the pass, making this route a better choice when the weather is poor. The tour ends when you reach the trestle, which is the last intact trestle of the many for which the Rio Grande was famous. It is obviously rickety and should not be walked or skied upon under any circumstances. Instead, stay on the new roadbed and admire this unique piece of history from the various angles it affords. Perhaps it will only be a few more years before the cumulative weight of a hundred winters' snows bring this one crashing down as well.

More advanced skiers could create any number of interesting tours in the vicinity of Lizard Head Pass. One of the most popular and interesting is to follow the general route of the Cross Mountain Trail into the Lizard Head Wilderness, where it eventually climbs above treeline and affords superb views of the San Miguel Range. Route-finding can be difficult, and there is high avalanche hazard once treeline is reached. The trail climbs steadily, and since it is often necessary to break trail through the latest snowfall, this tour can be quite strenuous. Furthermore, the rapid descent through thick forest on the return requires that you be able to control your skiing. This tour is not a good choice on stormy days, as high winds are common and limited visibility can cause even the experienced to become lost.

This tour starts from the Cross Mountain Trailhead, which is 2.2 miles south of the summit of Lizard Head Pass. The small parking area is often not plowed until a day or two after a snowstorm, so it may be necessary to

188

shovel out a parking spot. From the road, ski directly west toward the gully that is visible ahead. The trailhead signs, which are a few hundred yards from the highway, may not be visible above the snowpack. Climb onto the bank on the left side of the gully and climb gradually for less than 0.25 mile until reaching the bottom of a long meadow, which stretches up the slope to the left. Ski directly up this meadow until reaching the forest at its upper end. Just before entering the trees, turn sharply right and you should be able to see the trail right-of-way slicing into the forest. A second meadow is located 0.25 mile beyond the first. This time the trail skirts it to the left, so resist the urge to ski into its open expanse.

From this point on, the route should be easy to follow until you reach treeline. This portion of the trail is actually a long-abandoned logging road, and buried somewhere beneath the snow is the remains of an old sawmill. The grade is moderately steep and relentless, and it remains so throughout most of the tour. The trail officially enters the wilderness about 1.5 miles from the highway, though the sign may be buried beneath the snow. About 0.5 mile farther, the ascent eases temporarily as the trail enters a clearing, and the Lizard Head returns to view. Another 0.5 mile brings you to the actual timberline and the scenic reward for your journey: a view of the Lizard Head (named by early visitors who thought they saw a reptilian profile in the rock), Mount Wilson, and many other rugged peaks.

Though the views become more impressive as you climb higher, the avalanche hazard increases. If you choose to continue, do a snow-pit analysis first to determine the condition of the snowpack, as triggered avalanches are possible throughout the area. If it is safe, leave the route of the trail, which passes beneath the dangerous slopes of Point 12038, and ski farther west, where the slopes are gentler.

Sunshine Mesa

Extensive stands of mature aspen surrounded by exceptionally photogenic peaks make skiing on Sunshine Mesa a highly recommended winter experience. Deep snows bury the narrow road that leads to the mesa's rolling summit, which leaves skiers and snowshoers to enjoy both beautiful forests and majestic mountain panoramas in relative seclusion from the bustle at the nearby Telluride Ski Resort. Indeed, this route is only lightly traveled during

SUNSHINE MESA

DISTANCE: 3.5 miles round-trip

ELEVATION RANGE: 9,050 to 9,750 feet

TOTAL ELEVATION GAIN: 700 feet

TRAIL CONDITIONS: Steady, moderate grades on a snowbound roadbed

AVALANCHE HAZARD: None

SKILL LEVEL: Intermediate

SEASON: December through mid-April

USGS MAP: Gray Head (1953)

ADMINISTRATION: Uncompahgre NF; Norwood RD

TRAILHEAD: From the junction of CO 145 and CO 145 Spur just west of Telluride, drive west toward Placerville and turn left onto South Fork Road (signed Ilium) after 2.6 miles. Drive south on this road for 2.1 miles and turn right on Sunshine Mesa Road. Follow this road for 3.7 miles, then park at a small plowed area just outside a ranch entrance. The final 1.5 miles of Sunshine Mesa Road are steep and are usually icy and snowpacked. A four-wheel-drive vehicle with good snow tires or a car with chains will often be required to negotiate this road.

the winter months, owing in part to a previous lack of promotion as well as the somewhat white-knuckle drive to the trailhead. All the better, for the opportunity to experience solitude in such a scenic place is ample reward for the effort expended to access it.

Though named for the nearby peak rather than any climatic condition, Sunshine is an apt name for the mesa since it receives direct sunlight for most of the day. Because of this, the local climate is rarely bitterly cold, and with its moderate elevation, winds are typically light. With no avalanche hazard to be encountered, the mesa is a good destination on most winter days. One caveat is that the access road to the trailhead should be avoided during heavy snowfalls. The final 1.5 miles are steep and windy, and plowing is not usually done until such storms have dissipated. Even after plows have cleared the road, it is almost always snowpacked and often icy. A four-wheel-drive vehicle with good snow tires or a car with chains will most likely be required to safely reach the trailhead.

A long, flat-topped ridge that runs north from the San Miguel Range, Sunshine Mesa separates the waters of Bilk Creek from those of the south fork of the San Miguel River. The trailhead is situated on a small bench, about halfway up the mesa's eastern flank. From here, the tour follows the route of the snowbound upper portion of Sunshine Mesa Road, climbing steadily but not too steeply toward the top. Even within the first few feet, the view is incredible, as the craggy ridges of Palmyra Peak guard the eastern skyline while the high peaks of the Sneffels Range form a great wall to the north. A short distance from the trailhead, the road bends to the right, away from the entrance to another private ranch, and enters the dense aspen grove that covers the upper half of the mesa.

Aspen thrive in moist areas where temperatures are cool and there is an abundance of sunlight. The San Juans, which have a slightly moister climate and a longer growing season than other parts of the Rockies, feature some of the most extensive groves in the state. Though they occasionally form stable, multigenerational communities, aspen are more often just one step in the process of forest succession. Because they require direct sunlight, aspen are often the first tree

Patterns of light and shadow in a snowy aspen forest.

species to regenerate an area denuded by fire or avalanche. As the aspen grow, they shade greater portions of the forest floor, thus creating ideal conditions for the growth of conifers. As the conifers grow, they eventually create shadier conditions than the aspen can tolerate, thus the conifers become the dominant species once again. Eventually, fire or avalanche may destroy the conifer forest once more, and the process will repeat itself. The scattered presence of Engelmann spruce and subalpine fir demonstrates that forest succession does occur on Sunshine Mesa. It's a slow process, though—it may take as long as another one hundred fifty years for the conifers to become dominant in this forest.

The ecology of the aspen community is likely to be far from your mind as you ski through the forest; however, the beauty of these trees is hard to forget. Famous for their shimmering display of autumn gold, aspen are equally glorious in winter. The fall of sunlight through a dense grove creating artistic shadow patterns across the virgin snowpack, the texture of fresh snow on bare branches, and the glow of white aspen boles against a sapphire sky are but a few of the visual treasures to be appreciated in this most entrancing of Rocky Mountain forests.

The only place where the route may be confusing is about 0.5 mile from the trailhead, where a second road forks to the right. Stay to the left here and pass the Forest Service boundary signs that should be visible except in years of particularly deep snowpack. Another 0.75 mile of steady climbing brings you to a sharp switchback adjacent to a small pond. Another switchback within the next 0.25 mile leads you to the crest of the mesa, where the aspen forest gives way to meadow and a fascinating old homestead.

The site these homesteaders chose for their ranch is certainly scenic enough. Beyond the meadow and its blanket of glistening snow stand the majestic bastions of the San Miguel Range, including Sunshine Mountain and Wilson Peak. Imagine being able to gaze out your window each morning to watch the first rays of sunlight paint these peaks in a succession of pink, orange, and gold. Should you tire of this panorama, you could always look back to the north to admire the precipitous Sneffels Range, or east toward Palmyra Peak. Though the ranch house has been long abandoned and is in rapidly deteriorating condition, it is obvious that care and expense went into building it; notice the detail around the window frames. Several other buildings are scattered about the meadow, each of them built of hewn logs and each in poor condition. These buildings are private property—admire them, but do not enter or vandalize them.

The tour ends at this homestead, but extensions are possible. One option is to follow the meadows along the top of the mesa toward their western edge above Bilk Creek. By skiing to the far end of these meadows, you add about 1.5 miles (round-trip) to your excursion, but you are rewarded with an impressive view into Bilk Basin. A second option is to ski the forest-lined road that continues toward the Bilk Creek drainage; if you do so, be sure to turn back before entering this avalanche-prone area. A third possibility is to ski to the crest of one of the nearby hills in order to enjoy an aspen-lined telemark descent. Be aware that much of the land in this area is privately owned—please respect the owners' wishes by not trespassing. An alternate return to the trailhead for advanced skiers is to pursue a direct fall-line route through the dense aspen forest; otherwise, retrace your tracks and beware of the sharp corners.

East Dallas Creek

Draining directly from the towering spire of Mount Sneffels, East Dallas Creek flows northward through forests of spruce, fir, aspen, and juniper, which sweep down from the massive wall of peaks that make up the Sneffels Range. This country easily ranks among the most scenic in the West, and the ski tour up the creek's narrow valley is the best and easiest winter access into this stunning landscape. If that weren't enough, this tour provides access to Blue Lakes Hut, the most easily obtainable backcountry shelter in the spectacular San Juan Hut System. As either a base camp or a single stop on a continuing circuit, the hut allows reasonable access to some tremendous skiing terrain.

Though the glory of the tour comes from the grand vistas enjoyed en route, the valley's low elevation makes this one of the better stormy-day tours in the western San Juans. The route is easy to follow, and the one area of potential avalanche hazard is easily avoided. On warmer days, the snow conditions encountered in the first few miles can be mushy; however, the snowpack is generally deep throughout the winter season.

If at all possible, try to reserve a night at Blue Lakes Hut, which is about a mile beyond the end of this tour. The experience of overnighting deep in the winter wilderness is an unforgettable one, and while the accommodations are rustic, they are quite comfortable. Sleeping eight, the hut comes equipped with a wood-burning stove, propane cook stove, a complete set of cookware and utensils, lanterns, and foam pads. Blue Lakes Hut is located at the midpoint of a 28-mile, five-hut circuit across the western and northern flanks of the Sneffels Range. The routes between

---

EAST DALLAS CREEK

DISTANCE: 8 miles round-trip

ELEVATION RANGE: 8,200 to 9,150 feet

TOTAL ELEVATION GAIN: 950 feet

TRAIL CONDITIONS: Steady but overall gentle ascent of an unplowed road; snow can be mushy near the trailhead

AVALANCHE HAZARD: Low

SKILL LEVEL: Novice to intermediate

SEASON: December through March

USGS MAP: Mount Sneffels (1967)

ADMINISTRATION: Uncompahgre NF; Ouray RD

TRAILHEAD: From Ridgway, drive west on CO 62 for 4.9 miles and turn left onto Dallas Creek Road (CR 7). Follow this sometimes-muddy road for a total of 4.1 miles and follow the signs for the Uncompahgre NF access. Park where winter maintenance ends; there is space for several cars.

❀❀❀

the huts, which are spaced anywhere from 4 to 7 miles apart, are often challenging, and they should only be attempted by strong intermediate or advanced skiers. As with Blue Lakes Hut, most of the other shelters are
directly accessible via somewhat long but generally easier tours. Reservations are required, and as the system is becoming increasingly popular, it is
recommended that they be made well in advance—several months ahead if
you plan a weekend stay. Contact the San Juan Hut System at: P.O. Box
1663, Telluride, CO 81435; (970) 728-6935.

The route climbs at a very steady grade for the first 3 miles as the
snowbound road winds along the side of East Dallas Creek's narrow valley.
Until you reach the Uncompahgre National Forest boundary at mile 3.25,
the land surrounding the road is privately owned, so avoid wandering until
you enter public land. The initial 2 miles cross the upper fringe of the
pinon–juniper woodland ecosystem, which is common on the San Juans'
lower slopes. Typically, the snowpack is marginal at such elevations; however,
there always seems to be plenty of powder in this valley. The sight of snow-
covered juniper, Gambel oak, and ponderosa pine is pleasant, and while only
a portion of the Sneffels Range can be seen from here, it sets the stage for
the panorama to come.

As the East Dallas Creek valley bends toward the southeast, aspen become the predominant forest species. With this turn, more of the mountain
wall—dominated by the distinctive crest of Mount Sneffels—comes into
view. At the 2.5-mile mark, the road passes a gate and climbs a small rise to
arrive at a spectacular, unobstructed view of the Sneffels Range. Superlatives
just don't do these peaks justice. Lined up like the front line of an advancing
army of snow and rock, this panorama rivals any other in terms of sheer
awe-inspiring drama.

The flat, open expanse of the East Dallas Creek valley spreads before
you as you continue on the roadbed for another 0.5 mile, contouring above
the long, skinny meadow known as Willow Swamp. Once you reach the
forest boundary, you may choose to continue ahead on the road or drop
into the meadow. The road remains fringed by forest and shortly crosses the
bottom of a slope steep enough to present some avalanche hazard. The open
meadow is beyond the reach of any snowslides and offers an unimpeded
vista. The choice should be easy.

About 0.75 mile beyond the forest boundary, the little valley tapers to
an end, and the road crosses the creek just before it begins to climb into the

creek's narrowing ravine. The creek crossing is a suitable end point for the single-day tour, as the combination of snowy subalpine forest, jagged mountains, and rushing water create a scenic climax that is as great as any in the surrounding area. If you are staying at the hut, continue along the roadbed, which ascends more steadily for another mile. When the road enters a small glade and begins to curve up the western valley wall, you should be able to spy the shelter sitting atop a small knoll. While you are only 5.2 miles from your vehicle, this lonely little hut seems thousands of miles away from civilization. For many, this feeling of solitude is the ultimate reward.

Ironton Park/Red Mountain Nordic System

The inclusion of the Ironton Park/Red Mountain Nordic System ski routes is a bit out of character for this guide. While most of the tours described in this book are longer backcountry routes, this system includes several short, sometimes-groomed tracks through gentle terrain. The area is worthy of special consideration, though, as it features outstanding scenery in addition to a high degree of historical interest. The Ouray County Nordic Council (OCNC), a local organization that strives to provide quality cross-country skiing routes, maintains the trails. The OCNC has created this system with the cooperation of private landowners as well as several government agencies. Use of the area is free (though donations are appreciated), and the tracks are an ideal place for first-time skiers as well as anyone seeking a few hours of worry-free recreation.

One of the nicest features of this trail system is that it presents very few dangers—as long as you stay on the marked routes. There are no areas of avalanche hazard and no particular route-finding difficulties. Snowmobiles are prohibited on the trail system, and, in general, most of these trails can be skied in poor weather. The danger increases substantially if you ski off the marked routes. Not only would you be trespassing on private land (and thus be jeopardizing the continued use of these trails by the public), you could also be risking injury from the numerous abandoned mines and equipment found throughout the area. The OCNC also requests that you leave pets at home.

The trails that radiate from the Ironton Park Trailhead are the easiest and most popular routes in the system. Of these, the Townsite Loop is a

IRONTON PARK/ RED MOUNTAIN NORDIC SYSTEM

TOWNSITE LOOP

DISTANCE: 2 miles round-trip

ELEVATION: 9,700 feet

TRAIL CONDITIONS: Groomed ski track; flat terrain

AVALANCHE HAZARD: None

SKILL LEVEL: Novice

SEASON: December through mid-April

USGS MAP: Ironton (1955)

ADMINISTRATION: Ouray County Nordic Council

SILVER BELLE AND COLORADO BOY LOOP

DISTANCE: Approximately 1.5 miles round-trip

ELEVATION RANGE: 9,900 to 10,100 feet

TOTAL ELEVATION GAIN: 250 feet

TRAIL CONDITIONS: Ungroomed route across undulating terrain

AVALANCHE HAZARD: None

SKILL LEVEL: Novice to intermediate

SEASON: December through mid-April

USGS MAP: Ironton (1955)

ADMINISTRATION: Ouray County Nordic Council

IRONTON PARK TRAILHEAD: From Ouray, drive south on US 550 for 8 miles and turn left into a large plowed parking area.

SILVER BELLE TRAILHEAD: Travel on US 550 for 1.1 miles south of the Ironton Park Trailhead. Park in the large pullout on the east side of the road, near the small Silver Belle Trailhead sign.

❀❀❀

particularly enjoyable tour. The 2-mile loop winds through open meadows and sparse forest before it turns down what was once the main street of Ironton, which has been long abandoned. The OCNC maintains set track on this loop, and with little elevation change, this trail is a logical choice for first-timers. Snowshoers may use this trail, but please avoid walking in the ski tracks.

Pick up a trail brochure from the trailhead information board, then ski eastward parallel to the edge of the Idarado Mine's massive tailings—piles of worthless rock removed from the mine. The Idarado, which is the large complex adjacent to US 550 a few miles farther up valley, was one of the last operating mines in the San Juans. Operations ended in the early 1990s, though environmental cleanup is ongoing. Upon reaching the east edge of the valley, the track curves to the south and continues past the divergence of the North Pipeline route. For the next mile, the level track meanders through upper Ironton Park. The flat expanse of the park (in this case, *park* is used to describe a large meadow or grassy valley surrounded by mountains) seems out of place in this world of deep gorges and towering peaks. It was created at the end of the last Ice Age, when sediment-laden streams filled the bed of a shallow lake. Considering the surrounding panorama of beautiful peaks, it's easy to imagine what a spectacular lake it must have been.

Prior to the town site, a bridge across Red Mountain Creek makes a 1.2-mile version of the loop possible; however, this shortcut does not allow you to explore Ironton's remains. Continuing on the main route, the track crosses Red Mountain Creek 0.3 mile farther south and comes to a junction. The left branch continues southward, parallel to the creek, in order to tie into routes from the Silver Belle Trailhead. The right fork turns down Ironton's old main street and soon enters "town."

Ironton was one of the larger towns in the fantastically

A quiet day at the ghost town of Ironton.

rich Red Mountain mining district. Founded in 1883, the community had more than three hundred residents, and during its peak it boasted a post office, municipal water system, electric plant, and fire station. The town was an important supply center for the surrounding area and served as the northern terminus of the Silverton Railroad. The boom was short-lived, however, and as mining waned in the early years of the twentieth century, most residents moved on until only a handful of people remained. By the 1960s the town was abandoned. While many of the town's buildings have disappeared, several remain standing—albeit in various stages of decay. Admire the exteriors of these buildings, but please do not enter them. To complete the loop, simply continue skiing northward and follow the flat, straight track until you reach the trailhead.

The southern end of the Nordic System is accessible via the Silver Belle Trailhead, which is 1 mile south of the Ironton Park Trailhead. As equally scenic as those farther north, the trails here are somewhat more difficult and lack a set track. One of the best circuits combines the Silver Belle

Trail with the Colorado Boy Loop to create a fine 1.5-mile tour. Begin by skiing south from the trailhead sign and parallel to the old power line. After perhaps 100 yards, bear to the left and drop down to a bridge over Red Mountain Creek. Once across the stream, curve back to the north, climb steadily onto a small bench above the creek, and you'll soon reach the site of the Silver Belle Mine. The Silver Belle, which produced more than $1 million in silver ore, featured a shaft more than 700 feet deep. No surface buildings remain at the mine, and its large collection of tailings piles are hidden beneath the sparkling snow.

The tour continues onto the Colorado Boy Loop from the site of the Silver Belle. The loop, which winds through a mixture of forest and meadow on the slopes east of Red Mountain Creek, can be skied in either direction. Blue diamonds mark the route, which features marvelous vistas of the surrounding peaks. Upon closing the loop, either return to the trailhead via the Silver Belle Trail or explore the South Pipeline route as far as the edge of Corkscrew Gulch.

Cottonwood Gulch

Cottonwood Gulch is a fearsome-looking gorge that is tucked beneath the looming peaks near the headwaters of the Lake Fork River. Its rims barely a mile apart, the canyon has been cut to depths exceeding 3,500 feet. Nearly vertical walls sculpted from thick layers of volcanic rock present mighty cliffs broken only by a scattering of trees and numerous frozen waterfalls. An enjoyable yet little-known tour traverses this Yosemite-like setting. Meandering through groves of aspen and spruce, into small glades, and past massive boulders, the valley-floor route permits dramatic views of the surrounding cliffs and peaks. Seekers of solitude will find the gulch especially pleasing.

The tour traces the route of a snowbound four-wheel-drive route parallel to Cottonwood Creek. Because of the consistent grades as well as the variable snow conditions, this tour is more suitable for skiers of at least intermediate ability. Ranging from sun-crust to perfect powder, these variable snow conditions are largely the result of the widely varying temperatures that often occur in the canyon. Near its mouth, direct sunlight creates mushy snow, which often freezes into a thin crust atop a layer of "depth hoar." In such conditions, travel can be slow and tiring. Elsewhere in the canyon, the tremendously high and steep walls shade the canyon floor throughout the winter months. In such places, the cold temperatures help to produce the type of snow perfect for skiing. Further conspiring against novices, the canyon route is so lightly used that skiers are typically forced to break their own trail.

A number of avalanche paths are located in the canyon, and their run-out zones sometimes spread across its floor. Because the steep canyon walls prohibit significant snow accumulation, slides are typically less frequent here than in other San Juan valleys. The greatest danger exists after storms leave enough new snow to fuel slides. At such times, when the danger for natural avalanche activity is rated high, this tour should be avoided. At other times, be sure to use safe travel tech-

COTTONWOOD GULCH

DISTANCE: 6.6 miles round-trip

ELEVATION RANGE: 9,600 to 10,700 feet

TOTAL ELEVATION GAIN: 1,100 feet

TRAIL CONDITIONS: Snowbound road with moderate grades; variable snow conditions

AVALANCHE HAZARD: Moderate

SKILL LEVEL: Intermediate

SEASON: December through mid-April

USGS MAP: Redcloud Peak (1964)

ADMINISTRATION: BLM; Gunnison RA

TRAILHEAD: From Lake City, drive south on CO 149 for 2.3 miles and turn right onto the road signed Lake San Cristobal and Alpine Loop Scenic Byway. Drive on this road (which turns to gravel after 4 miles) a total of 13.1 miles from the highway, and park at the Cataract Lake Trailhead. The latter half of this road is usually icy and snowpacked.

niques when crossing avalanche-hazard areas. The other weather phenomena for which you should be prepared is the often bitterly cold temperatures that occur in the shaded portions of the canyon. Not only is there no solar energy to warm the surrounding air, cold air often spills from the surrounding peaks and pools in the canyon bottom. In short: dress warmly.

From the trailhead, the snowbound road continues into the confines of the impressive gorge. For the first 0.5 mile or so, the deep incision of Cataract Gulch to the south allows the sun to leak into the otherwise shaded valley. The result is the sometimes-difficult snow conditions described above. While you'll soon miss the warmth of the sun, the snow conditions improve dramatically once the sun becomes hidden behind the canyon's wall.

The grade eases somewhat as the walls close in even further, and then it continues to ascend in a stair-step fashion. The first of the avalanche paths is located on the left side of the canyon, though it rarely deposits snow as far as the road. Numerous frozen falls cling to the ravine's rocky face, while the mixture of meadow, aspen, and spruce keep the scenery varied and interesting. Your neck can easily become cramped as you gaze at the immense buttresses lining the gorge, and it may come as a surprise that the south-facing cliffs are often bare of snow—such is the intensity of the sun at this latitude and elevation. These towering cliffs block the sun from reaching the road, however, and the crispness of the snow is matched by the crispness of the air. The skiing and the scenery continue in much the same manner for the next few miles.

Geologists have determined that many of the deep valleys and canyons in this corner of the San Juans match the edges of great calderas formed during the height of the region's volcanic history. When violent eruptions emptied their magma chambers, many of the San Juans' volcanoes collapsed into massive depressions, much like what happened at Oregon's Crater Lake. Though continuous volcanic activity filled the calderas with debris thousands of feet deep, the caldera rims remained weak zones that were exploited by stream and glacier erosion to form these canyons. If you trace the valleys of the Lake Fork River and Henson Creek on a large-scale map, it is easy to identify the elliptical shape of one such caldera. It is likely that Cottonwood Gulch follows either another caldera rim or an associated fracture.

The mouth of Boulder Gulch is about 2.5 miles from the trailhead. Beyond this landmark, the valley floor opens somewhat, and direct afternoon sunlight makes a welcome return. The willow flats and beaver ponds of summer are usually deeply buried beneath the snow, making the area easy to traverse. While there is little chance of a skier-triggered avalanche, the run-out zones of canyon-wall slide paths become larger and more numerous. Such is the terrain as far as the mouth of Cuba Gulch, which is about 0.75 mile above Boulder Gulch. The tour ends at this point, as the gentle valley floor ends in a barricade of mountain flanks and steep ravines.

When spring snowpack consolidation reduces the high avalanche hazard, experienced telemarkers may wish to explore the upper reaches of Cottonwood Gulch in search of potentially exciting terrain. The mountainsides are steep and forested on much of their lower flanks, so the routes are not easy; however, a decent snowpack can usually be expected until sometime in June. Of particular interest are the more rolling slopes found near the Continental Divide at the head of Cuba Gulch. Though the hazard may be reduced during spring, the potential for avalanches is there all the same, so exercise prudence if you choose to tackle this terrain.

Rambouillet Park

Few San Juan ski tours offer the variety of terrain and scenery found on the various routes to Rambouillet Park. Enjoying a gentle, stream-side glide; rocketing down a steep, twisting ravine; inching across a vast, open park; traversing a long alpine ridge—this is all possible in this scenic area. Further separating Rambouillet Park from the ranks of the average is the existence of an extensive yurt system—the Hinsdale Haute Route. By utilizing these basic but comfortable backcountry shelters, a fine day of skiing can be turned into a memorable weekend—or week—of winter adventure.

Rambouillet (pronounced RAM-bow-lay) Park is part of the undulating plateau country that separates the La Garita Range from the craggier heart of the San Juans. The park lies on the east side of a broad ridge that veers north from the Continental Divide. While the slopes west of this ridge drop steeply in the Lake Fork Valley, the east flank slopes more gently and is broken by a series of shallow ravines that form the headwaters of Cebolla Creek. One of the more enjoyable

RAMBOUILLET PARK

CEBOLLA CREEK LOOP

DISTANCE: 9 miles round-trip

ELEVATION RANGE: 10,450 to 11,700 feet

TOTAL ELEVATION GAIN: 1,250 feet

TRAIL CONDITIONS: The ascent to and descent from the park utilize a pair of ravines, while the park itself is a broad, gently sloped meadow. Grades are gentle to moderate, though the descent is steep in places. A part of the Hinsdale Haute Route, much of the route is regularly traveled and often marked with wands. Route-finding in the park itself could be difficult when visibility is low.

AVALANCHE HAZARD: Moderate

SKILL LEVEL: Intermediate

SEASON: Late November through mid-April

USGS MAP: Slumgullion Pass (1986)

ADMINISTRATION: Gunnison NF; Cebolla RD

SLUMGULLION POINT

DISTANCE: 7 miles round-trip

ELEVATION RANGE: 11,500 to 12,200 feet

TOTAL ELEVATION GAIN: 1,200 feet

TRAIL CONDITIONS: The unmarked route traverses an alpine ridge, with significant wind exposure. Grades are moderate, but there is quite a bit of up-and-down travel. Avoid this route during stormy weather.

AVALANCHE HAZARD: Moderate

SKILL LEVEL: Intermediate to advanced

SEASON: Late November through mid-April

USGS Map: Slumgullion Pass (1986)
Administration: Gunnison NF;
Cebolla RD

Cebolla Creek Access: From Lake City, drive south on CO 149 for 14.5 miles (2.4 miles north of Spring Creek Pass) until you reach a pair of plowed pullouts on either side of Cebolla Creek. The trail starts from the parking area on the creek's south side.

Slumgullion Pass Access: This trailhead is located where CO 149 crosses Slumgullion Pass, about 10.6 miles south of Lake City or 6.3 miles north of Spring Creek Pass. A large parking area is available at the summit and is adjacent to a large snow stake. Coming from Lake City, a sign that marks the pass is located at least 0.25 mile prior to the parking area.

tours in this vicinity ascends the west fork of Cebolla Creek, crosses the heart of the park, and descends to create a sizable loop. Skiers who can handle the moderately steep terrain will enjoy forests, open meadows, and fine views throughout much of the route. This tour provides the primary access to both the Jon Wilson and Rambouillet Yurts, the first two shelters in the Hinsdale Haute Route's four-yurt system. A very scenic "highline" tour is possible if you start at Slumgullion (slum-GUL-yun) Pass and traverse the crest of the ridge above Rambouillet Park. The terrain is interesting, though it is the vast panorama of saw-toothed peaks that make the route superlative. Additionally, telemarkers can use the ridge to gain access to a series of shallow bowls. If there is a strike against Rambouillet Park, it is its popularity with snowmobilers (a maintained snowmobile route winds through it); however, the Cebolla Creek drainage is off-limits to the machines, and the ridge-line route is infrequently buzzed.

With such varied terrain, a wide range of weather, snow, and avalanche conditions can be expected in this area. When skiing the Cebolla Creek Loop, you'll usually find good snow and calm weather in the lower portions of either ravine, though frequent gusty winds can create areas of crust in the upper half of either drainage. In the open meadows of the park, the snow is usually very good, though it can be breezy here, as well. When whiteout conditions occur, route-finding in the park can be very difficult, and the skiing treacherous. Though generally infrequent, avalanches are possible in several areas of the loop in Cebolla Creek. The upper half of the west fork ravine has steep, open slopes that could be prone to slides, while the same hazard exists in the parallel ravine to a slightly lesser degree. When a natural avalanche cycle is forecast for the eastern San Juans, it is best to avoid these gullies. At other times, triggered slides are only possible if you stray from the primary route, but still be cautious. The ridge traverse, which crosses a knob known as Slumgullion Point, should be reserved for days of calm weather. Obscured visibility and high winds make for treacherous travel conditions on this exposed ridge. While the snow is often deep, it varies from pillowy soft to hard crust, with some areas swept bare by the persistent winds. You can avoid avalanche terrain if you stay on the ridge crest; however, the slopes below—so inviting for telemarking—are wind-loaded almost daily and are often steep enough to present a serious hazard. Careful route selection is mandatory.

While either route is an excellent single-day tour, staying a night or two in one of the yurts is highly recommended. The yurts, which are modeled after the traditional shelters of Mongolian nomads, are large canvas structures that rest on top of wooden platforms. Clear plastic panels serve as windows and skylights, which make the yurt a bright, airy place to relax while allowing a great deal of passive solar heating. Each yurt, which sleeps up to eight, is equipped with a wood-burning stove for heat, a propane stove for cooking, all kitchen utensils, lanterns, sleeping pads, and bunks. The Jon Wilson Yurt is the easiest to reach; at only 1.75 miles from the Cebolla Creek Trailhead, it is accessible to even novice skiers. The Rambouillet Yurt is more isolated, though stronger parties can reach it from either trailhead in about three hours. The Colorado Trail Friends Yurt, which is spectacularly situated atop the Continental Divide, and the Fawn Lakes Yurt are true backcountry shelters, and skiing to either requires advanced skills, careful preparation, and a multiday investment of time. For information and reservations, contact the Hinsdale Haute Route at P.O. Box 771, Lake City, CO 81235; (970) 944-2269.

The Cebolla Creek Loop initially follows Cebolla Creek upstream from CO 149. The first few miles to the Jon Wilson Yurt is likely to be well packed and easily followed. Indeed, this section, which crosses the creek several times via small bridges, is an enjoyable tour for skiers of all abilities during all weather conditions. It winds through subalpine forest, across willow flats, and passes several interesting rock walls. The creek is usually free-flowing by early March, and its musical descent enlivens the scenery.

After about 1.5 miles the ravine splits; keep to the left and begin to ascend the west fork of Cebolla Creek. After you pass the Jon Wilson Yurt after 0.3 mile, the drainage narrows, and the existence of the packed trail becomes less predictable. Stay on the floor of the ravine as it twists and turns in a westerly direction. The grade is quite reasonable, while the scenery is peaceful. Patches of forest decorate the ravine walls, leaving broad, open slopes to divert the attention of turn-seekers, though the avalanche hazard should be considered before climbing these slopes.

Two miles above the Jon Wilson Yurt, the ravine flattens as it enters the southern end of Rambouillet Park. Ski past a small gully on the north, and continue directly west for another 0.5 mile until you reach a second north-trending drainage. Skiers with a reservation at the Rambouillet Yurt will find it tucked behind a line of trees 0.25 mile directly northwest of this point. Otherwise, turn north here and ski directly toward the lightly forested knob of Slumgullion Point to reach the flat portion of the park. The groomed snowmobile route, well packed and marked by orange wands, is intercepted at this point, and it can be followed to the head of the return route in the ravine if you don't desire to break your own track. (Actually, snowmobile tracks are likely to vector in all directions throughout the park, so they can be utilized when you come across them.) While their noise can be annoying, keep in mind that the park has been popular with snowmobilers much longer than it has with skiers.

As you traverse the park in a northeasterly direction, you'll enjoy nice views of the La Garitas and the adjacent mass of Snow Mesa, with the distant line of the Weminuche Wilderness section of the Continental Divide visible far to the south. If time and energy allow, climb to the ridge to the west to gain an eye-filling panorama of the San Juans' most rugged corner, which includes Uncompahgre Peak and the Wetterhorn. Otherwise, continue across the meadows for about 1.5 miles, until another ravine begins an easterly descent out of the park. Turn down this ravine and begin a fairly steep descent. This narrow gully—made narrower by an occasional patch of forest—fairly plummets off the plateau in places. If you can maintain control, this ravine is great fun—it's akin to an intermediate slope at a downhill area. However, if you question your ability to stay in control, return via the much gentler West Fork. After a very quick 1.5 miles, the ravine joins with a small tributary from the north and flattens considerably. Another 0.25 mile returns you to the West Fork confluence. Turn left here and retrace the original 1.5 miles to gain the trailhead.

The Slumgullion Point route is straightforward, and it's perhaps the easiest winter alpine traverse in the San Juans. From the parking area at

Slumgullion Pass, ski into the dense subalpine forest on the south side of the highway and pass a snowpack-measuring stake on the left. Continue south/southwest and climb steadily along the broad crest of the ridge, quickly pass a larger monitoring station, and follow the occasional marker until you reach treeline after about 0.5 mile. From this point, simply stay on the undulating crest and enjoy the magnificent vistas.

A mile from the trailhead is Point 12047, which can either be directly crossed or skirted to the east. After you descend from this point and cross a smaller rise 0.5 mile farther, a choice of routes presents itself. Either stay on the ridge and climb gradually to gain the summit of Slumgullion Point, a total of 3 miles from the trailhead, or drop down a shallow bowl into Rambouillet Park. Once in the park, you may ski in almost any direction or head directly to the Rambouillet Yurt, if that is your destination. You can either make the summit of Slumgullion Point the tour's turnaround point or continue west along the ridge until reaching the top of a large, shallow bowl. Descend through this bowl, then traverse beneath Slumgullion Point to enter Rambouillet Park. Traverse northeast across the park, then climb back onto the ridge to close an enjoyable loop. From here, simply retrace your original tracks back to the trailhead.

Snow Mesa

One of the most unique topographic features in the San Juans, Snow Mesa is a massive, nearly level plateau that sits adjacent to the La Garita Range. Its smooth summit extends for more than 20 square miles, while its average elevation exceeds 12,000 feet. As the name suggests, the mesa is an ideal place for skiing, and as one might suspect, the scenery from this alpine platform is stunning. Perhaps Snow Mesa's most attractive quality is its sense of vastness. Though it may sound far-fetched, Snow Mesa's wide openness can be compared to the emptiness of Antarctica. The immense and unbroken field of wind-blown snow stretches to a seemingly endless panorama of distant peaks. Below the azure sky, the only sound heard is that of the wind blowing the ice crystals into ever-changing patterns.

What keeps Snow Mesa from being a true wilderness world is its use by snowmobilers—in fact, the primary route onto the mesa follows a track maintained by the Lake City Continental Divide Snowmobile Club. While

SNOW MESA

DISTANCE: 4 miles round-trip to the mesa; unlimited additional mileage atop the mesa

ELEVATION RANGE: 10,900 to 12,300 feet

TOTAL ELEVATION GAIN: 1,400 feet

TRAIL CONDITIONS: The primary route follows a groomed snowmobile track with moderate to steep grades. Atop Snow Mesa, the terrain is flat and open, though disorientation can occur during reduced visibility

AVALANCHE HAZARD: Moderate

SKILL LEVEL: Intermediate

SEASON: Late November through mid-April

USGS MAPS: Slumgullion Pass (1986); Baldy Cinco (1986)

ADMINISTRATION: Rio Grande NF; Divide RD

TRAILHEAD: From Lake City, drive south on CO 149 for 16.9 miles until you reach the summit of Spring Creek Pass (6.3 miles south of Slumguillion Pass). From Creede, drive north on CO 149 for 31.1 miles until you reach Spring Creek Pass. Park at the plowed lot atop the pass.

this may discourage some skiers, others will realize that the route onto the mesa is simply a means to an end, with the "end" being the nearly limitless opportunities for solitude and unexcelled touring atop the mesa. For this pleasure, it is an easy compromise to share a couple of miles of trail with the machines.

Actually, it is the snowmobilers who are doing the sharing—snowmobile registration fees fund the maintenance of the track. For this reason, snowmobilers should be given every consideration, and skiers and snowshoers should yield the right-of-way. Don't let this dampen your interest too much; the reality is that there are so many miles of maintained snowmobile routes and so few snowmobilers, that crowds are extremely rare. It is uncommon for more than a handful of snowmobilers to use this route on any given day, with few if any skiers and snowshoers likely to be present. In other words, don't shun Snow Mesa, because the likelihood is that the vast majority of your tour will be conducted in quiet solitude, and with a packed trail to boot.

Though skiing a groomed track would usually indicate an easy tour, it actually takes a great deal of effort to reach the mesa's summit. The steepness of the route (as well as the speeds possible on the packed trail) makes well-developed skiing skills a must—particularly on the return descent. Furthermore, the unbroken vastness of the mesa makes it easy to become disoriented when visibility is reduced. Skiers must be able to identify potentially dangerous situations and react accordingly. Finally, the final 0.5 mile of the ascent onto the mesa traverses potential avalanche terrain. While skier-triggered slides are unlikely, the cornices that overhang the lip of the mesa could be dangerous. As this hazard is unavoidable, do not attempt this route under such conditions.

A number of snowmobile routes converge at the meadows of Spring Creek Pass, but it should be easy to locate the correct route to Snow Mesa. Cross the highway and follow the wide, groomed path that leads southeast into the meadows. A number of signs identify the route, as do orange markers. Very quickly, a track diverges to the left and begins to climb out of the meadow to the east. Follow this route, and use care to avoid any individual snowmobile tracks that may lead hither and yon. Follow this track for the remainder of the distance to the mesa. When the snowpack is shallow, these markers may not be present. In this situation, finding the route may be more difficult. Carefully studying your topographic map, however, should keep you traveling in the right direction.

The track begins a steady ascent into a shallow ravine just south of the ridge that carries the Continental Divide onto Snow Mesa. Subalpine forest encloses the trail for much of the first mile, while the grade is fairly steep. At the end of the first mile, the grade relents as the track enters a meadow, where the blocky slopes below the mesa suddenly appear much closer. The ascent steepens as the track passes through another 0.25 mile of forest before it emerges rather abruptly at treeline. The climb seems even steeper as the track enters a narrow bowl carved into the otherwise smooth west flank of Snow Mesa. The vista westward across the expanse of Jarosa Mesa and Rambouillet Park encompasses a greater quantity of beautiful peaks with each upward step. Impressive cornices line both sides of the bowl, which discourage prudent skiers from seeking turns on these beautiful slopes. The track stays squarely in the middle of the bowl as it shifts to the left and makes the final ascent onto the mesa. Though this is the safest route through the avalanche terrain, the possibility of a slide does exist—caution should definitely be exercised.

With a final steep push, the mesa top is attained, and the terrain changes dramatically. Gone are the cloaking forests and confined vistas; instead, the flat expanse of the mesa seems to stretch forever before it melts into the surrounding panorama, which stretches from the rolling summits of the La Garita Range to the saw-toothed line of the Weminuche and Uncompahgre Wildernesses. The opportunities for exploration are limited only by your level of interest, energy, and the quality of the weather. The slopes that lead to the crest of the La Garitas, including the 13,383-foot summit of Baldy Cinco, are rather easily attained and offer a significant feeling of accomplishment. Be wary of avalanche-prone areas, though most slopes are less than 25 degrees, and the hazard is generally low. Skiing southward atop the mesa is another possibility; in about 2 miles, it tapers into a narrow point, much like a rocky headland jutting into a sea of space. Don't stray too close to the mesa's edge, lest you find yourself tumbling down the back of a collapsed cornice. Finally, the truly intrepid could simply continue along the route of the snowmobile track, which continues eastward across the mesa before it eventually descends to the town of Creede, about 20 miles distant.

Ivy Creek

Ivy Creek is essentially the only easy and safe winter access into the vast Weminuche Wilderness east of the Continental Divide. Its gently sloped lower valley offers winter explorers the opportunity to experience winter at its most primeval, when even the few hints of human existence that appear during summer are hidden beneath the cold, snowy silence. The beautiful scenery, which includes rich subalpine forests, extensive meadows, and glimpses of the Continental Divide, is made more enticing by the fact that the wilderness designation offers refuge from the hoards of snowmobilers that converge on the Rio Grande Valley's snowbound roads and trails.

The valley can be a pleasant place to ski during stormy weather as it is often sheltered from strong winds and there is no avalanche danger. However, the road that accesses the trailhead is not a high priority for Mineral County road maintenance crews, so if it is snowing heavily, be sure not to get snowed in at the trailhead. In fact, because the road is only plowed for the residents of the single home that is in the vicinity of the trailhead, it is a good idea to check with the county to ensure that winter maintenance will still be done at the time of your visit. In the worst-case scenario, it may be necessary to park near Spar City and ski an additional 2.6 easy miles to the trailhead.

To begin the tour, it is necessary to first find the beginning of the Ivy Creek Trail, which is at the rear of the campground and directly east of the parking area. Ski directly east toward the mouth of Ivy Creek's valley, which is less than 0.25 mile distant, and you should soon be able to identify the trailhead signs behind the campground's outhouse. This initial distance can be windy, and the snow is sometimes hard-packed, but rest assured that once you enter the valley's protective fold, the snow will be soft and the winds will be mellow. The only tricky part of the tour is to locate the trail behind the sign, as few traces are visible. Ski a few yards to the right behind the sign, then, as you approach a small footbridge over Ivy Creek, veer left away from the bridge. In a few feet, the cleared right-of-way should be obvious, which is up on a small bench to the left of Ivy Creek and leads into the forest. From this point until the meadows, the trail's route is easy to follow.

The trail climbs gradually and remains near the left bank of the creek as the valley curves southward. The valley here is narrow, with somewhat steep walls that are blanketed by a dense forest of conifers. Solitude is virtually assured: relatively few cross-country skiers visit the Rio Grande Valley in winter, and this route has not been publicized in the past. As a result,

IVY CREEK

DISTANCE: 5 miles round-trip
ELEVATION RANGE: 9,200 to 9,900 feet
TOTAL ELEVATION GAIN: 700 feet
TRAIL CONDITIONS: Gentle grades and few obstacles; snowbound hiking trail in open meadows
AVALANCHE HAZARD: None
SKILL LEVEL: Novice
SEASON: December through early April
USGS MAPS: Spar City (1986); Workman Creek (1964)
ADMINISTRATION: Rio Grande NF; Divide RD

TRAILHEAD: From Creede, drive 6 miles west on CO 149 and turn left onto Middle Fork Road just before the second Rio Grande River bridge. After 4 miles, bear left onto FR 528 (Lime Creek Road) and continue another 2.5 miles until a junction just before the old town of Spar City. Bear to the right at this junction and drive 2.6 miles, passing several snowed-in roads. Just before you cross a bridge over a small creek, park at the small pullout adjacent to the Ivy Creek Campground sign. Because the route that begins at Middle Fork Road is usually icy and snowpacked, good snow tires or chains are recommended.

breaking trail through the most recent snowfall is a likely chore, and though novice skills are sufficient for the route, this tour can be a workout.

If it's not buried beneath the deep snow, you'll come across a sign that marks the entrance to the Weminuche Wilderness about 1 mile from the

The beauty and solitude of winter in the subalpine forest.

parking area. Though slightly steeper for a short distance, the grade soon eases as the valley widens. Aspen become more prevalent, and the first small meadows appear as the trail passes the mouth of a small tributary drainage not far into the wilderness.

Soon, the true attraction of this tour appears as the trail enters the lower edge of a long meadow, which extends along the valley floor for nearly 1.5 miles. With little more than 100 feet of additional elevation gained in this distance, the meadow is an easy and exceptionally beautiful place to enjoy an hour or two of skiing. The often-virgin snow of the meadow is surrounded by a subalpine forest of spruce, fir, and aspen that has been untouched by the hand of humankind. In the distance, the high crest of the Continental Divide stands like an unconquerable fortress at the heart of the wilderness, its steep flanks defended by an army of avalanches and high winds prepared to repel any intruders.

This meadow, like others found in subalpine valley bottoms, is largely the result of denser cold air pooling at the floor of the valley, which keeps winter temperatures colder than even the subalpine forest species can tolerate. Studies suggest that the air temperature changes in as small a distance as a few hundred feet up the valley walls—on average, it may be as much as 5°F to 10°F warmer than at the valley bottom. Regardless of their location in the valley, living creatures—both plant and animal—have made a variety of adaptations in order to survive the harsh winter climate. Physiological adaptations, or the changing of physical structure, is one of the most common, and a prime example of this is the conifers—primarily subalpine fir and Engelmann spruce—that grow in this ecosystem. Unlike lower-elevation conifers such as ponderosa pine, which tend to have a spreading crown, these species have developed distinctly "pointed" forms that allow them to shed heavy accumulations of snow and withstand strong winds. Another adaptation is migration, which is common to most animal species. Deer, for example, cannot survive long periods in a snowpack deeper than 18 inches, so they move down to lower elevations from late autumn until spring. The deer that live in this area congregate in large herds along the Rio Grande River. Elk, a species that can tolerate deeper snows, may remain in this valley throughout the winter.

The tour ends at the southern edge of the meadows, though the distance can be shortened as desired. More intrepid skiers may wish to continue beyond the meadows, where the trail reenters dense forest and climbs at a steeper rate. A smaller set of meadows, located about 2 miles beyond the end of the lower meadows, is a possible destination. Note that these 2 miles are much rougher and are suitable only for advanced skiers. Also, the avalanche hazard increases as the valley narrows and its walls steepen, so use caution. Otherwise, retrace your path to your vehicle, and enjoy the easy glide through the silent and beautiful setting.

Cumbres Pass

Though *vertical* may accurately sum up the most common perception of the San Juans, there are portions of this great range that lack the massive peaks and deep gorges that made the area famous. Cumbres Pass is one such place. At this southern extreme, the San Juans taper into a landscape of high plateaus, shallow valleys, and rolling hills. Though less dramatic than the cathedral-like peaks found elsewhere in the San Juans, the area does not lack for beauty, especially in its rich forests and open meadows. One of the snowier locales in Colorado, Cumbres Pass features the type of topography and the quality of snow that make for prime winter touring.

Cumbres Pass, with adjacent La Manga Pass, forms a watershed divide between the Rio Chama and the Rio Grande river basins. Storms that churn across the southwest United States strike this area throughout the winter, creating a snowpack that easily exceeds 10 feet in an average year. Small valleys that radiate outward from the passes offer extensive touring opportunities, while the surrounding ridges offer potential telemarking terrain. Few slopes in this vicinity are steep enough to present significant avalanche hazard, and where such hazard does exist, it is often easily avoided. Because of its open exposure and high elevation, strong winds and blinding snow discourage backcountry travel on stormy days. Though the area is popular with the snowmobile crowd, the existence of a well-developed backcountry hut system more than atones for this detraction.

One of the most intriguing tours in the Cumbres Pass area is to the crest of Neff Mountain, a broad-shouldered summit that rises about 1,000 feet above the surrounding valleys. Neff Mountain is a good destination for skiers of all abilities: A marked route (courtesy of the Southwest Nordic Center, proprietor of the area's hut system) follows an old logging road up the northern side of the mountain and presents novices the opportunity to enjoy miles of beautiful forest and meadows, while intermediate skiers can tackle the smooth northern slope that leads to Neff Mountain's summit in order to appreciate the full-circle vista of the surrounding highlands. Sitting midway up the northeast side of the mountain, the Neff Mountain Yurt—a circular canvas structure built atop a wooden platform—is an ideal base camp for anyone who wishes to linger for more than a day.

From the trailhead, cross the highway and pick up the snowbound road that climbs very gradually in a northwesterly direction. The road alternates between patches of forest and open meadow for the first 0.5 mile. Though rarely difficult to locate, the route is marked by blue diamonds, which are strategically hung from trees at regular intervals. Soon, the track turns to the west and begins to climb the lower slopes of Neff Mountain. With the meadows of the Los Pinos River (same name, different river from that in the Weminuche Wilderness) a couple of hundred feet below, the road maintains this course for about a mile and passes several very large trees.

CUMBRES PASS

DISTANCE: 7.5 miles round-trip
ELEVATION RANGE: 9,800 to 10,880 feet
TOTAL ELEVATION GAIN: 1,088 feet
TRAIL CONDITIONS: First 3 miles of route follow snowbound roads at gradual grades; final mile climbs the gladed flank of the mountain on the path of least resistance, at generally moderate grades
AVALANCHE HAZARD: None, though some hazard exists off-route
SKILL LEVEL: Novice to Neff Mountain Yurt, intermediate to the summit
SEASON: Late November through mid-April
USGS MAP: Cumbres (1967)
ADMINISTRATION: Rio Grande NF; Conejos Peak RD

TRAILHEAD: Cumbres Pass is 11.7 miles east of Chama, New Mexico, and 34 miles west of Antonito, Colorado, via CO 17. La Manga Pass is 7 miles east of Cumbres Pass via CO 17. The Neff Mountain Trailhead is 3.4 miles east of the Cumbres Pass summit. The plowed parking area is opposite the trail, which is marked by a large blue disk.

After curving through a small ravine, the road continues westward for another 0.3 mile until it reaches a junction. The route to the Neff Mountain Yurt and the top of Neff Mountain forks to the left (marked by blue diamonds) and climbs more steadily into the forest. The right fork, which is marked by yellow diamonds, continues along the Los Pinos Valley toward Trujillo Meadows and the other two Southwest Nordic Center yurts. After a short distance, the Neff Mountain route switchbacks to the left and continues to climb across the northern flanks of the mountain. The forest in this section is particularly scenic, with noble conifers piercing the deep blue sky.

About a mile from the junction, the road eases onto a flat bench perched at the 10,400-foot level of the mountain. The Neff Mountain Yurt sits in this opening, tucked into the deep snow and scattered trees in an unassuming manner. As with all yurts in the Southwest Nordic Center system, it can be reserved on a nightly basis throughout the winter. Sleeping from four to six individuals, the shelter includes a wood-burning stove for heat, a propane cook stove, lanterns, cooking utensils, and an ample supply of firewood. For information and reservations, call the Southwest Nordic Center at (505) 758-4761, or write to P.O. Box 3212, Taos, New Mexico 87571.

Though novices will need to return to the trailhead at this point, more skilled skiers can continue ahead to the summit of the mountain, which is about 1 mile southwest and 500 feet higher than the yurt. Though there is no marked trail for this final mile, route-finding during clear weather should present no difficulties—simply ski directly southwest along the path of least resistance until you reach the summit. Though not steep enough to avalanche, the climb can be tiring—especially since you'll probably have to break trail. Perseverance pays off when you arrive at the broad summit. Open valleys encircle the mountain, and forested ridges that lead to the barren, windswept plateaus are observed farther beyond. Cars driving along the winding highway over Cumbres Pass appear minuscule, while the keen eye may pick out the snow shed of the Cumbres & Toltec Railroad peeking out of the snow at the pass.

From the summit, telemarkers will find slopes worth exploring, especially on the northern slope, which presents the best snow and terrain. Its shadier exposure keeps the powder drier, though its slopes are the most gradual. This side of the mountain features several large, open meadows as well as forests of moderate density. Immediately east of the summit are Neff's steepest slopes, though these become much gentler below 10,400 feet. Some avalanche hazard could be encountered here; the south and west flanks of the mountain present slopes of a steady and fairly steep grade. Though there are some open bowls just below the summit, the forests are denser on these sides of the mountain, making them less attractive for telemarking. Whichever route you choose, always keep an eye out for forest hazards, and be observant of possible avalanche terrain, especially in gullies.

Wolf Creek Pass

Wolf Creek Pass is another of the San Juan locales held in the highest regard by Colorado's backcountry skiers. The variety of terrain attracts much of the attention, as the ridges and valleys in the vicinity are ideal for both telemarking and touring. Even more legendary is the quantity and quality of snow at the pass. A check of the ski report on nearly any day reveals that the adjacent Wolf Creek Ski Area boasts the deepest snowpack in the state—often by a wide margin.

One of the more interesting routes in the vicinity is Wolf Creek Road, which winds through forested and gladed terrain on the west side of the pass. The road, which ends on a saddle that separates Treasure Mountain from the Continental Divide, is suitable for intermediate touring and offers access to several potential telemarking routes. The overall avalanche danger is low, but as you near the saddle, steeper slopes could endanger those who venture from the road. Small but steep banks are also scattered throughout the area, though these potential avalanche areas are all easily avoided. The lower portions of the road are a fine choice for stormy-day touring, as the forest is particularly scenic amidst falling snow (not to mention sheltered from the gustiest winds).

The sign for Wolf Creek Road marks the trailhead, though deep snows can obscure it from view at times. Once you locate the trailhead, ski down the road as it descends some 50 feet in order to cross Wolf Creek. A short distance after it crosses the creek (less than 0.25 mile from the highway), Wolf Creek Road veers to the left and begins to climb in an easterly direction parallel to a tributary of the creek. The road switchbacks through some fairly recent clear-cuts, and the tremendous snowpack often makes the exact route of the road impossible to follow. The saddle that is the ultimate goal is easily discerned toward the southeast, so if the roadbed route is not visible, simply choose the path of least resistance up the moderately sloped valley. The forested sections of this route are very enjoyable because the moist local climate has encouraged the luxuriant growth of subalpine trees. When the forest opens into a small glade or meadow, the vista expands to include the rugged ridge that forms the valley's north wall—the Continental Divide.

The road crosses the tributary of Wolf Creek near the 10,600-foot contour and continues to ascend at a moderate pace. As you approach the

WOLF CREEK PASS

WOLF CREEK ROAD

DISTANCE: Approximately 6 miles round-trip

ELEVATION RANGE: 10,100 to 11,150 feet

TOTAL ELEVATION GAIN: 1,100 feet

TRAIL CONDITIONS: Route follows snowbound roads, though the exact roadbed may be difficult to discern at times; forested and gladed slopes make up the remaining terrain; grades are moderate

AVALANCHE HAZARD: Low to moderate

SKILL LEVEL: Intermediate

SEASON: Late November through April

USGS MAP: Wolf Creek Pass (1984)

ADMINISTRATION: San Juan NF; Pagosa RD

LOBO OVERLOOK

DISTANCE: 5 miles round-trip, though this can be easily shortened with route variations

ELEVATION RANGE: 10,800 to 11,750 feet

TOTAL ELEVATION GAIN: 950 feet

TRAIL CONDITIONS: Primary route follows a snowbound road with moderate grades; alternate routes include moderate to steep grades through open meadow and scattered forest; high winds are common at the overlook

AVALANCHE HAZARD: Moderate

SKILL LEVEL: Intermediate to advanced

SEASON: Late November through April

USGS MAP: Wolf Creek Pass (1984)

ADMINISTRATION: Rio Grande NF; Divide RD

saddle, be wary of approaching the steep slopes on either side of the narrowing ravine, as the avalanche hazard increases in these areas. Once at the saddle, admire the view of the Divide, which wraps around the headwaters of Wolf Creek in a great arc. To the south, the slopes drop away into the broad valley of the San Juan River's east fork. Farther yet are the peaks of the South San Juans. While touring skiers will want to retrace their route back to the highway at this point, telemarkers can begin their search for perfect powder. This area is well suited for novice to intermediate telemarkers. Denser sections of forest can be challenging, but the many open slopes are ideal for practicing the art of the telemark turn.

The terrain immediately north of Wolf Creek Pass offers some of the most easily accessible, quality telemarking in southern Colorado. A pair of rounded summits feature open, gladed, and forested terrain on a variety of aspects. While the snowpack in this corner of the San Juans tends to be more stable than that farther west, the potential for avalanches must still be carefully considered before you tackle these slopes. Though it might be tempting to ski immediately after one of Wolf Creek's epic snowfalls, it is best to wait a day or two before you head into this area. Don't worry about missing out on first tracks—there is plenty of powder here for everyone. If telemarking is not your interest, the road that winds to the Lobo Overlook, which is atop the higher of the two hills, is still a very enjoyable tour.

The tour's initial destination is the gentle saddle located at the head of the ravine that is directly north of the trailhead. There are two possible routes by which to gain this saddle. One is to follow the snowbound road that eventually climbs to the overlook. Easily identified by the reflector posts poking above the snow, this longer but gentler route gradually ascends in an easterly direction for 0.5 mile, then switchbacks sharply to the west to reach the saddle in another 0.75 mile. The less patient may halve this distance by climbing directly up the ravine toward the saddle. If this steeper route is your choice, be sure to climb the ravine's right flank in order to avoid potential avalanches from the slopes to the west.

Once at the saddle, telemarkers must decide which summit will be their objective. If it is to be the somewhat lower hill to the southeast, diverge from the road here and climb directly up the mostly forested slope— it is perhaps 0.5 mile, with an elevation gain of about 300 feet, to the top. The large clearing on the west flank of the hill offers the most attractive skiing, though densely forested, steep slopes will have to be negotiated if you descend too far to the west. Instead, aim for the saddle, and either ascend to Lobo Overlook for another run or continue down the ravine to the highway.

Continuing toward Lobo Overlook, you are again presented with two choices. The easiest is to simply proceed up the snowbound road, which winds around the north side of the hill and gains its summit after a long mile of gradual ascent. This is the best choice for touring since the ease of the route allows you to enjoy the surrounding vistas. Across a vast foreground of forested ridges, the bald summits of the La Garitas may be spied far to the north, while on clear days the eastern panorama extends to the Sangre de Cristo Range, some 75 miles distant. The shortcut route proceeds along a power line right-of-way, which vectors away from the saddle and toward the radio antenna adjacent to the overlook. Though the distance is

WOLF CREEK ROAD ACCESS: Located on US 160, 2.2 miles west of the Wolf Creek Pass summit (or 20 miles east of Pagosa Springs). Parking is available on the shoulder of the highway.
LOBO OVERLOOK ACCESS: Located on US 160, a short distance east of the Wolf Creek Pass summit. A large plowed parking area is located opposite the SCENIC OVERLOOK sign.

shorter, this direct route is ultimately more taxing since the rate of ascent is significantly steeper.

Lobo Overlook sits atop the summit of an 11,750-foot mountain, in close proximity to a large radio-communications antenna complex. The overlook is a satisfactory destination for touring skiers, as the aforementioned northern and eastern vistas are matched by those to the south and west. The rugged heart of the South San Juans stands in bold relief above the undulating terrain south of Wolf Creek Pass, while to the southwest, the mesas of northern New Mexico can be seen fading toward the horizon.

The most popular telemarking descents are on the east-facing slopes below the overlook. A broad, open bowl comprises the first 200 vertical feet, followed by open meadows separated by islands of forest and small glades. In all, there is about 500 feet of vertical to be enjoyed before you arrive back at the aforementioned saddle. Simply be sure not to head too far toward the south-facing slopes, which feature narrow cliff bands and more dangerous avalanche conditions. The northeast flank also has some nice terrain. A short but fairly steep bowl is located on this side, between the crest of the hill and the snowbound road below. Several runs down this bowl could easily be enjoyed in a few hours' time, and with its tapered slope, it offers descents of varying steepness.

Williams Creek

Upon exiting an impressive canyon, Williams Creek winds through an idyllic valley at the southern foot of the Weminuche Wilderness. Nearly flat, the floor of the upper valley is covered in snowy meadows, while the lower end is submerged beneath the iced-over waters of Williams Creek Reservoir. A mixed forest of aspen, Douglas fir, blue spruce, and ponderosa pine blankets the surrounding walls and craggy cliffs of dark volcanic rock, forming a striking battlement to the north and east. Sheltered from all but the fiercest storms and free from avalanche hazard, this landscape creates the perfect setting for long, easy ski tours.

The tour follows the unplowed road to the far end of the valley and passes a pair of summer campgrounds en route. The elevation gain is minimal, and the entire tour remains between the 8,300- and 8,400-foot contours on the west side of the valley. While cold air pools here at night, its relatively low elevation and location on the south side of the San Juans ensures that temperatures are usually mild on sunny days. The warmer temperatures and sunny exposure can create mushy snow conditions, however, and the best touring is usually found only from late November until early March. Though a highly enjoyable tour in its own right, this valley is an especially fine choice when storms or avalanche conditions render higher-elevation tours unsafe.

Little route description is necessary for this tour—simply follow the road as far as you please. The road stays somewhat above the valley floor to start, which allows a nice overview of the reservoir, a popular ice-fishing venue. The road bends through a shallow ravine after 0.5 mile and passes beneath stands of young aspen and conifers, which compose the diverse montane ecosystem forests. (The ponderosa pine is also an important member of the montane coniferous forest. Its orangish-red bark; long, green needles; and sweet vanilla aroma make it a favorite.) Compare these conifers to those of the subalpine ecosystem found in places like Ivy Creek, which is 1,000 feet higher, and on the north side of the range. These trees have broad crowns, which means that they have not had to adapt to heavy snow accumulation. Storms at these lower elevations deliver less snow, while warmer temperatures melt the snow that does fall at a quicker pace.

The gently rising valley floor meets the level road at the 1-mile mark, and from this point forward, the tour remains mostly on the fringe of the

WILLIAMS CREEK

DISTANCE: 6 miles round-trip

ELEVATION RANGE: 8,300 to 8,400 feet

TOTAL ELEVATION GAIN: 150 feet

TRAIL CONDITIONS: Wide, snowbound road with nearly flat grades

AVALANCHE HAZARD: None

SKILL LEVEL: Novice

SEASON: Late November through early March

USGS MAP: Cimarron Peak (1973)

ADMINISTRATION: San Juan NF; Pagosa RD

TRAILHEAD: From Pagosa Springs, drive west on US 160 for 2.6 miles and turn right onto Piedra Road, which is at the crest of the long hill out of town. Follow this road, which soon turns to gravel, for a total of 21.3 miles, being sure to stay left at all major junctions and follow the signs to Williams Creek Reservoir. Turn right onto Williams Creek Road and proceed for 1.7 miles. Park near an unplowed road adjacent to the entrance of the reservoir's boat ramp. Portions of Williams Creek and Piedra Roads can be slick, as a combination of snowpack and mud commonly exists during winter.

forest. At about 2 miles, the road splits into two forks. The primary route continues ahead on the valley floor for another mile and ends at the Williams Creek Trailhead at the mouth of the creek's narrow canyon. The left fork provides an interesting diversion for skiers who seek a longer tour. It climbs steadily up a forested hillside for several miles and eventually reaches the open meadows of Poison Park, which sits atop the broad ridge that separates Williams Creek Valley from the equally lovely Weminuche Creek Valley. Whichever route you choose, you can retrace your tracks to return to the trailhead when you're ready.

Chimney Rock

Sitting atop a narrow ridge in the shadow of an isolated rock spire, the thousand-year-old Anasazi ruins at Chimney Rock are one of the most spectacularly situated archaeological sites in the Southwest and are the destination for one of America's most unique ski tours. The long, winding road that climbs to the ruins is unmaintained during winter months, leaving it the domain of the self-propelled. While the snow itself isn't always on par with the light, dry powder so prevalent elsewhere in the San Juans, the opportunity to experience this mystical place in quiet solitude makes this a tour not to miss.

Chimney Rock is located in the southern foothills of the San Juans and is at an elevation that is lower than any of the other winter tours described in this guide. As a result, the "winter season" here is shorter and less predictable than at the higher terrain. In general, there should be sufficient snow from December until early March, though daytime temperatures that commonly reach into the forties can make the snow sloppy, even within these months. Your best bet is to ski this route within a few days of a storm, before the sun has made inroads into the snowpack. Because the primary attractions of this tour are the scenery, history, and solitude of the ruins—not the skiing terrain—the warmer temperatures, lesser snowfalls, and a lack of avalanche terrain make this tour a nice choice during storm cycles.

From the highway, ski west across the flat floor of the Stollsteimer Creek valley and enjoy the open meadows and dwarf forest of the pinon-juniper woodland ecosystem. Because the winter climate is relatively mild and the snowpack only a foot or two deep, this ecosystem is a critical winter

 220

habitat for a great variety of Rocky Mountain wildlife. Throughout the tour, keep an eye peeled for deer, elk, coyote, hawks, and golden eagles. The spires of Chimney Rock and the slightly smaller Companion Rock serve as sentinels for the surrounding countryside. A fire tower that is visible just south of Chimney Rock is adjacent to the ruins—use this landmark to gauge your progress.

After 0.5 mile of effortless gliding, the road begins to climb steadily up the southeast flank of the ridge, curving south at first, then switchbacking sharply at mile 1.25 to bring the road onto a northwest heading. As elevation is gained, the forest makes the transition into that of a more montane character, with ponderosa pine, fir, and aspen becoming increasingly predominant. Aside from a short switchback just prior to mile 2.0, the road continues directly along the tapering ridge until it reaches a high rim at mile 3.0. A quarter mile farther along the crest is a parking area at the end of the road and a lower group of ruins. The most impressive ruin—Great House—sits another 0.25 mile above the parking area, on the crest of the ridge immediately south of Chimney Rock. Beyond the parking area, the ridge is only a few feet wide, with precipitous drops on either side and a steeper grade. Because of this, less-experienced skiers should walk the final distance to Great House and trace the summer footpath as much as possible.

There are many questions surrounding the history of Chimney Rock, with speculation more prevalent than concrete evidence. It is known these ruins were constructed by the Anasazi, who developed an agricultural society throughout the Southwest between about A.D. 500 and 1300. The Anasazi are generally grouped into one of three cultural districts: the Mesa

CHIMNEY ROCK

DISTANCE: 7 miles round-trip

ELEVATION RANGE: 6,550 to 7,600 feet

TOTAL ELEVATION GAIN: 1,050 feet

TRAIL CONDITIONS: Long, steady climb on a snowbound road

AVALANCHE HAZARD: None

SKILL LEVEL: Novice

SEASON: December through early March

USGS MAP: Chimney Rock (1968)

ADMINISTRATION: San Juan NF; Pagosa RD

TRAILHEAD: Drive on US 160, for either 15 miles west from Pagosa Springs or for 42 miles east from Durango, until you reach the junction of CO 151. Turn south here and proceed 3.2 miles until you reach the beginning of Chimney Rock Road. There should be space for several cars to park on the shoulder of the highway.

Verdean, famous for the cliff dwellings found in the southwest corner of Colorado; the Kayenta, who lived in northern Arizona and southern Utah; and the Chacoan, who developed the most advanced culture of the three, based upon a great city built in a New Mexico canyon. Archaeologists believe that the adjacent Piedra River valley had been the domain of people of the Mesa Verde culture for about one hundred fifty years, until approximately A.D. 1076, when a group of Chacoans migrated here to build this large pueblo. Once consisting of about fifty-five rooms and two kivas, Great House was obviously the result of meticulous planning. Built directly on bedrock, most of the structure's rock and adobe components had to be hauled from elsewhere. The efficient use of limited space on the ridge crest is impressive, while the exacting detail found in the ruin's stone walls demonstrates highly skilled masonry techniques.

Far removed from the other Chacoan communities, the purpose of this outpost remains unclear. Some archaeologists speculate that this complex served as an important trading center for the accumulation of resources—particularly timber, which couldn't be obtained from the arid, barren canyon that was home to the central Chacoan empire. Others believe that Chimney Rock was meant to be a religious sanctuary, and that this high-altitude site was chosen for its closer symbolic proximity to the gods. Perhaps most intriguing is the theory put forth by archaeo-astronomers, who have determined that a "lunar standstill" phenomenon occurs here once every eighteen years, when the full moon that rises on the night of the winter solstice appears to stand still between the towers of Chimney and Companion Rocks. Could it be that Chimney Rock was built solely for the observance of this mystical and awe-inspiring event? The truth will likely never be fully understood, for the Anasazi left Chimney Rock and each of their other communities within just a few generations, leaving their exquisite buildings to stand in cold silence for the next eight hundred winters.

Chimney Rock, especially in the solitude found on most winter days, is a truly spiritual place. Take the time to sit and soak in the accomplishments of this ancient culture. Of course, the future integrity of the ruin is in your hands. Please do nothing to compromise this: Do not climb on the rock walls, climb into the kivas, or alter the site in any way. Admire the astounding panorama as the Anasazi certainly did, for the eye can wander from high San Juan peaks to vast New Mexico mesas. Should your schedule allow, this journey is ideal on an evening when a full moon lights the sky. The route is safe and easy to follow, and even if it is not the night of the winter solstice, the joining of human art and celestial wonder creates a very special experience.

RESOURCES AND INFORMATION

Land Management Agencies:

SAN JUAN NATIONAL FOREST
15 Burnett Court, Durango, CO 81301
(970) 247-4082
www.fs.fed.us/srnf

Columbine Ranger District
376 South Pearl Street, Bayfield, CO 81122
(970) 264-2268
Dolores Ranger District (East)
100 North Sixth, Dolores, CO 81323
(970) 882-7296
Pagosa Ranger District
180 Second Street, Pagosa Springs, CO 81147
(970) 264-2268

RIO GRANDE NATIONAL FOREST
1803 West US 160, Monte Vista, CO 81144
(719) 852-5941
www.fs.fed.us/srnf

Divide Ranger District
13308 West US 160, Del Norte, CO 81132
(719) 657-3321
Conejos Peak Ranger District
15571 County Road T-5, La Jara, CO 81140
(719) 274-6301
Saguache Range District
46525 CO 114, Saguache, CO 81149
(719) 655-2547

UNCOMPAHGRE AND GUNNISON NATIONAL FORESTS
2250 US 50, Delta, CO 81416
(970) 874-6600

Norwood Ranger District
1760 Grand Avenue, Norwood, CO 81423
(970) 327-4261
Ouray Ranger District
2505 South Townsend, Montrose, CO 81401
(970) 240-5300
Cebolla Ranger District
216 North Colorado Street, Gunnison, CO 81230
(970) 641-0471

BLM—SAN JUAN RESOURCE AREA
15 Burnett Court, Durango, CO 81301
(970) 247-4082
www.co.blm.gov/sjra/sjra.html

BLM—GUNNISON RESOURCE AREA
216 North Colorado Street, Gunnison, CO 81230
(970) 641-0471
www.co.blm.gov/gra/gra-hmepge.html

Weather, Avalanche, and Road Conditions

THE NATIONAL WEATHER SERVICE (COLORADO STATE INFORMATION):
http://iwin.nws.noaa.gov/iwin/co/co.html

THE WEATHER CHANNEL
www.weather.com
(Specific forecasts are available for Alamosa, Cortez, Durango, Gunnison,
Montrose, and Telluride.)

COLORADO AVALANCHE INFORMATION CENTER
(970) 247-8187 (Durango hot line)
www.caic.state.co.us

COLORADO DEPARTMENT OF TRANSPORTATION
(303) 639-1111 (statewide hot line)

(970) 247-3355 (Durango hot line)
www.dot.state.co.us/public/index.htm

COUNTY SHERIFFS
(In an emergency, always dial 911)

Archuleta County (Pagosa Springs): (970) 264-2131
Conejos County (Antonito): (719) 376-5921
Dolores County (Dolores): (970) 677-2257
Gunnison County (Gunnison): (970) 641-1113
Hinsdale County (Lake City): (970) 944-2291
La Plata County (Durango): (970) 247-1157
Mineral County (Creede): (719) 658-2600
Montezuma County (Cortez): (970) 565-8441
Ouray County (Ouray): (970) 325-7272
Rio Grande County (Del Norte): (719) 657-4000
Saguache County (Saguache): (719) 655-2525
San Juan County (Silverton): (970) 387-5531
San Miguel County (Telluride): (970) 728-3081

USGS MAP SALES
USGS Information Services
P.O. Box 25286
Denver Federal Center
Denver, CO 80225
(800) HELP-MAP
(Note that USGS maps can also be purchased from individual retailers throughout the region.)

REGIONAL TOURIST INFORMATION
Southwest Colorado Travel Region:
(970) 247-9621 or (800) 933-4340
www.swcolotravel.org

APPENDIX: ADVENTURE LOCATOR

The San Juans cover a vast area. It's not easy to drive from one corner of the range to another—especially if you plan to explore the backcountry and then return to your base camp. This is particularly true during the winter when dirt-road shortcuts are snowed in and a journey from, say, Durango to Lake City can take a half day. Also consider if you plan to spend a weekend in Telluride, it does you no good to ponder a hike in the South San Juan Wilderness. Or, if you plan to take a short biking trip close to your home in Phoenix, you'll want to know which rides are in the southwest corner of the San Juans—not the northeast.

The Adventure Locator will help you meet these and other trip-finding challenges. In the Adventure Locator, the region is divided into four logical quadrants: southwest, northwest, northeast, and southeast. The quadrants have maps and tables that correspond with all of the trails in this book. The quadrant maps point you in the right direction. The easy-to-use tables classify the type of adventure; identify the trails' names, locations on the maps, and page numbers for the descriptions; offer approximations of how long it takes to complete each trail; suggest base camps; and provide driving distances between the trailheads and base camps.

This will hopefully make it easy to enjoy the perfect San Juan adventure.

SOUTHWEST QUADRANT

BEST BASE CAMP: Durango
ACCESS: Albuquerque: 212 miles
Denver: 379 miles
Salt Lake City: 400 miles

Phoenix: 455 miles
OTHER NEARBY TOWNS: Cortez, Pagosa
Springs, Silverton, Dolores

TYPE	TRIP NAME	LENGTH OF TIME	NEAREST TOWN	TRAILHEAD DRIVING DISTANCE FROM DURANGO	MAP ID #	PAGE #
Hike	San Miguel Traverse	Full day or weekend	Dolores	84 miles northwest	H8	52
Hike	Indian Trail Ridge	Quarter day	Durango	23 miles northwest	H7	50
Hike	Emerald Lake	Half day or weekend	Durango	25 miles east	H13	111
Hike	Needles Range Circuit	Multiday	Durango	D&SNGRR access in Durango	H1	30
Hike	V-Rock Trail	Half day	Pagosa Springs	86 miles east	H8	97
Hike	Quartz Lake	Half day	Pagosa Springs	75 miles east	H9	102
Hike	Rainbow Hot Spring	Half day	Pagosa Springs	76 miles east	H10	104
Hike	Palisade Meadows	Full day	Pagosa Springs	83 miles east	H11	107
Hike	Piedra River	Full day or weekend	Pagosa Springs	73 miles east	H12	109
Hike	Arrastra Basin	Half day	Silverton	53 miles north	H4	42
Hike	Ice Lake Basin	Half day	Silverton	57 miles north	H5	45
Hike	Columbine Lake	Half day	Silverton	56 miles north	H6	48
Hike	Crater Lake	Full day	Silverton	43 miles north	H2	36
Hike	Colorado Trail– Molas Highlands	Full day or weekend	Silverton	45 miles north	H3	38
Bike	Echo Basin	Quarter day	Durango	29 miles west	B6	130
Bike	Hermosa Creek	Half day	Durango	35 miles north	B1	116
Bike	La Plata Canyon	Half day	Durango	16 miles west	B5	127
Bike	Treasure Mountain	Half day	Pagosa Springs	79 miles east	B7	165
Bike	Lime Creek Road	Quarter day	Silverton	29 miles north	B2	119
Bike	Placer and Picayune Gulches	Quarter day	Silverton	62 miles north	B3	121
Bike	Black Bear Pass	Quarter day	Silverton	64 miles north	B4	123
Ski	Wolf Creek Pass	Half day	Pagosa Springs	80 miles east	S7	215
Ski	Williams Creek	Half day	Pagosa Springs	78 miles east	S8	218
Ski	Chimney Rock	Half day	Pagosa Springs	45 miles east	S9	220
Ski	The Meadows	Full day	Rico	90 miles northwest	S6	184
Ski	Lime Creek	Half day	Silverton	29 miles north	S1	170
Ski	Coal Creek	Half day	Silverton	35 miles north	S2	172
Ski	South Mineral Creek	Half day	Silverton	52 miles north	S4	178
Ski	US Basin	Half day or weekend	Silverton	64 miles north	S5	181
Ski	Molas Pass	Varied	Silverton	42 miles north	S3	175

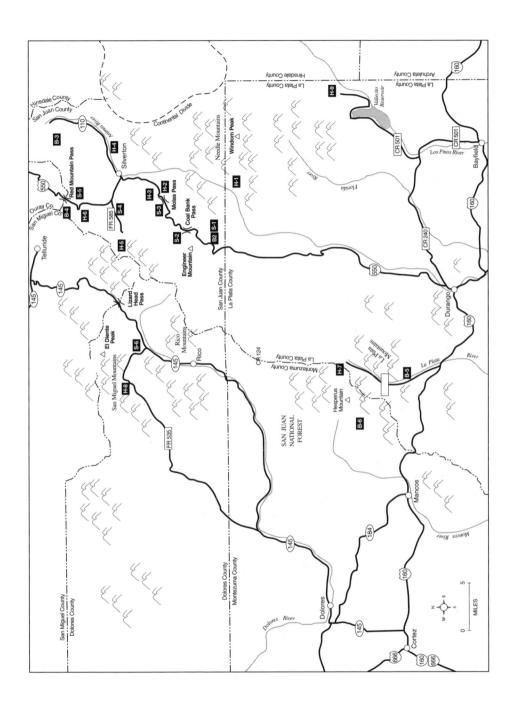

BEST BASE CAMP: Telluride
ACCESS: Denver: 265 miles
      Albuquerque: 321 miles
      Salt Lake City: 417 miles

Phoenix: 480 miles
OTHER NEARBY TOWNS: Ouray,
Ridgway, Montrose

TYPE	TRIP NAME	LENGTH OF TIME	NEAREST TOWN	TRAILHEAD DRIVING DISTANCE FROM TELLURIDE	MAP ID #	PAGE #
Hike	Wasatch Trail	Half day or full day	Telluride	In Telluride	H3	60
Hike	Lizard Head Trail	Full day	Telluride	15 miles south	H2	56
Hike	Sneffels Highline	Full day	Telluride	3 miles west	H4	63
Hike	San Miguel Traverse	Full day or weekend	Telluride	25 miles south	H1	52
Hike	Bear Creek– American Flats	Half day, full day, or weekend	Ouray	52 miles east	H6	67
Hike	Blaine Basin	Half day	Ridgway	46 miles north	H5	66
Hike	Wetterhorn Basin	Full day	Ridgway	60 miles east	H7	72
Hike	Cimarron Headwaters	Weekend or multiday	Ridgway	65 miles east	H8	74
Bike	Cimarron Valley	Full day	Montrose	86 miles northeast	B6	148
Bike	Black Bear Pass	Quarter day	Ouray	63 miles east	B1	123
Bike	Red Mountain District	Quarter day	Ouray	60 miles east	B5	144
Bike	Galloping Goose Trail	Quarter to full day	Telluride	In Telluride	B2	131
Bike	Wilson Mesa	Half day	Telluride	10 miles west	B3	139
Bike	Last Dollar	Half day	Telluride	5 miles west	B4	141
Ski	Sunshine Mesa	Quarter day	Telluride	8 miles west	S3	189
Ski	Lizard Head Pass	Half day	Telluride	15 miles south	S2	185
Ski	The Meadows	Full day	Telluride	20 miles south	S1	184
Ski	East Dallas Creek	Full day or weekend	Ridgway	39 miles north	S4	193
Ski	Ironton Park/Red Mountain Nordic System	Quarter day	Ouray	58 miles east	S5	195
Ski	US Basin	Half day or weekend	Ouray	63 miles east	S6	181

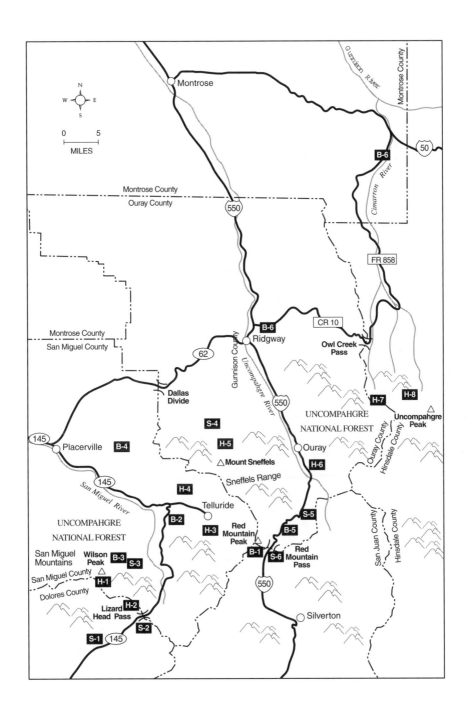

NORTHEAST QUADRANT

Bᴇsᴛ ʙᴀsᴇ ᴄᴀᴍᴘ: Lake City

Aᴄᴄᴇss: Denver: 251 miles

Albuquerque: 318 miles

Salt Lake City: 453 miles

Phoenix: 627 miles

Oᴛʜᴇʀ ɴᴇᴀʀʙʏ ᴛᴏᴡɴs: Gunnison, Saguache

TYPE	TRIP NAME	LENGTH OF TIME	NEAREST TOWN	TRAILHEAD DRIVING DISTANCE FROM LAKE CITY	MAP ID #	PAGE #
Hike	American Basin–Handies Peak	Quarter day or half day	Lake City	20 miles west	H3	83
Hike	Uncompahgre Peak	Half day	Lake City	9 miles west	H1	78
Hike	Cataract Gulch	Half day	Lake City	14 miles west	H2	81
Hike	Powderhorn Lakes	Half day, full day, or weekend	Lake City	35 miles north	H4	86
Hike	San Luis Peak	Full day or weekend	Gunnison	102 miles east (much closer via forest roads)	H5	88
Bike	Saguache Stagecoach Road	Half day	Gunnison	85 miles east (much closer via forest roads)	B2	156
Bike	Jarosa Mesa	Half day	Lake City	17 miles south	B3	159
Bike	Alpine Loop Backcountry Byway	Full day	Lake City	1 mile west	B1	151
Ski	Cottonwood Gulch	Half day	Lake City	14 miles west	S1	198
Ski	Snow Mesa	Half day	Lake City	17 miles south	S3	205
Ski	Rambouillet Park	Full day or weekend	Lake City	15 miles south	S2	201

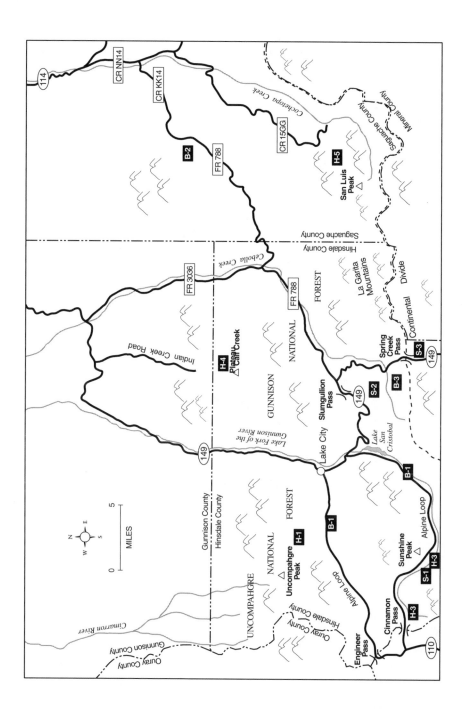

SOUTHEAST QUADRANT

BEST BASE CAMPS: Monte Vista (MV) or Pagosa Springs (PS)

ACCESS: Denver: 243 miles (MV)/303 miles (PS)

Albuquerque: 214 miles (MV)/208 miles (PS)

Salt Lake City: 532 miles (MV)/462 miles (PS)

Phoenix: 587 miles (MV)/517 miles (PS)

OTHER NEARBY TOWNS: Creede, South Fork, Del Norte, Alamosa, Antonito, Chama (New Mexico)

TYPE	TRIP NAME	LENGTH OF TIME	NEAREST TOWN	TRAILHEAD DRIVING DISTANCE FROM MONTE VISTA	MAP ID #	PAGE #
Hike	Conejos Peak	Half day	Del Norte	45 miles southwest	H1	95
Hike	Conejos Headwaters	Quarter day, full day, or weekend	Del Norte	45 miles southwest	H1	91
Bike	Jarosa Mesa	Half day	Creede	84 miles northwest	B1	159
Bike	Bachelor Historic Loop	Half day	Creede	55 miles northwest	B2	161
Bike	Treasure Mountain	Half day	South Fork	56 miles west	B3	165
Ski	Cumbres Pass	Full day or weekend	Antonito	80 miles south	S3	212
Ski	Snow Mesa	Half day	Creede	84 miles northwest	S1	205
Ski	Ivy Creek	Half day	Creede	70 miles northwest	S2	208
Ski	Wolf Creek Pass	Half day	South Fork	55 miles west	S4	215

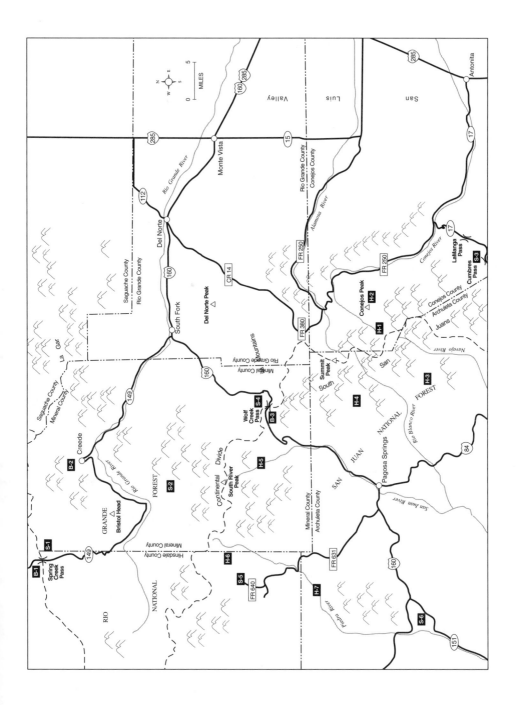

INDEX

Bold-faced items refer to trip descriptions listed in the contents. Bold-faced numbers refer to the first pages of the trails' descriptions. Italicized numbers refer to pages with photographs.

239